WORLD WAR II
IN THE AIR

THE PACIFIC

WORLD WAR II
IN THE AIR
THE PACIFIC

EDITED BY

Colonel James F. Sunderman, U.S.A.F.

 VAN NOSTRAND REINHOLD COMPANY
NEW YORK   CINCINNATI   TORONTO   LONDON   MELBOURNE

This book is dedicated to my cousin

First Lt. David E. Koenig

who took a B-25 from New Guinea to Rabaul one day in 1943

and never came back . . .

when we were kids we used to tramp the woods and
ford the streams of northwest Ohio for
rabbit and pheasant and quail and
revel in the wide, eternal world of
nature that was a boy's life
down on the farm . . .

First published in paperback in 1981
Copyright © 1963 by Litton Educational
Publishing, Inc.
Library of Congress Catalog Card Number
80-13027
ISBN 0-442-20044-7

Van Nostrand Reinhold Company
A division of Litton Educational
Publishing, Inc.
135 West 50th Street, New York, NY 10020

Van Nostrand Reinhold Ltd.
1410 Birchmount Road, Scarborough,
Ontario M1P 2E7

Van Nostrand Reinhold Australia Pty. Ltd.
17 Queen Street, Mitcham, Victoria 3132

Van Nostrand Reinhold Company Ltd.
Molly Millars Lane, Wokingham, Berkshire,
England RG11 2PY

Cloth edition published 1963
by Franklin Watts, Inc.

16 15 14 13 12 11 10 9 8 7 6 5 4 3 2 1

Library of Congress Cataloging in Publication Data

Sunderman, James F   ed.
    World War II in the air.
    Reprint of the 1962-63 ed. published by F. Watts,
New York, in series: The Watts aerospace library.
    Includes indexes.
    CONTENTS: [1] The Pacific.—[2] Europe.
    1. World War, 1939-1945—Aerial operations—
Addresses, essays, lectures. I. Title.
[D785.S9 1981]   940.54′4   80-13027
ISBN 0-442-20044-7 (v. 1)
ISBN 0-442-20045-5 (v. 2)

ACKNOWLEDGMENTS

The selections in this book are used by permission and special arrangements with the proprietors of their respective copyrights who are listed below. The editor's and publisher's thanks to all who made this collection possible.

The editor and publisher have made every effort to trace the ownership of all material contained herein. It is their belief that the necessary permissions from publishers, authors, and authorized agents have been obtained in all cases. In the event of any questions arising as to the use of any material, the editor and publisher, while expressing regret for any error unconsciously made, will be pleased to make the necessary correction in future editions of this book.

University of North Carolina Press and Air Force Aid Society (copyright holder) for "A Quiet Sunday Morning" by Clive Howard and Joe Whitley. This selection is from the book ONE DAMNED ISLAND AFTER ANOTHER by Clive Howard and Joe Whitley. Reprinted by permission.

Random House, Inc. for "Tallyho! Bandits Over Clark!" by John Toland. This selection is from the book BUT NOT IN SHAME by John Toland. Copyright © 1961 by John Toland. Reprinted by permission of Random House, Inc.

Little, Brown and Company for "Episode at Vigan" by Walter D. Edmonds. This selection is from the book THEY FOUGHT WITH WHAT THEY HAD by Walter D. Edmonds. Reprinted by permission of the publishers.

Air Force Magazine for "The Bamboo Fleet" by Capt. Roland Barnick. Reprinted by permission of *Air Force* Magazine.

Official U.S. Air Force Historical Files for "Angels With and Without Wings."

The Airpower Historian for "The Tokyo Raid — An Avenging Call" by Col. Jack A. Sims, USAF. This selection is from the October 1957 issue. Reprinted by permission of *The Airpower Historian* and the author.

Duell, Sloan & Pearce, an affiliate of Meredith Press, for "The Setting — Into a Strange, Weird World" by Capts. Donald Hough and Elliott Arnold. This selection is from the Introduction to the book BIG DISTANCE by Capts. Donald Hough and Elliott Arnold. Copyright 1945 by the authors. Reprinted by permission of the publishers.

Air Force Magazine for "Southwest Pacific Boomerang" by Col. B. B. Cain. Reprinted by permission of *Air Force* Magazine.

E. P. Dutton & Co. and Martin Caidin for "Saburo Sakai: King of Jap Aces" by Saburo Sakai with Martin Caidin and Fred Saito. This selection is from the book SAMURAI! by Saburo Sakai with Martin Caidin and Fred Saito. Reprinted by permission.

Harper & Brothers for "The Cactus Bumblebees" by John A. DeChant. This selection is from the book DEVILBIRDS by John A. DeChant. Copyright 1947 by John A. DeChant. Reprinted by permission of the publishers.

Air Force Magazine for "Henderson Tower" by Capt. J. E. Roberts and S/Sgt. John R.

Dunn. Reprinted by permission of *Air Force* Magazine:

Harper & Brothers for "Maj. 'Mad' Jack Cram and His Wild Blue Goose" by John A. DeChant. This selection is from the book DEVILBIRDS by John A. DeChant. Copyright 1947 by John A. DeChant. Reprinted by permission of the publishers.

Duell, Sloan & Pearce, an affiliate of Meredith Press, for "Down in and at 'Em" by Capts. Donald Hough and Elliott Arnold. This selection is from the book BIG DISTANCE by Capts. Donald Hough and Elliott Arnold. Copyright 1945 by the authors. Reprinted by permission of the publishers.

Duell, Sloan & Pearce, an affiliate of Meredith Press, for "Vignettes of New Guinea's Jungle Air War" by Gen. George C. Kenney, USAF (Ret). These selections are from the book GENERAL KENNEY REPORTS by Gen. George C. Kenney. Copyright 1949 by the author. Reprinted by permission of the publishers.

G. P. Putnam's Sons for "Two Can Play" by Maj. Gen. Claire Lee Chennault, USAF (Ret). This selection is from the book WAY OF A FIGHTER by Claire Lee Chennault. Copyright 1949 by the author. Reprinted by permission of the publishers.

U.S. Air Services Magazine for "The Password Was Mandalay" by Lt. Col. James W. Bellah, USA (Inf). This selection is from the May issue of 1944. Reprinted by permission.

Harold Matson Co. for "Over the Hump" by Eric Sevareid. Copyright 1945 by Eric Sevareid. Reprinted by permission of Harold Matson Co.

Air Force Magazine for "Bombs for Paramushiru" by Maj. Louis C. Blau and Maj. Frank T. Gash. This selection was from the November issue of 1943. Reprinted by permission of *Air Force* Magazine.

G. P. Putnam's Sons for "Courage—Guts—Skill" by Capt. Gene Gurney, USAF,

edited by Lt. Mark P. Friedlander, Jr., USAFR. This selection is from the book FIVE DOWN AND GLORY: A HISTORY OF THE AMERICAN AIR ACE by Gene Gurney and Mark P. Friedlander, Jr. Copyright 1958 by the authors. Reprinted by permission.

Duell, Sloan & Pearce, an affiliate of Meredith Press, for "Balikpapan" by Capts. Donald Hough and Elliott Arnold. This selection is from the book BIG DISTANCE by Capts. Donald Hough and Elliott Arnold. Copyright 1945 by the authors. Reprinted by permission of the publishers.

Air Force Magazine for "Into Hidden Valley" by Capt. Manford Susman. This selection is from the January issue of 1945. Reprinted by permission of *Air Force* Magazine.

The authors for "A Gooney Gets a Zero" by Lt. Col. Carroll V. Glines, USAF, and Lt. Col. Wendell F. Moseley, USAF. This selection is from the book THE INCREDIBLE DC-3 by Carroll V. Glines and Wendell F. Moseley, published by Van Nostrand Reinhold. Reprinted by permission.

G. P. Putnam's Sons for "Hankow, China: The First Fire-Bomb Raid" by Maj. Gen. Claire Lee Chennault, USAF (Ret). This selection is from the book WAY OF A FIGHTER by Claire Lee Chennault. Copyright 1949 by the author. Reprinted by permission of the publishers.

Duell, Sloan & Pearce, an affiliate of Meredith Press, for "Back to the Philippines" by Gen. George C. Kenney. This selection is from the book THE SAGA OF PAPPY GUNN by Gen. George C. Kenney. Copyright 1959 by the author. Reprinted by permission of the publishers.

Duell, Sloan & Pearce, an affiliate of Meredith Press, for "I Take Bong Out of Combat" by Gen. George C. Kenney. This selection is from the book DICK BONG by Gen. George C. Kenney. Copyright 1960 by the author. Reprinted by permission of the publishers.

Air Force Magazine for "A Stroll on Luzon" by Lt. Russell D. Giesy. This selection is from the August issue of 1945. Reprinted by permission of *Air Force* Magazine.

United States Naval Institute for "Philippine Exodus: The Kamikazes of Mabalacat" by Capt. Rikihei Inoguchi, Comdr. Tadashi Nakajima and Roger Pineau. This selection is from the book THE DIVINE WIND by Capt. Rikihei Inoguchi, Comdr. Tadashi Nakajima and Roger Pineau. Copyright © 1958 by United States Naval Institute, Annapolis, Md. Reprinted by permission.

University of North Carolina Press and Air Force Aid Society (copyright holder) for "Prayer, Guts and Yankee Resourcefulness" by Clive Howard and Joe Whitley. This selection is from the book ONE DAMNED ISLAND AFTER ANOTHER by Clive Howard and Joe Whitley. Reprinted by permission.

Holt, Rinehart and Winston and U.S. Navy Dept. for "The Marianas 'Turkey Shoot'" by Capt. Walter Karig, USNR, Lt. Comdr. Russell L. Harris, USNR, and Lt. Comdr. Frank A. Manson, USN. This selection is from the book BATTLE REPORT: THE END OF AN EMPIRE by Capt. Walter Karig, USNR, Lt. Comdr. Russell L. Harris, USNR, and Lt. Comdr. Frank A. Manson, USN. Copyright 1948 by Holt, Rinehart and Winston, Inc. Reprinted by permission of the publishers and U.S. Navy Dept.

Air Force Magazine for "The Spirit of Attack." Reprinted by permission of *Air Force* Magazine.

Duell, Sloan & Pearce, an affiliate of Meredith Press, for "No Screen to Hide Us" by Wilbur H. Morrison. This selection is from the book HELLBIRDS by Wilbur H. Morrison. Copyright 1960 by the author. Reprinted by permission of the publishers.

Air Force Magazine for "Banzai!" This selection is from the July issue of 1945. Reprinted by permission of *Air Force* Magazine.

Maj. Gene Gurney, USAF, for "The Giant Pays Its Way" by Maj. Gene Gurney. Written especially for this volume by the author.

Air Force Magazine for "Direct Wire." This selection is from the November issue of 1945. Reprinted by permission of *Air Force* Magazine.

University of North Carolina Press and Air Force Aid Society (copyright holder) for "The Sun Also Sets" by Clive Howard and Joe Whitley. This selection is from the book ONE DAMNED ISLAND AFTER ANOTHER by Clive Howard and Joe Whitley. Reprinted by permission.

Air Force Magazine for "Our Power to Destroy War" by Gen. Henry H. Arnold. This selection is from the October issue of 1945. Reprinted by permission of *Air Force* Magazine.

Editor's and publisher's grateful thanks are due the United States Air Force which supplied the majority of the photographs included in this volume. Thanks are also due the following sources who were generous suppliers of photographic materials:

United States Navy for official photos on pages 5, 9, 59, 60, 61, 64 (top), 98, 109, 154, 208, 220, 222 (top), 233, 247, 281.
United States Army for official photos on pages 25, 58 (bottom), 281, 283.
Douglas Aircraft Company for the photo on page 183.
Martin Caidin for the photos on page 92.

Contents

PART THREE: THE HOMESTRETCH AND VICTORY

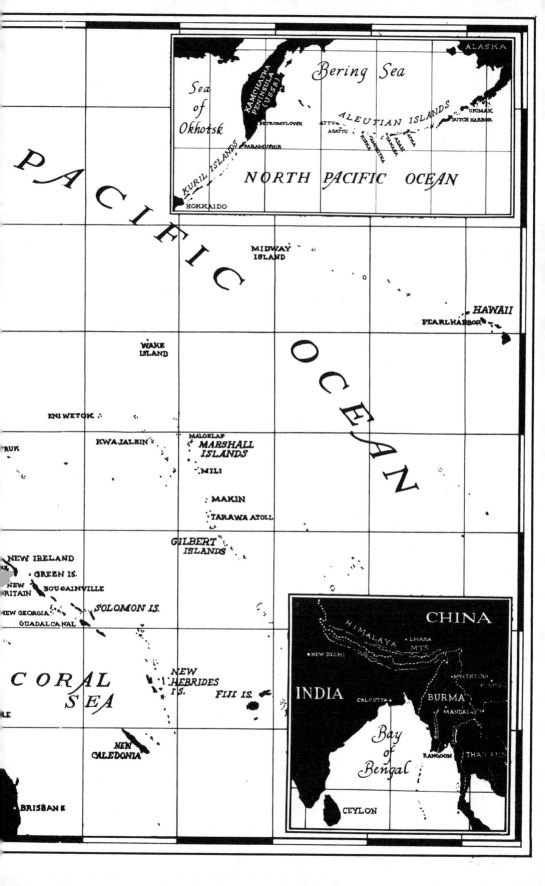

The Pacific War could not have been avoided, but we could have been better prepared to meet it. Unheeded were the signs of the times and the words of men as far back as the mid-1920's.

Prologue: Pacific Prophecy

IN APRIL 1926, 15 years before Pearl Harbor, Gen. William "Billy" Mitchell, outspoken advocate of air power, publicly warned of Japanese plans to seize Alaska, Hawaii and the Philippines. Amid jeers, laughs, and condemnations from his military superiors and private citizens he proclaimed that Japan was planning war against the United States.

A surprise aerial attack on Pearl Harbor, he said, would take place while Japanese negotiators would be talking peace with our officials behind closed doors. Moreover, it would come on a Sunday morning.

Two years previous to this, the controversial Mitchell completed a tour throughout the Pacific Ocean area and the Far East and, on October 24, 1924, he submitted a 325-page SECRET report* to the War Department. In view of history as it happened, the document is sadly prophetic. For here, 17 years before the Japanese sneak attack on Pearl Harbor, General Mitchell foresaw the war and spelled

out for his superiors how he thought the Japanese would start it.

Nobody paid any attention to Mitchell at the time. A year later he was court-martialed and forced to resign from the service. For 34 years this SECRET document lay buried in official files.

Here, from the yellowing, aged pages of the report, recently declassified, are brief excerpts of his 1924 Pacific prophecy:

". . . The rumblings of this coming strife have ceased to be audible whispers, but are the loud protests of the Japanese people, the vanguard of the Asiatic . . . Sooner or later the diplomatic means . . . will fail and a physical means of impressing our will on the hostile state will be the only recourse. In other words, war."

". . . The Japanese have specialized on their air force since 1918. They have taken the best European models and copied them, both in organization, training, and materiel. It now appears that the Japanese are probably the second air power

* *Report of Inspection of United States Possessions in the Pacific and Java, Singapore, India, Siam, China, and Japan* by Brig. Gen. Wm. Mitchell, Assistant Chief of Air Service, October 24, 1924.

1

in the world with between 600 and 800 airplanes in the hands of troops and reserves of personnel, materiel, and industry to maintain them. Their airways extend from their main islands to Korea, Manchuria, Formosa, north along the Kuriles and south via the Bonin Islands to the vicinity of Guam and possibly through the Palau, Caroline, and Marshall islands."

". . . Japan estimates that, if war comes, America will begin the war with the methods and systems of the last war. She is, therefore, preparing her whole war-making powers so that every advantage can be taken of new developments in the art of war. Her aviation is receiving first consideration as are also her submarines and light cruisers. All her plans are carefully worked out and kept up-to-date. She knows that war is coming some day with the United States and that it will be a contest of her very existence. The United States must not render herself completely defenseless by, on the one hand, thinking that a war with Japan is an impossibility, and on the other, sticking to methods and means of making war as obsolete as the bow and arrow is to the military rifle."

". . . I am convinced that the growing air power of Japan will be the decisive element in the mastery of the Pacific."

". . . Air operations for the destruction of Pearl Harbor will be undertaken . . . Aeronautical siege will then be inaugurated against all the Hawaiian Islands, and all vessels approaching will be attacked through the air or under the water."

". . . The [air] attack to be made on Ford's Island at 7:30 A.M. Route to be direct. Group to move in column of squadrons to vicinity of targets then to attack in column of flights in 'V'. . . . Actually nothing can stop it except air power. Oahu would be attacked from two sides."

"At the conclusion of the attack, bombardment will return . . . to make similar attack . . ."

"Japanese pursuit aviation will meet bombardment over Ford's Island. It will proceed by squadron, one at 3,500 feet altitude approaching Ford's Island from Kaena Point (west), one at 5,000 feet altitude from the east and down the sun's rays. Should hostile pursuit fail to appear or be destroyed, airdromes will be attacked with machine guns. The squadron on the alert will be held to defend the airdromes on Niihau. Listening and observation posts will extend as far as the coast of Oahu on submarines and sampans. Rallying point for pursuit: Barbers Point. Pursuit will be sure that bombardment has completed its mission before leaving the island of Oahu . . ."

". . . The defense of the Hawaiian Islands [1924] involves merely the defense of the island of Oahu alone against an attack by small boats landing troops from the ships. In this day and age it is an utterly ineffective method of defense because the shore defenses and the things useful in a military way can be easily destroyed by an enemy possessing control of the air. An attack of this kind would involve comparatively little effort and only a small part of the war-making resources of Japan."

". . . The Philippines would be attacked in a similar manner."

". . . The initial successes, as things stand now, would probably be with the Japanese."

The controversial air pioneer, Brig. Gen. William Mitchell, shown here in the cockpit of his plane at the Dayton Air Races in 1922 — two years before his prophetic prediction of the war with Japan.

3

Battleship Row, Pearl Harbor, several hours after the first Japanese attack.

PART ONE

RETREAT AND DEFEAT

America's military air arm lagged in the 1930's due to small budgets and officials who were unconvinced of the importance of military air power. Bulk of our heavy bomber force was the twin-engine B-18 shown above. It could not live in the air with Japanese fighters.

A Curtiss P-36. It comprised the bulwark of American fighter aircraft prior to Pearl Harbor. It was no match for the far superior Japanese fighters.

Introduction

GENERAL MITCHELL's prediction of the war with Japan seemed farfetched to most people in the early 1920's, but by the late 30's it was hardly fancy anymore.

Japanese armies and air forces invaded Manchuria in 1931 and the next year began to pour into China. Soon after, the Empire drew up ties with two militant and aggressive world powers, Germany and Italy. By this time Japanese arsenals bulged with air, sea, and ground forces fully equipped with weapons for war. Especially strong and modern were the carrier-and-land-based air forces.

In 1939, the Rome-Berlin-Tokyo Axis became a vibrant and dynamic military and political alliance with the implicit purpose of defeating the United States.

It was then, too, that the Japanese government announced a new national foreign policy called "The Greater East Asia Co-Prosperity Sphere," aimed at bringing all of Asia, Southeast Asia and the Pacific Islands under Japanese economic and political control. This bold and arrogant plan threatened the most vital American policies, interests, and holdings in the Far East and ran counter to U. S. "Open Door" China policy. The repercussions were immediate. Sale of U. S. aircraft to Japan was halted and

U. S. commercial treaties with the Empire were abrogated. The two great powers were heading pell-mell for a showdown. Every sign pointed to what Mitchell had predicted in 1924, and America was unprepared for it.

In the summer of 1939, Hitler invaded Poland. The clouds of war enveloped Europe and drifted menacingly across the horizons of the Far Pacific. Yet, when Maj. Gen. Henry H. "Hap" Arnold, Chief of the Army Air Corps, went up before Congress at that time to plead for more aircraft to bolster his puny Air Corps, he met the "$64 question":

"I want to ask you," shot a Congressman, "who are we going to fight?"

No statement could better illustrate our unpreparedness for war. Two decades of peace had lulled America into apathy and shortsightedness. Since World War I, air technology had projected a new element — air power — into military thinking, strategy and tactics. Surface forces could not exist in battle without control of the air overhead. Air power could play a decisive role in war. And if our leaders did not recognize it, there were those in other countries who did. America, the country that had discovered the mysteries of flight, was a fifth-rate world power in the air, trailing Germany, Japan, Italy and England.

Hap Arnold's Air Force of 1939 consisted of 26,000 men, 2,000 of whom were pilots, 2,600 mechanics. Of the 800 first-line aircraft, 700 were standard models all approaching obsolescence and unfit for combat. They were B-18 twin-engine bombers, A-17 light attack bombers and P-36 pursuits. In contrast, Japan had nearly 3,000 and Germany 4,100 first-line modern combat-ready aircraft. The September 1939 Air Corps had only 23 B-17 Flying Fortresses — our only modern air weapon! The Navy's air arm was no better off.

True, there had been plans and programs in military files, but precious little money to carry them out. A small step forward had been taken on January 12, 1939, when President Franklin D. Roosevelt called for a $300 million Air Corps expansion to include a limit of 6,000 planes. But it would take time to translate money and Congressional authorization into rolling assembly lines and trained aircrews.

Fortunately, American technological know-how had not lapsed between the two great wars, and on the drawing boards in the pre-World War II era were advanced models of modern combat aircraft. These included the P-39 "Aircobra," the P-40 "Kittyhawk and Tomahawk," the P-38 "Lightning," the gull-winged F4U "Corsair," the F4F "Wildcat," the SBD "Dauntless" dive bomber, the TBF "Avenger," and the TBF "Devasta-

tor"; the A-20 "Havoc" attack bomber; the B-25 "Mitchell" and B-26 "Marauder" tactical light bombers; the 4-engine B-17 "Flying Fortress," and B-24 "Liberator" — heavy bombers; and the C-47 "Skytrain" and the C-54 "Skymaster" transports. It is a tribute to our aeronautical scientists and engineers that many of these proved equal and some superior to the most advanced Japanese and German models, and would carry the brunt of the air war to successful conclusion.

Some of these aircraft would be ready by December of 1941, assuming money became available for their manufacture. Others would follow in the early years of the war. Still others, such as the P-47 "Thunderbolt," P-51 "Mustang" and the F6F "Hellcat" fighters and the B-29 "Superfortresses" would be largely "born" of the war and enter combat no earlier than 1943.

It was fortunate indeed that the war did not begin for America in 1939 as it did for Europe. We had time to change our attitudes toward military preparations, and change we did in a hurry, as the German Luftwaffe spearheaded the Nazi conquest of Europe.

In May of 1940, President Roosevelt called for a 50,000-plane Army and Navy Air Force, backed up by a 50,000 annual military aircraft production program. And in June, 1940, when Hap Arnold went back to Congress things had changed.

"All you have to do is ask for it,"

he was told, as Congress handed him a blank check.

Naval air chiefs met the same reception and the airmen of both services rolled up their sleeves and got to work. There were production contracts of all kinds to let, pilots to be trained by the tens of thousands, technical schools to be set up and manned, bases and facilities to be built, strategic and tactical plans to design. Ahead was a Herculean job and so little time left in which to do it, for the affairs of men were rapidly drifting toward the inevitable brink of war.

By December of 1941, the Army Air Corps was far from being ready to fight, yet it showed results of the emergency expansion. Sixty-seven combat groups had been developed with 18 deployed overseas; 28½ in the U. S. and 20½ in training. Officers and men had risen to 354,000, including 9,000 pilots and 69,000 mechanics. Aircraft strength had reached 2,846 first-line combat planes, although only 1,157 were equipped with modern weapons.

The Navy's air arm could muster only seven large and one small aircraft carrier, five patrol wings, two Marine aircraft wings, 5,900 pilots, 21,678 enlisted men and 5,233 aircraft of all types including trainers.

While the air buildup was beginning to show results, commitments to the Pacific took second place over the war in Europe.

Facing Japan on all fronts around the Pacific rim were but between 600 and 800 U.S. military aircraft.

The bulk of these were concentrated at two places, Hawaii and the Philippines, and on three Navy aircraft carriers of the Pacific Fleet, the *Lexington, Enterprise,* and *Saratoga.*

Bulwark of naval air power in the Pacific at the time of Pearl Harbor were the carriers *Lexington* (below), *Enterprise* and *Saratoga.* The Japanese erred greatly in not destroying them. It was the "Lex" and "Big E" that gave them their first defeat in the Coral Sea six months after Pearl Harbor.

In the Philippines, mainly at Clark and Nichols fields, Maj. Gen. Lewis H. Brereton, General MacArthur's Air Commander, had about 265 combat aircraft of which only 35 B-17's and 107 P-40's were first-line equipment. The remainder of the force was made up of 123 obsolete B-18's, P-35's, O-46's, O-52's, and a miscellaneous assortment of trainers. In addition there were the 1,200 officers and men of the 27th Bomb Group whose planes had not yet arrived.

Across the China Sea, on Formosan airfields alone, were more than twice this number of Japanese craft: 150 army bombers and 300 naval aircraft including 184 Zero fighters — a highly maneuverable 350 mph heavily armed fighter. Shrouded in oriental secrecy, the Zero was to become one of the greatest surprises of the war for U. S. flyers.

In Hawaii, on the island of Oahu, Maj. Gen. Frederick L. Martin's Hawaiian Air Force comprised some 231 aircraft — half of which were modern by combat standards of the time. The organizations included the 18th Bomb Wing at Hickam Field (B-17's), and the 14th Pursuit Wing (P-40's) at Haleiwa Field. Other types of planes included A-20's, P-36's, O-47's and B-18's — all largely obsolescent. An additional 169 shore-based naval observation and patrol aircraft added up to a total U. S. air strength in Hawaii on December 7, 1941, of about 400 aircraft.

Of the three Navy aircraft carriers of the Pacific Fleet, the *Lexington* and *Enterprise* were in Hawaiian waters, and the *Saratoga,* just out of dry-dock repairs, lay at anchor in San Diego.

The Japanese had a clear-cut 6 to 1 superiority in combat aircraft. However, considering the antiquity of most American planes, the odds were better than that. Little wonder they struck before the tremendous American production plans could get into high gear and massive reinforcements could pour onto Pacific air bases.

They had seen the first trickle begin. On May 13-14, 1941, Lt. Col. Eugene L. Eubank had brought 21 of the 19th Bomb Group's big B-17's to Hawaii on a record mass-overwater flight. In September of 1941, nine B-17's of the 14th Bomb Squadron (19th Bomb Group) under Maj. Emmett "Rosey" O'Donnell, Jr., arrived at Clark Field from Oahu, via Midway, Wake, New Guinea and Australia, in a historic route-pioneering flight which zigzagged around and occasionally through Japanese-held island territory. Following the same route, the whole 19th Group (35 B-17's) made the flight from California to Clark Field between October 22 and November 6, 1941. America's newest P-40 fighters, transported to the Philippines and Hawaii by Navy ships, began appearing on airfields in increasing numbers. Though small, these air reinforcements for the Pacific had begun, and they quickly showed up in Japanese intelligence reports.

Their arrival held ominous meaning for the Japanese. Formosa was within easy range of the B-17's. And the P-40's were far superior to the P-35's and P-36's which previously lined Philippine airfields.

The Japanese warlords now knew that they had to move before these newly arrived units were joined by others and became fully operational. They had to strike suddenly and decisively. Their master plan called for military conquest of the Pacific and without control of the air it could not succeed.

And so it was that in the early morning of December 7, 1941, a Japanese carrier task force, which had secretly moved to a position 200 miles north of Oahu, Hawaii, launched 183 planes at 6:00 A.M. At 7:55 this first wave struck Hickam and Wheeler fields, the naval bases at Kaneohe and Ford Island, and the seven battleships tied up like ducks in a row at Pearl Harbor. An hour later the second wave of 170 planes swept down upon the bases.

Ten hours later, flying from Formosa, 108 Japanese bombers accompanied by 84 Zero fighters repeated their brilliant surprise performance in the Philippines. In a quick one-two punch, masterfully planned and executed, Japan destroyed the major American air strength in the Pacific.

Fortunately, the two Navy aircraft carriers, *Lexington* and *Enterprise,* were on the high seas between Hawaii and Wake and Midway islands. The enemy would have done well to plan their destruction too, for it was these two flattops which handed the enemy their first major defeat in the South Pacific within six months, and set the pattern for fast-striking Navy carrier air task forces.

In lightning-like fashion the flood of conquest began. For six months the Japanese swept everything before them with ease. Air attack spearheaded advances on land and sea. American-held islands of Guam and Wake fell within a few days of each other. The British battle cruiser *Repulse* and the battleship *Prince of Wales,* were ignominiously sunk off the Malayan coast by swarms of Japanese land-based bombers and torpedo planes when they ventured out of the British naval base of Singapore — victims of Japanese air superiority. Americans, British, Dutch and Australians were driven south from one line of defense to another as the Japanese military machine swept into the Dutch East Indies, Java, Borneo, the Celebes, and southeast into the Admiralty Islands, New Guinea, and the Solomons up to the very gates of Australia. Filtering through Malayan jungles, they captured the "impregnable" fortress of Singapore on February 15, 1942. Japanese armies and air forces poured into Indochina, through Thailand, and seized Rangoon, Burma on March 8, 1942. Heading northward they overran most of Burma, cut the Burma road and isolated China from her supply lifeline.

In six months the Japanese warlords had carved out a rich and sprawling empire — rich in the oil and natural resources which an industrial society needed, and sprawling over hundreds of sparsely populated islands into which could stream the bursting population of the homeland.

These were the dark days of the war, the days of defeat and retreat for America and her Allies. But the expanded Empire, accrued through a string of brilliant tactical victories, contained one basic strategic flaw. The long sea-lanes which held it together were vulnerable to air attack. Unless the Japanese could maintain air supremacy over all their gains and the air and shipping lifelines which held them together, the Empire would inevitably disintegrate under them. It was a flaw that would prove fatal.

Thus was the Pacific War tailormade for air power, and air power would play a decisive role in winning it.

"The initial success," wrote Mitchell in 1924, "would be with the Japanese."

It was in the initial Japanese successes that our airmen fell back. They fought courageously with what they had, but it simply wasn't enough.

Bound for Pearl Harbor, a Japanese torpedo plane takes off from its carrier's deck as ground crew waves from bridge.

12

Despite repeated warnings from Washington in November, 1941, that the Japanese were planning a surprise attack somewhere in the Pacific, military life and duty in Hawaii remained largely on a "business and pleasure as usual" basis. No one in Hawaii dreamed the Japanese would strike an island 3,500 nautical miles from their own homeland. Certainly, they reasoned, if further Japanese aggression did take place, it would be in Southeast Asia somewhere.

The only airplanes which the Duty Officers in Hawaii expected on early Sunday morning, December 7, 1941, were two flights of 12 B-17's (six in each flight) of the 38th and 88th Reconnaissance Squadrons arriving from California. These air reinforcements for the Philippines were being ferried without ammunition, with their armor replaced by extra fuel tanks necessary for the 2,392-mile leg from California, and with their guns still packed in manufacturer's cosmoline.

Little did the two flight commanders, Maj. Truman Landon (later a four-star Air Force general) and Maj. Richard H. Carmichael, realize as they left California with their formations on the evening of December 6, that they were off on a combat mission. The pilots and crews looked forward to a short stopover in beautiful Hawaii, 14 hours away.

A Quiet Sunday Morning

Clive Howard and Joe Whitley

AT SUNSET, on the evening of December 6, 1941, a formation of Flying Fortresses soared out over San Francisco, wheeled slowly like giant birds and gradually settled on a course straight across the Pacific toward far-flung Manila; first stop, Hawaii.

Some 6,000 miles of sky flecked with clouds and sea specked with islands bridge the space between California and the Philippines. The rock and coral and jungle buttresses of this vast and invisible structure lie so far apart that a long-range bomber on an island-to-island flight, even with miraculous navigation and no head winds, was scraping the bottom of its fuel tanks when it landed.

But the longest gap of all is between San Francisco and Honolulu, 2,392 miles, with not a rock, not so much as a coral reef, to mar one of the greatest stretches of unbroken blue water on the earth.

The B-17's were airborne more than 12 hours when the fingers of dawn ripped through the cellophane of night. The bomber crews peered eagerly through the clouds scudding beneath them for a sight of land. There was nothing but the tumbling horizon. Far to the west, Oahu, like its sister islands, was still wrapped in darkness and silent in slumber.

Yet, even at this early hour, some men on the island were awake and active. One of these was an engineer in a Honolulu broadcasting station who, throughout the night, had been playing records of Hawaiian music to provide a homing beam for the incoming bombers.

Another was Col. William E. Farthing, base commander at Hickam Field. It was a new thing in December, 1941 — this mass flight of giant land planes across 2,000 miles of black ocean between sunset in California and sunrise in Hawaii; new enough to keep a busy, worried base commander awake most of the night and to send him down to the control tower before full daylight, just to see the big ships come in.

It was a few minutes past five when Colonel Farthing stepped from his quarters into the morning freshness. Except for the eternal mists rolling along the towering Koolau Range, the sky was cloudless. A soft wind stirred the palm leaves. The Colonel thought never in the Islands had he seen a dawn so beautiful as this one promised to be.

It was Sunday, the seventh day of December, 1941.

On a lonely hill called Opana, high above the lush green table of land that rises in gentle terraces to the Koolau Ridge, two young soldiers rubbed their eyes and yawned sleepily. The luminous dial of the alarm clock in their tent showed it to be 3:45 A.M. Except for the mynah birds, scolding from the bushes, they were the only evidence of life in that vast panorama of sea and land.

But to Tech. Third Class Joe Lockard and Pvt. George Elliott, nothing was beautiful. They had, to their way of thinking, one of the worst jobs in the Army.

They had slept the night, as they had slept every other night for the past three months, in a tent beside a paneled Army truck containing the instrument known technically as an SCR 270-B Radio Direction Finder. Before the first faint flush of dawn, the two men were grumbling through the business of the day, which was to probe a wide area of the sea with radio waves sent out from their finder. The theory was that, up to a certain distance, if the radio waves encountered anything that shouldn't have been there — like a Japanese battleship, say — they would bounce back again and make a disturbance called a "pip" on a screen called an oscilloscope. At five other widely separated spots on the island, other grumbling members of the Signal Aircraft Company (Hawaii) went about similar duties.

Nobody in Hawaii knew much about SCR 270-B. On Thanksgiving Day, an alert had been called and, by superhuman efforts, all six stations had been kept in continuous operation until December 3. Then, as men grumbled and parts began to break down, it was decided to man all stations from an hour before daylight to an hour after sunrise, from four o'clock to seven o'clock. That made it just perfect for griping.

Shortly before six o'clock, Private Elliott walked over to Lockard who was staring into the oscilloscope.

"Any pips today?" he asked brightly.

Lockard stared at him sourly. No pips today. No pips yesterday. Not a single pip, in fact, in the three months Lockard had spent sweating out the oscilloscope.

By now, full daylight had come, and the few people who were abroad to see the sun, as it burst brilliantly through the swirling Hawaiian mists, met more than their number of stragglers coming in from leave. Military duties had been cut to a minimum consistent with the alert. It was the first Sunday after payday and Honolulu was a good liberty town.

The minute hand of the clock on the wall of the Hickam Control Tower stood at exactly forty-five minutes after five when Colonel Farthing came up the stairs at a lively clip. Besides the regular crew, Col. Cheney L. Bertholf, adjutant general of the Hawaiian Air Forces, was in the lookout post this particular morning.

"Morning, Cheney!" Farthing exclaimed. "What's the matter? Couldn't you sleep either?"

"No, Bill. I wanted to see them come in, too. They should be in around eight-thirty," Bertholf said.

An Army sedan which bore the markings of the base hospital moved down the hangar line and pulled up near the tower. Inside was Capt. Anthony D'Alfonso, medical officer of the day. "This will do," he said yawning. "Got the guns loaded?"

The driver, an enlisted man, reported the guns ready for use.

The "guns" were flit guns. It was the duty of the medical officer of the day to spray incoming planes against insect pests. D'Alfonso, too, was waiting for the Fortresses. He settled back luxuriously against the sedan cushions for a nap until the bombers came.

It was exactly seven o'clock when, on Opana Hill, Lockard and Elliott banged shut the last panel door of their radar truck, turned the last key and looked around for the truck that was to take them down the mountain and to breakfast. No truck. They looked down the narrow, rutted road that they and other members of the signal company had built with their hands and sweat on Thanksgiving Day. Still no truck in sight. Therefore, no breakfast.

Lockard swore. "Of all the stinking jobs in this man's Army — " He turned back toward the radar truck.

"Hey," Elliot exclaimed. "Where you going?"

"I'm supposed to give you training, ain't I?" Lockard growled over his shoulder. "Well, here's your chance."

It was two minutes after seven by the time the generator had turned up to operating efficiency. Lockard peered into the 6-inch cathode ray which forms the oscilloscope. He couldn't believe what he saw.

For the first time in three months of waiting and watching, something was happening. A "pip" jumped up, so big it seemed to hit him right in the eye.

"George!" Lockard yelled. "Hey, George! Lookit here!"

Elliott came running in from outside. He didn't know much; he didn't have to. There it was. A baby would have dropped his bottle and reached for that shadowy image shooting up and down.

"What is it?" he gasped.

"What do you think it is, coming in at 150 miles an hour — a fleet of milk wagons? It's planes, lots of 'em."

"Mark!" Lockard commanded.

Elliott ran for a sheet of transparent paper and placed it over the map which lay beside Lockard.

"Mark! Time, 7:02. Miles 136. That's where I caught it first."

Elliott made quick notations on the transparent paper.

"Joe, what d'ya s'pose they are, those planes?"

"How should I know? Navy planes, maybe — off a carrier."

Lockard reached for the telephone. It wasn't, as he knew, his business to worry about what caused the disturbance. In the language of the soldier, whoever was looking into the 'scope when a pip occurred would know that something was happening and would telephone a place over at Fort Shafter called the Information Center, and something would be done about it by somebody else.

Lockard jiggled the hook of the telephone furiously. No one answered and he took another look into the 'scope.

"Mark! 7:04. 132."

"7:04. 132."

Lockard banged the receiver hook up and down. "Somebody's got to answer," he bellowed.

"Joe! Joe McDonald!" he yelled into the mouthpiece. "Joe! Joe McDonald."

Sweat greased the palm of Lockard's hand and the telephone slid almost from his grasp. "Joe!" he shouted. "Joe McDonald!" Then, as the instrument on the other end clicked into life, Lockard sighed with relief: "Is that you, Joe?"

"Yeah, this is McDonald," an unexcited voice came back over the telephone.

"Joe, it's Joe Lockard! Lockard, at Opana! I gotta get someone at the Information Center. It's important."

"There ain't nobody there," McDonald's voice came calm and unconcerned. "They closed at seven."

"Listen Joe," Lockard pleaded, "I got to talk to an officer. I may get in trouble for this. Be a pal. Grab somebody. Anybody! Any officer at all!"

There was a silence while Lockard and Elliott watched the 'scope, fascinated. The pip continued to flare violently up and down, the intervals lessening as whatever caused it to appear sped closer and closer toward the station.

Suddenly, the telephone came to life. A new voice, crisp and authoritative, cut in: "This is Lieutenant Tyler, the watch officer."

"Sir," said Lockard in a rush, "this is Opana SCR. A large fleet of planes appeared on the 'scope, time 7:02, miles 136, azimuth zero to 10 degrees. They have been coming toward this station ever since. At 7:04, our last reading, they were at 132.

"7:04. 132."

There was a long silence, then: "I see."

Lockard and Elliott waited tensely. Then the voice again. "OK. It's OK. That's all."

The Hickam Field Control Tower rose about 50 feet above the ground and from this height the crew had a broad view of Pearl Harbor and the channel which swept down past Fort Kamehameha to the sea, now clearly visible in the morning light.

Colonel Farthing was standing against the tower window, idly scanning the sky with a pair of binoculars. He swung the glasses momentarily over into Pearl Harbor and picked up the dark outlines which crowded the water — more battleships, cruisers and destroyers than, in his 15 months at Hickam, he had ever seen in Pearl Harbor. The Colonel's glasses moved out to sea and paused on a freighter, dark against the water, which crept in from the direction of Barbers Point. The glasses moved over the horizon, then swung abruptly back to the freighter.

"Hello, what's that?"

"What?" asked Bertholf.

"That freighter. She got her landing gear swung outboard and there's a destroyer heading for her, blinking her lights. What's she saying?"

"W——h——o?" spelled out a radio operator of the tower crew. "The destroyer's blinker is saying "W——h——o!"

"That's funny," said Farthing, watching through the glasses. "That destroyer is rushing in as though she meant business."

At their radar truck near the tip of the island, Lockard and Elliott plotted the incoming flight until, 22 miles out, they lost it in the permanent "echo" of their own radio. Until then, the radar showed the planes speeding directly toward them, straight as bullets truly aimed.

At 7:30 exactly, the truck came to take them down to breakfast. As Lockard and Elliott hurriedly shut up shop again, the planes they had been plotting must have passed directly over their heads, high in the air. They neither saw nor heard them.

At 7:55, from their eyrie high in the control tower, Colonel Farthing and Colonel Bertholf saw a long thin line of planes approaching from Kauai way.

Navy peashooters? Marine planes?

On the third attack, 16 enemy planes hit the barracks, parade grounds and other buildings at Hickam Field in an eight-minute foray. Photo was taken during the attack. Japanese pilots tried to destroy the flagpole but narrowly missed. Ripped by machine-gun fire, the American flag continued to fly throughout the holocaust.

Farthing was startled out of his first observation by the sharp dart-like plunge of the line toward Pearl Harbor.

"Darned realistic maneuvers! Wonder what the Marines are doing to the Navy so early today?"

Farthing was following them with his binoculars. They weren't Marine planes. Nor Navy. Nor Army. These were single-engined with fixed undercarriages!

A short, thick, black object fell from the first plane. Another.

Bombs!

The plane zoomed and two orange-red disks flashed in the glare of the morning sun.

"Japs."

The word was drowned in the roar as the first bomb exploded the battleship *Arizona*.

EDITOR'S NOTE: The two flights of B-17's approached Hawaii around 8:00 on the morning of December 7, 1941, completely oblivious of what was happening there.

Coming out of an overcast, 150 miles

18

The price of unpreparedness. This shattered P-40 was one of some 70 planes destroyed on the line at Wheeler Air Base.

Most of the B-17's arriving from San Francisco during the height of the attack landed safely, but crew members were strafed as they ran to shelter. Here some of them sort out baggage at Hickam Field after the attack.

north of Oahu, Landon's plane ran smack into a flight of eight dive bombers, heading north. These curious craft had "red meatball" insignia and they made a firing pass at the B-17, raking it with a hail of bullets. Landon was stupefied, frozen with disbelief. Japs! This close to Hawaii! He poured full throttle, pulled back up into the overcast. The other B-17's in the two flights met similar startling Japanese reception. With no advance warning, low on gas, without armor, there was nothing to do but let down and land on the battered airfields in the midst of the attack. This they did. Nine landed at Hickam, two at Haleiwa, and one on a golf course after being chased around the island of Oahu by a Japanese fighter. On landing, the crews leaped from their aircraft as the big birds rolled to a stop and ran for anything that offered protection. One of the B-17's was completely destroyed, two badly damaged.

Following the attack, confused intelligence flashes reported the Japanese carrier fleet at various points around Hawaii. Flyable AAF aircraft (P-40's, O-47's, P-36's, A-20's) made 48 sorties between 9:30 A.M. and 3:20 P.M. without finding the Japanese fleet. Major Landon's report of the Jap planes he encountered 150 miles north of Oahu suggested the fleet lay in that direction. It was noon, however, before nine Navy dive bombers were finally sent on a scouting patrol 200 miles to the north, but by then the Japanese fleet was long gone, speeding back to the safety of the Inland Sea of Japan.

The Japanese had left behind a scene of destruction. The attack had destroyed 87 out of 169 naval aircraft; 152 out of 231 AAF planes. Personnel casualties were tragic: 2,086 Navy officers and men killed, or fatally wounded, 749 wounded; 218 Army personnel killed. One hundred and sixty-three Air Force men were killed, 43 missing, and 336 wounded.

Japanese statistics were brighter: 324 aircraft returned to their carriers; 29 planes and 55 Jap flyers had been lost in the attack, although an additional 50 of the returning planes had crash-landed on the carrier decks.

It was a brilliantly executed plan that called for high rejoicing in Japan. In America it was a day that had come apart at the seams.

The vaunted Japanese Zero fighter appeared in every major battle of the Pacific War. First flight-tested in 1939, it had many model variants, most famous being the carrier-based which appeared over Pearl Harbor. The Zero controlled the skies until the Battle of Midway in June, 1942.

Ten hours after the first Japanese bombs had fallen on Hawaii, a "second Pearl Harbor" occurred, this time in the Philippines.

From Number 1 Victoria Street in the walled portion of the city of Manila, General MacArthur commanded American ground and air forces in the Pacific.

It was here that Gen. Lewis Brereton, Commander of the Far East Air Forces under MacArthur, headed several hours after the first word of Pearl Harbor hit the Philippines. It was 5:00 A.M., December 8, 1941. He asked MacArthur for permission to send his entire two squadrons of B-17 Fortresses (based at Clark Field near Manila) against Japanese airfields on Formosa — from whence, in all probability, air attacks on the Philippines would come.

Since news of scattered Japanese air strikes on outlying Philippine Islands had not yet reached MacArthur's headquarters, General Brereton's request was denied. MacArthur declared we couldn't attack until fired upon. To General Brereton and his staff of air officers, this was incredible.

Shortly after 10:00 A.M. on December 8, warning of an approaching Jap air armada of 192 bombers and fighters reached Clark Field. Lt. Col. Eugene Eubank ordered all B-17's and the two squadrons of P-40 fighters to get airborne immediately so that they would not be caught on the ground as were the planes at Pearl Harbor. The crews took off and flew aimlessly around the local area. About an hour later the alert was dubbed "false alarm." As the bombers and fighters landed, word came to Clark field from MacArthur's headquarters authorizing a strike against Japanese airfields on Formosa.

Plans got under way immediately for a strike at dusk, but hardly had they begun when Iba Field, a small grass fighter strip on the coast 40 miles across the mountains from Clark, spotted on their radar a Jap bomber and fighter force approaching from the direction of Formosa. Iba flashed the message immediately to all fields in Luzon. But for reasons, including confusion, bad radio and teletype communications and sabotage, Clark Field never got the word. At other bases, however, such as Nielson and Nichols, fighter pilots were ordered into the air or on cockpit alert at the end of the strip. There was one exception — Del Carmen Field. Here a squadron of P-35's failed to receive orders to patrol over Clark Field.

The fighters that did get aloft, restlessly orbited their home fields, waiting for the Japs. Suddenly a message crackled through the earphones, "Tallyho! Bandits Over Clark." Twelve P-40's from Nichols swung around and headed for Clark, only to be called back by their commander. A flight of Iba Field P-40's, in sight of Clark, saw nothing unusual, and headed toward home.

So it was that on December 8, 1941, at 12:30 P.M., noon hour at Clark

21

Field, not one fighter was flying cover for the neatly parked rows of B-17 Flying Fortresses and the P-40 fighters.

No one at Clark could know that hell would descend from the heavens in ten minutes. And in the mess hall, mechanics and aircrews were enjoying a meal, satirically joking about the "rumors" going around that the Japanese had attacked Pearl Harbor.

"Tallyho! Bandits Over Clark!"

John Toland

THE FIRST of the two flights of Japanese bombers were then within sight of Clark. In fact, their crews had spotted the mass of B-17's shining in the bright sun, from Tarlac. Their prey was ridiculously obvious, sitting out in the great, unprotected central Luzon plain. As an extra guidepost, Mt. Arayat, 15 miles east of the field, stuck up like a huge traffic marker. No one could miss this 3,867-foot lonely peak standing in the middle of miles of plain, its cone dented, according to native lore, when Noah's Ark landed.

Now, the neat outlines of Fort Stotsenberg became distinct to the bomber pilots with its white buildings, lines of acacia and mango trees and the big polo field. A mile east stretched Clark Field. Not a single protecting pursuit plane was above it. At first the Japanese pilots couldn't believe what they saw: rows and rows of parked P-40's and Flying Fortresses. It was incredible luck. Almost ten hours after Pearl Harbor every plane based at Clark was a helpless, sitting target.

The second flight of 27 old-type "Nell" bombers swung in behind the leading Bettys. Suddenly 36 Zero fighters were hovering above the bombers like shepherds. Everything was working with precision. It was 12:35 P.M.

George Setzer, who had the taxi concession at Fort Stotsenberg, was just driving out the gate. Hearing a growing roar, he stopped the car. He and his daughter, Stella, got out. They saw a mass of silver planes coming from the northwest.

"It's about time they came to help us," he said joyfully.

On the perimeter of the airfield, New Mexican National Guardsmen of the 200th Coast Artillery were having lunch or just loafing around their 37-mm. and 3-inch antiaircraft guns. They, too, thought the approaching bombers were friendly. At the cry, "Here comes the Navy," Sgt. Dwaine Davis, of Carlsbad, grabbed the movie camera bought from company funds and began taking pictures.

"Why are they dropping tin foil?" asked someone.

"That's not tin foil and those are Japs!"

Just then there was a sound as of rushing freight trains.

At the west end of the field, a crew chief of the 20th Pursuit Squadron was standing in front of the operations tent. He looked up. "Yonder they come!" he shouted.

Hearing this, Lt. Joe Moore, the squadron commander, raced for his P-40. Followed by six others, he quickly taxied into position. He shot into the air, swung wide and started a maximum power climb. Two others got into the air, but the last four planes were hit by bombs.

Corp. Douglas Logan, a B-17 gunner and cameraman, was at Headquarters Building watching Maj. Birrell Walsh conduct the briefing for the photographic mission over Formosa at a blackboard. Just left of Logan stood Colonel Eubank, the bomber commander. Logan saw him look absently out the window at the sky and turn away. The corporal looked out and saw men running frantically on the field.

Eubank, realizing what he had seen, jumped back to the window, then yelled, "Take cover, men! Here they come!"

As everyone headed for the rear door a stick of bombs exploded. The last to reach the door was Logan. Suddenly the floor pitched. Logan flopped. As he rolled toward a corner he in-stinctively put his hands up to cover his face.

The air-raid siren was now wailing. Someone shouted to get out of the hangars. Men began to saunter out. Above they saw planes in a great V. It was such a beautiful formation, they were thrilled — until they realized bombs were falling on the P-40's and B-17's at the far end of the field. They dove for the trenches, recently built by the base commander, Lt. Col. Lester Maitland, and till now chidingly referred to as "Maitland's Folly."

At the west end of the runway, Corp. Durwood Brooks, a combat radio operator, was sprawled on his bunk when he heard the first bombs fall. He sprang up and ran into the latrine. Then he yelled and ran outside toward a row of slit trenches. They were filled with white-clad cooks. He looked up and saw three V's, forming one great V. It was so perfect it was beautiful. He watched in fascination until a bomb hit 100 yards away. He was shocked. Someone was trying to kill him. He ran to the library and hid behind a heavy wooden piling. Every time a bomb hit he seemed to rise a foot in the air.

Except for the bombs dropped on the pursuit planes about to take off, the raiders were concentrating on hangars, shops and buildings. Anti-aircraftsmen of the New Mexico National Guard were shooting 37-mm. and 3-inch guns at the passing formations. It was the first time most of the men had fired live ammunition. Much of their training in the United States had been with broomsticks and boxes or wooden models. And even if their bursts were exploding far below the targets, it was satisfying and somehow exhilarating to shoot finally in earnest.

At Fort Stotsenberg, cavalrymen were standing under mango trees with their horses. They were proud of their mounts. Not one had panicked even though the ground shook from reverberations, and flak from Clark Field clattered down on all sides.

Maj. Gen. Jonathan "Skinny" Wainwright was watching the bombing from outside his headquarters. His houseboy ran to him, eyes big with terror. He was wearing the General's steel helmet. "General, what shall I do?" he asked.

"Go get me a bottle of beer," yelled the General above the din. A moment later his aide, Capt. Tom Dooley, drove up.

"Tom, you darn fool," shouted Wainwright angrily. "You didn't drive past Clark during this bombing, did you?"

"You sent me orders to report as fast as I could."

Wainwright walked into his headquarters and wrote Dooley an order for a Silver Star.

Abruptly the bombing of Clark stopped. Corporal Brooks dazedly walked toward the flight line. The idea of war was new and terrifying. Bodies and parts of bodies were lying all over. In a slit trench he saw two Filipino pin boys. They were good friends, killed by someone who hadn't even seen them. Brooks couldn't figure it out. Then he saw another friend, a Polish boy of 19. By some freak he was blown up like a balloon by an explosive bullet and to Brooks looked almost transparent.

Others staggered from the trenches. In the sudden silence the groans of the wounded could be heard. Many of the buildings were burning. The big oil dump blazed, sending dark rolls of smoke across the field.

As Colonel Eubank started a hurried inspection of the group, the two B-17's being painted were taxied unharmed out of their burning hangar. Eubank learned only a few of the Flying Fortresses parked on the field were damaged. His bombers had been saved by a miracle.

Lt. Joe Moore was now about 20,000 feet above Clark in his P-40 with Lt. Randall Keator on his tail. Trailing half a mile behind and 3,000 feet below was Lt. Edwin Gilmore, the third of the pursuit pilots to take off successfully from Clark. Nine Zeros suddenly swooped down on Gilmore. Moore and Keator jumped the Japanese. Almost instantly Keator shot down a Zero. It was the first American kill over the Philippines. A moment later, Moore found a Japanese in his sights. As Moore pulled the trigger, he wondered how it would feel to shoot live ammunition. Up until now it had been forbidden because of its scarcity. A Zero blew up in his face. He dove

These Republic P-35's, shown here on maneuvers in the Philippines before Pearl Harbor, were no match for the speedy, highly maneuverable Japanese Zeros.

on another target. There was a second explosion.

Pilots of the 34th Pursuit Squadron in Carmen, 14 miles to the south, saw smoke rising from Clark Field. Without orders they took off in their worn P-35's. Before they reached Clark several Zeros confidently attacked the much larger American group. Easily outmaneuvering the outdated 35's, the Japanese drove them off.

At 12:40 P.M. the 12 P-40's of Flight A and C were still circling over their field at Iba, looking anxiously for raiders. Suddenly over their radios they heard a hysterical voice shouting,

"All pursuits to Clark Field! All pursuits to Clark! Enemy bombers overhead!" Then they heard the crash of bombs in their headsets. They raced to the east.

Standing near the strip at Iba, Second Lt. Glenn Cave watched the P-40's disappear. A moment later at 12:44 P.M. another pilot said, "Look at that pretty formation of B-17's."

Cave looked to the west. He counted 52 planes in perfect formation at 13,000 feet. "You're crazy," he said, "there aren't that many B-17's in the Philippines." Black objects started wobbling from the planes. The two pilots dove into one of the few fox-holes on the beach. Cave landed first, the other man on top of him. As bombs exploded and the earth shook he was glad he was the man on the bottom.

At that moment the six Iba planes of B Flight which had flown to Manila and returned when they heard the mysterious false alarm from Clark were innocently approaching their home field for landing. The control tower frantically called the incoming planes, warning of the bombers high overhead, but the radios of the P-40's were jammed.

As the first plane touched down, Second Lt. Andy Krieger, pilot of the plane flying cover for the other five, saw the field explode in a great blinding flash. Krieger climbed away so fast he had to level off at 10,000 feet to let his engine cool. Looking down he saw what looked like a squadron of P-35's circling the field. They were crazy to try and land on that bombed-out strip. Then he saw they had big red spots on the wings — Japanese! He dove into their circle, and shot at the plane ahead. When tracers suddenly zipped past him, he turned and saw three Zeros on his tail.

On the field below, Cave also thought the planes swooping down were P-35's. Red lights on the wings were blinking. Cave was puzzled. Suddenly bullets spattered in the sand. He finally realized he was being strafed. He heard a deep rumble. Another flight of bombers was making its run. This time the other man got to the bottom of the foxhole first. Cave looked at his legs sticking up and wondered if they'd be hit.

Halfway to Clark, the other Iba pursuit planes heard Lieutenant Krieger call, "All 3rd Pursuit to Iba." Half of the 12 planes turned back. But Lt. Fred Roberts and five other Iba pursuit pilots flew headlong into the Zero fighters preparing to dive onto Clark Field. Almost out of gas, three Americans were quickly shot down. To Roberts' amazement the Japanese planes were faster, more maneuverable and climbed at a terrifying rate. How could these possibly be Japanese? He and other pilots had been told there was no such thing as a good Japanese fighter plane.

He didn't know, of course, that exact data on these Zeros had been sent to the War Department by the brilliant, unorthodox Claire Chennault in the fall of 1940. The chief of the Flying Tigers had also revealed how the heavier P-40 could master the faster Zero, but this information, which could have saved the lives of bewildered American pilots dying that moment, had been filed and forgotten. Chennault was not at all popular with Air Corps commanders.

Holes appeared in Roberts' wings. Suddenly a cable at his feet was shot out. He felt a sting in his leg, then numbness. The needle of his gas gauge wobbled near empty. He pulled sharply to the west, heading for Iba.

As he crossed the Zambales Mountains, smoke was rising from his home field. Tiny objects, obviously Japanese strafers, were diving and circling, but he had to come in. As he approached the field he tried to lower his wheels. Something was wrong. As he swung in behind a two-place Japanese fighter, the man in its rear began blinking a red light at him. Roberts loosed a burst and turned out to sea. With only ten gallons of fuel, he decided to beach his plane. He headed toward the water at 120 miles an hour, then realized he'd misjudged the distance. He was too high. He quickly nosed down, crashing into the surf 50 yards from shore.

He swam to the beach. The barracks was burning. So were other buildings, and a gas truck. He heard a pig squeal and looked toward what had been the village of Iba. All the nipa shacks were blazing; palm trees were mowed down; carts were tipped over; horses lay dead, feet in the air. Children screamed in terror. Filipinos were moaning, "Help me, Joe."

The strip was a mass of craters. Several P-40's were crackling. The radar shack was a shambles, its operators killed. The control tower was riddled with bullets, its crew of four dead.

Disaster had struck suddenly. Iba was completely destroyed and most of the survivors were in a state of shock. The coolest man was not a combat pilot but the young flight surgeon,

Lt. Frank Richardson. Taking charge, he commandeered a bus, quickly loaded the wounded, and headed for Manila.

Back at Clark, as the survivors stared unbelieving at the wreckage, there was a cry, "Here come the strafers!"

The Zeros which had been circling far above the bombers were diving. Their main targets were the big Flying Fortresses and P-40's parked on the field. Soon they were joined by 44 of the 53 Zeros from Iba, now looking for new targets. One by one the parked Fortresses exploded with great roars as tracers ignited their gas tanks.

"Get in the woods," shouted an officer to men in the big ditch near the main hangar. Several dozen men scrambled out of the deep straight ditch and headed for the nearby woods as three Zeros swept over, riddling the area.

A score of white-coated Chinese dashed out of Charlie Corn's PX restaurant. A Zero swooped and the ground was instantly white with their bodies. Close by, Corporal Brooks was looking helplessly for quick shelter. He threw himself at a shallow ditch, digging frantically with hands and feet as two Zeros dove at him, their bullets squealing past. He ran to a deeper ditch and jumped onto a master sergeant.

"Excuse me," he said.

"Never mind," said the sergeant. "That's just one more it has to go through to get at me."

In a nearby trench an antique water-cooled .30-caliber machine gun was pitting bullets at the strafers. A youthful mechanic was pumping it to keep it cool. After the first wave passed, the young man still kept pumping frantically as if in a trance.

A truck swung by, blood dripping out of the sides. It was filled with wounded heading for the Fort Stotsenberg Hospital. Other wounded were talking dazedly, eyes blank.

The Zeros now had little opposition except from the machine guns of the 200th Field Artillery, and the 192nd and 184th Tank Battalions. When the water-cooled barrels of the artillerymen's old Brownings burned out, the gunners grabbed rifles and shot at the swooping Zeros.

As suddenly as it started the attack was over. Great black clouds of smoke covered the field. All the parked P-40's and 30 medium bombers and observation planes were burning. All but three of the Flying Fortresses were completely destroyed. In one raid the Japanese navy airmen had knocked out half of MacArthur's Far East Air Force.

The P-40 was America's best in the air at the outbreak of war. Although not as fast or maneuverable as the Zero, better trained American pilots capitalized on its armor and speed. There were just not enough of them in the early days of the war.

Wind and rain the next day prevented Japanese follow-up attacks on Clark Field, and during the night of Dec. 9, 1941, 14 B-17's flew into Clark from Del Monte Field, Mindanao Island. The next day these Fortresses struck at large Japanese invasion convoys headed for the Philippines, and that night returned to Del Monte Field.

On the 10th, Jap Zeros strafed Del Carmen, destroying all the fighters on the field. Less than an hour later, an overwhelming force of 100 bombers and 150 fighters swept over Nichols Field and the Cavite Naval Base. By the night of the 10th, General Brereton had only 17 B-17's left out of 35 originally; 12 were operational, all now at Del Monte Field in Mindanao (out of range of Jap Formosa-based bombers). In fighters there were only 22 P-40's and 15 P-35's, based mainly at Clark and Nichols fields. In addition, about 25 miscellaneous aircraft had escaped the Japanese bombing, mainly B-10 and B-18 bombers — all old obsolescent equipment.

Episode at Vigan

Walter D. Edmonds

THE PURSUITS were no longer flying under squadron organization; but two pools of flyers and planes had been set up at Clark and Nichols fields respectively. The ground crews serviced the planes as they came in and the pilots took the missions in rotation. They were, for the most part, the older, more experienced men, and the missions were mainly reconnaissance. The whole of Luzon was covered each day: the planes from Clark Field taking care of the northern section and those from Nichols flying the southern beats, to Legaspi, out over the island passages, and Mindoro.

The P-40's generally went in pairs but many missions had to be undertaken by a single plane; and these long and solitary flights through skies dominated by the enemy put a heavy strain on the pilot. Even when he was well clear of areas of Japanese activity, the mountains with their sudden storms, the strangeness of the green jungle, and the little nipa-roofed shacks suddenly encountered in their tiny clearings, served to emphasize the pilot's own loneliness. But for many of them it was the overwater flying that was hardest to get used to. If a pilot went down then, it was for keeps; for even if he managed to get free of his plane, there were the sharks. Some pilots never got over this uneasiness but all of them had more than a taste of it before they were done. Then, at times, the sight of men working in a rice field on a steep mountain terrace, the motionless shapes of carabao standing beside their square and blocky shadows, or a native cart raising its delicate feather of dust along an open country road, lent unreality to the plane's flight; and the pilot, unless he was on guard, would relax his watchfulness. Most of them learned quickly that unending vigilance was the price of their survival, and that sixth sense of awareness that belongs to both the hunted and the hunting and is only latent in civilized and peaceful men became the instinct by which they lived.

But a few men at each field developed the ability to capitalize on the very lack of support that made these flights hazardous, striking when the Japanese least expected aggressive action from a lone plane. Grant Mahony, on reconnaissance out of Nichols Field to Legaspi, suddenly went in to strafe the Japanese-held radio station and some of their parked planes. When nine pursuits came diving down on him, he led them off on a chase round the 8,000-foot peak of Mount Mayon. Mahony had learned that the P-40 at low altitudes could pull away from the Zero; but this was one thing that as yet the Japanese did not know and they went after Mahony like yelping hounds. The whole pack of them were still in hot pursuit as he brought them round full-circle back across

their own airfield at tree height for a second strafing attack. Only then, with the radio station demolished, several planes burning on the field, and the fuel dump ejaculating rolls of black smoke, did he set out for home. He lost the Japanese in the creases of the mountain valleys and returned to Nichols Field to make a difficult landing on the patched-up airstrip with some of his bombs still dangling from their faulty releases underneath his wings.

On the same morning Boyd D. Wagner, flying out of Clark Field on a similar, solitary reconnaissance, was jumped north of Aparri by five Zeros. Like Mahony, instead of hightailing it for cloud cover, he took his ship right down to wave level and headed inland. Two of the Japanese pilots had evidently been detailed to take care of the lone American pursuit plane, for when Wagner looked back, he saw them sticking hot on his tail. He found that they weren't to be shaken off, so he tried a maneuver that no Japanese pilot had ever had worked on him before.

Men often spoke of Wagner as a "born" flyer, because there was nothing that he couldn't do with a plane; but he was more than that. Like many skillful people, he was not satisfied with the skill he had, but worked indefatigably to improve it. His nickname of "Buzz" came from his habit of buzzing other planes in the air. Long before the war he had begun to use unsuspecting and frequently out-

"Buzz" Wagner.

raged commercial jobs as his figurative clay pigeons, working out on them the best angles of attack and the handling of his own ship and an endless and often spectacular variety of evasive tactics. As he was also a trained aeronautical engineer, he undoubtedly knew as much about the performance characteristics of the P-40, when war came, as any other man.

Now, with the two Zeros still chasing him, Wagner suddenly throttled back and let the astonished enemy flash past over his head while he poured his own machine guns into their tails. Before either of the Japanese pilots could think up any evasive tactics for his own benefit, both Zeros were flaming and on their way into the ground. Wagner then turned back and, still hedgehopping, came in across the airfield at Aparri, catching the Japanese there completely by surprise. They had 12 planes on the line. Wagner strafed them as he roared

down the field and when he zoomed up at the far end, five of them were burning. Then, to quote his own laconic report: "My gas was running low, so I returned home."

Results like these were heartening to the whole Army, yet to the pursuit pilots they did not mean the same thing as an actual attack mission staged as such. They chafed under their confinement to reconnaissance, for, with each passing day, as the Japanese established more and more airdromes, first principally round Aparri, then at Legaspi, and finally at Vigan, the American pilots could see for themselves the gradual constrictive process that would ultimately mean the extinction of their own air effort. The hit-and-run tactics, developed in sporadic attacks like Mahony's and Wagner's and in other unreported brushes, became the basis of the combat tactics by which the P-40 was finally turned into an effective airplane.

31

But it was increasingly evident on Luzon in December that our dwindling number of pursuit planes could less and less afford to be risked in an offensive strike.

However, when the report came in on the evening of December 15 that there were 25 new Japanese planes on the airstrip at Vigan, it was decided to stage a dawn attack on them, and three of the most experienced flyers at Clark Field were assigned to the mission. They were Lieutenants Wagner, Church, and Allison W. Strauss, all members of the 17th Squadron.

The airfield [at Vigan] was a single, north-south strip, close to the beach, about four and a half miles southwest of Vigan, and the three P-40's came to it from the sea as dawn was breaking. Strauss stayed up in the paling sky to furnish top cover, while Wagner went in with Church on his wing. Each of the P-40's carried six 30-pound fragmentation bombs, three under each wing. As they neared the field they saw the 25 Japanese airplanes lined up beneath them on the turf. It was darker down there, where the gray, predawn shadows were creeping toward the mountains. The air was perfectly still as Wagner put his plane over and started down.

Wagner went through without a scratch; but by the time Church started, the Japanese antiaircraft guns were going full blast, and they now had only the one plane to concentrate on. At the very beginning of the dive,

the nose of the P-40 burst into flame. It was then that Church had to make his split-second choice, for he could still have let the plane go. But the P-40 did not waver in its dive. Even with the fire pouring back over the cockpit, Church controlled his ship through its full run, dropped his bombs on the target, and went strafing down the line like a comet. From where they circled above and beyond the field, Wagner and Strauss followed the flaming course of his ship. It never rose, but carried as straight as though the controls were locked until it crashed, about a mile away, in the flatland toward Vigan.

Church's death touched off a spark in Wagner. In spite of the heavy antiaircraft fire, he made five more strafing runs across the field. Only one Japanese plane succeeded in getting off the ground. The pilot tried to take it up just as Wagner was coming in. The Zero was half hidden from Wagner by his own wing, so to get a clear view of the whole strip he rolled his plane over on its back. No other pilot in the Philippines could have done it with a P-40 at strafing altitude. When he saw the Japanese plane, Wagner righted his ship and throttled back to let the other gain headway, and then shot it down.

Ten planes were destroyed and seven more left burning when Wagner and Strauss finally gave over and turned home. Even the Japanese had been impressed. They buried Church with full military honors.

Within two weeks after the devastating Japanese air raids on Luzon air-fields, organized American air forces in the Philippines were completely wiped out. Japanese troops swept ashore in numerous places, the largest landing occurring at Lingayen Gulf, and quickly overran the island of Luzon. Dozens of Japanese air bases sprang up.

Maj. Gen. Jonathan M. Wainwright, MacArthur's chief commander in the Philippines, could offer but token resistance with his pitifully small army. Without an air force overhead his situation was hopeless and on December 24 he retired with his forces to the island of Corregidor in Manila Bay, and to the rugged peninsula of Bataan on the northwest side of the Bay.

Among the Americans in this retreat were thousands of airmen — flyers, ground crews and support personnel — whose planes had been destroyed or flown to Australia, and whose units no longer existed. They now picked up rifles to fight a last ditch stand with their army compatriots. Plagued by starvation, wracked with dysentery and lacking medical supplies, these gallant men on Bataan held out until April 9, and on Corregidor until May 6, 1942. Their stubborn resistance upset the Japanese timetable for Philippine conquest. The tragic story of their last days and the brutal treatment given them by the Japanese after their surrender will never be forgotten.

Out of the dismal last days of Bataan and Corregidor comes a tale of American ingenuity in the air. A handful of airplanes were resurrected on Bataan and Corregidor, maintained and flown by our airmen under the most trying circumstances until the very last. This was a crude, make-shift, ten-plane air force whose clandestine operations brought a small measure of aid and comfort to dying men. It air-dropped medical supplies to isolated units from Mindanao to Bataan, evacuating personnel when-ever possible. One by one this tiny force fell to the overwhelming enemy.

The Bamboo Fleet

Capt. Roland Barnick

THEY called me The Admiral of the Bamboo Fleet.

That's because I flew a resurrected Navy amphibian between Bataan and Mindanao during the closing days of the Philippines battle.

The amphibian had a nickname, too. We called her "The Duck."

There were eight of us in the Bamboo Fleet — Capts. Jack Caldwell, Joe Moore, Jack Randolph, Bill Bradford, Harvey Whitfield and Dick Fellows, Sgt. Bill Strathern, and myself.

We were all Army Air Force pilots who had come over with P-36's or P-40's long before Pearl Harbor. Four of us were serving our third year in the Philippines and all of us had been there at least 18 months when war broke out.

Our P-40's, after the Japanese attack, were all busy in combat but they didn't last too long. Some were shot down, some were riddled on the ground, some cracked up in operation.

But we still needed men and planes to maintain air transport communication between the islands of the Philippines.

That's where the Bamboo Fleet came in. It was organized in February, 1942, by the late Brig. Gen. Harold H. George to fly personnel out of Bataan and Corregidor, and to bring in food, quinine, and other supplies from Mindanao for the wounded among General MacArthur's ground forces.

Three, of more than four planes, were patched-up civilian ships that had never been meant for war zone flying. The other was The Duck, a three-place Navy Grumman amphibian that had 700 hp. and could do 90 miles an hour when the wind was right. The Duck was my plane and that's how I got dubbed The Admiral.

We found The Duck in Meriveles Bay at the foot of Bataan, across from Corregidor. She had been sunk there by Jap strafing about three months before the fall of Bataan.

When we decided to lift her out she was awash clear up to the propeller hub and had been that way for six weeks. But we finally got her up. We did it by means of a barge with a crane on it, a little ingenuity, and a lot of hard work. Dripping wet, The Duck didn't look too flyable.

The other three planes were commandeered by the U. S. Government from civilians, natives of the Philippines.

One was a three-place Waco of ancient vintage with about 250 hp. when it was feeling right and could have made 90 mph if it had been new.

Another was a three-place Bellanca of about the same power and speed — so old and shaky that it had been condemned for private flying when we got it.

The other plane was our "speedster." It was a four-place Beechcraft that turned out 450 hp. and could do about 170 mph, if pushed.

That was the Bamboo Fleet.* And it was appropriately named. The planes were all patched together with native bamboo and what other odds and ends we could find. Where there were no airplane tires around, we used truck tires. On one ship a caster from a wheelbarrow was used as a tail

* EDITOR'S NOTE: In addition there were two Navy PBY's, a Fairchild, another Beechcraft, and two decrepit P-35's.

wheel. There wasn't a gun in the fleet.

The Duck was particularly lame. After we dug her out of the bay, we tied her wings on with baling wire, patched the fuselage with native wood, and fixed up the power plant with parts taken from other engines of different types and with miscellaneous parts from various aircraft.

I guess The Duck was held together mostly by faith. Repair of the Fleet, of course, was quite a problem. There were no spare parts to be had and there were few mechanics available. All pilots pitched in on service and repair work, and somehow we got by.

All of our flying was over enemy-held country or water. We would hop off from Bataan or Corregidor fields, fly to Cebu about 300 miles south, refuel at hidden bases there and then fly on to Mindanao — a total of 550 miles.

The planes were built to carry 250 to 600 pounds pay load. We carried from 500 to 1,400 pounds on every trip, with extra passengers going out, extra freight coming in.

We made about 35 round trips in all, evacuating 100 to 120 personnel and bringing in tons of supplies.

The little planes of the Bamboo Fleet finally went down fighting.

The Waco got hers between Cebu and Del Monte in Mindanao. She had taken off from Cebu with three of our men aboard. But she didn't quite get away. Two Jap navy patrol planes caught her in the air and literally burned her right out of the sky. The crew went with her.

Just about that time the Beechcraft got caught by the Japanese in the air over Mindanao, had its landing gear wrecked, and made a crash landing. A Jap plane came in and shot it up on the ground.

The Bellanca was lost trying to get away from Corregidor. She had landed there somehow at night and had been hidden in a cove during the day; the next night she tried to take off down a sloping, unlighted runway that was badly pockmarked with shell craters. The Bellanca got off the ground all right but she was too old and too overloaded. She crashed in the bay just a few hundred yards offshore.

That left The Duck. The Duck and I were still on Bataan at midnight on April 8, 1942, the last night before the peninsula capitulated.

On April 9, at 12:30 A.M., five passengers and myself crowded into the two-seated amphibian. We took off while the area was under heavy Jap artillery and machine-gun fire, and got away only 15 minutes before the field surrendered.

Ours was the last plane to leave Bataan.

When we got in the air I found we were so heavily overloaded that we could only make 75 feet altitude. To help us climb I had the passengers throw out their parachutes, extra clothing and baggage, together with the floorboards from the plane's hull and everything else we could strip out.

That gave us another 50 feet.

With no instruments, very little fuel, and a prayer, we headed in the general direction of Cebu. We made Iloilo. The next day we ripped some more stuff off The Duck and adjusted the propeller. We made it, too, and that's where I left The Duck, on April 25. Shortly after I was off for Australia.

I left The Duck intact. There were a few other pilots around who might have flown her after that.

EDITOR'S NOTE: There were other punitive air operations conducted by the retreating airmen as they moved south before the onrushing Japanese conquest. One in particular and perhaps the largest single effort was a direct hit against Jap-held targets in the Philippines from Australia; it was made in hopes that the enemy blockade of Corregidor might be broken long enough to allow quick shipment of supplies to reach General Wainwright and his beleaguered forces there. On April 11, 1942, ten B-25's, with auxiliary long-range gas tanks attached, and three B-17's left Darwin, Australia, on a 1,500-mile flight to the southern Philippine island of Mindanao, where Filipino guerrillas were strongest. All 13 planes arrived at Del Monte and secretively dispersed to scattered adjacent airstrips. For two days this force hammered Japanese shipping and docks at Cebu, harbor facilities at Davao and Nichols Field on Luzon. Six battered-up pursuit planes left on Mindanao supported the bombers by trying to pin down enemy fighters at nearby Davao airstrip, but the Japs were too strong. The three B-17's were seriously damaged by Japanese air attack on Del Monte Field. The B-25's fared better. Flying from concealed airstrips they sank three enemy transports in Cebu harbor and shot down three enemy aircraft.

The B-25's all returned to Darwin after a record-breaking operation of 6,000 nautical miles. Left behind were the gallant ground crews who had serviced the planes on Mindanao during this daring two-day strike. These men faced the doom of eventual capture and death or imprisonment, for there was no way to evacuate them from their isolated strips deep within the Japanese-controlled territory.

Strikes such as this one were largely ineffective, merely hit-and-run tactics, using to the hilt the few remaining aircraft available to American airmen in Australia.

While the Japanese swept to victory across the Philippine skies, elsewhere there was a different story unfolding.

Deep in the interior of China, at an air base near Kunming — the city in which the harassed Chiang Kai-shek government had taken refuge — the Japanese felt the first sting of defeat at the hands of a small group of pilots. This unit was the American Volunteer Group (AVG), better known as the "Flying Tigers."

For nearly a decade before Pearl Harbor, Japanese military aircraft had roamed at will over China, virtually unopposed in the air, dropping their lethal bombs on highly populated cities, indiscriminately slaughtering innocent Chinese by the tens of thousands. Jap bombers and fighters, nestled at some 200 bases on the China mainland, ranged out ahead of advancing Japanese armies to strike the ill-armed, ill-supplied, retreating Chiang Kai-shek forces.

The situation in China was indeed desperate when this band of American flyers (the AVG) landed in Rangoon in the summer of 1941 to begin training under the supreme tactician of fighter air war, Claire Chennault. Chennault was a retired U.S. Army Air Corps captain whom Chiang Kai-shek had brought to China in 1937 as an air adviser.

In the steaming tropical jungles of Burma during the summer and fall of 1941, Chennault and this band of volunteers tirelessly studied the strength and weaknesses of the Japanese. Here they trained for six months while their P-40B (Tomahawk) fighters arrived from the United States, and precious fuel was brought in at great sacrifice across the towering Himalaya Peaks to Kunming Field in the valley of the She-Shan mountains.

In early December, 1941, two AVG squadrons moved to Kunming, China, and one remained at Rangoon, Burma. When the Japanese struck Pearl Harbor, the men of the AVG were ready to go to work, nor did they have long to wait.

Angels With and Without Wings

United States Air Force Historical Files

THE SKY above Kunming, China, was crystal-clear blue that bright-washed morning of December 20, 1941. The ruins of long-previous bombing raids stood out in jagged contrast to the ancient shops and hovels of the capital city of Yunnan Province. The untold thousands of Chinese in this eastern terminus of the Burma Road were following the sing-song pattern of their daily anonymous lives, resigned to the inevitability of Jap-brought horror and destruction.

Only in the bellies of an odd score of foreigners was there the knotted strain of expectant waiting. Only these few Americans were tense with prayerful hope in their untried hearts. Sprawling and crouching in the ready shack on their newly built airdrome outside Kunming, they smoked and cursed and waited.

One hundred miles to the south, Chinese coolies halted the rhythmical monotony of their rice planting and stared skyward at the ten twin-engine planes droning relentlessly toward Kunming. Back in the ready shack, Bob Sandell, of San Antonio, Texas, was lighting another cigarette, glancing at his watch and shrugging his shoulders wearily. It was beginning to seem as if today, like yesterday, would be another washout. He cursed, quietly and satisfyingly.

Fifteen minutes later, the endless cigarettes and curses were forgotten. Hemmed in by the crowding, eager pilots of the American Volunteer Group, Claire L. Chennault crisply read the radio message they had all been waiting to hear: "Ten Jap medium bombers are heading for Kun-ming from the south; just sighted 60 miles away."

Fat, dumb and happy, the ten Nakajima bombers were approaching their I.P. (Initial Point of bomb runs) when Scarsdale Jack Newkirk, leading Bert Christman, Don Bernsdorf and Gil Bright, intercepted them. Newkirk radioed that the Japs were less than 30 miles to the south. With hardly a pause for taxiing, Bob Sandell and 14 of his Adam and Eve Squadron were off for the kill.

For years, bombing the Chinese had been a safe and honorable way for the Japs to serve their Emperor. There was never any effectual opposition, and, with the rest of the world tied up in a huge-scale European war, there was no reason to believe that the lush targets of China's densely peopled cities would ever be adequately defended. With their customary complacency, the Japs were flying at a contemptuously low and accurate altitude. There was no protective screen of fighters escorting them, and their gunners were merely along for the ride.

With the abruptnesss of sudden death, all the smugness of the loose Jap formation was shattered. Roaring in on them from all angles, the P-40's of the AVG had a picnic of destruction. The Nakajimas passed their scheduled I.P., forgotten in their frantic efforts to escape; the bombs, a few minutes before destined for the heart of Kunming and its 500,000 defenseless people, were scattered harmlessly

(Left) The shark-mouthed P-40's of the Flying Tigers. Here a flight crosses mountain ranges looking for enemy targets. (Right) The great Claire Chennault. With only a handful of planes he held the entire China-based Japanese air force at bay for years.

over the countryside as the .50-caliber slugs of the P-40's transformed the Jap bombers into infernos of exploding gas and ammunition. In a matter of as many minutes, six of the Naka-jimas were strewn in flaming bits among the rice paddies of the Yunnan plateau. The other four Japs disap-peared over the horizon, but they never reached their base.

The people of Kunming were de-lirious in their joyous gratitude and surging hope; the news mushroomed out into the villages, the farms, the mountainsides. Everywhere the people asked the same questions: Who were these American flyers who, in their outmoded P-40's, had struck the first

blow of vengeance for the years of un-opposed slaughter? Why were they here?

Until the late spring of 1941, these same flyers had been instructor pilots, test pilots, patrol-bomber pilots in the Army, Navy and Marine Corps. Then, to their various bases, had come a group of civilians with a bizarre prop-osition. Headed by a hard-eyed ex-U.S. Army pilot, Claire Lee Chen-nault, these civilians had offered the pilots high adventure, high pay and combat experience in the Orient.

The story behind that appealing offer properly starts with Claire Lee Chennault. A former Louisiana schoolteacher who had taken flight

39

training and won his wings at an age that today would be declared far too advanced, Chennault had seen 20 years of Army service and had earned an unparalleled reputation not only as a superb precision flyer but as a master tactician and theorist of modern pursuit warfare. American aviation enthusiasts had long marveled at the incredibly intricate acrobatics flown by Chennault and his two wingmen, Luke Williamson and Haywood S. Hansell. Billed as the "Three Men on a Flying Trapeze," they had performed every acrobatic maneuver in the books with their wing tips tied together by 20-foot spans of rope.

As the years passed, however, Chennault's hearing became increasingly impaired. Although his insistence on the necessity of radical revisions in the stale, World War I conceptions of aerial warfare had become annoying to the more conservative Army powers, he was retired in 1937 with the rank of captain not because of those theories, as has been suggested by many historians, but because, in addition to his partial deafness, he himself decided that he had outlived his usefulness to the Army Air Corps. Reluctantly, he prepared to resign himself to the comparatively dull routine of life as a gentleman farmer.

Although his theories may have failed to impress the U.S. Army, those same theories and demonstrated tactics had strongly attracted the attention of at least two foreign governments. Russia, after viewing Chennault's demonstration of airborne invasion, had bid for his services, offering him complete freedom to develop and expand his theories with well-trained pilots and modern aircraft. But because acceptance of such an offer would have meant the loss of his citizenship, Chennault refused. Russia went ahead and started the first large-scale experimental training of paratroops.

Shortly after his retirement from the Army, Chennault was also asked by the Chiang Kai-shek government to come to China as a civilian adviser of air training — with no loss of citizenship involved. Chennault's restless interest was immediately aroused, and within a few weeks he was on his way to China.

Madame Chiang Kai-shek had been appointed National Secretary of Aviation. Chennault, upon first meeting her, predicted: "You and I will get along all right in building up your air force." And they did get along all right, but building up a Chinese air force was a task requiring infinitely more than good will.

Upon his arrival, Chennault was given a ready-made nucleus of pilots. On the whole, however, these men of various nationalities, were nothing more than international adventurers who were more adept at "hangar flying" than at actual aerial performance. With heart-sickening monotony, they crashed and smashed up the scarce new planes allotted to Chennault. In the simple routine of landing, they totally destroyed 11 fighters and four bombers and completed the destruction of the remaining force soon after during an air raid when, panic-stricken, they wildly took off the field in every direction. Fifteen more fighters and the only remaining bomber, were destroyed; the Japanese never fired a shot.

Three years passed, and Chennault gradually built up another international air force that proved so effective against the heretofore unmolested Japanese bomber raids on Nanking that the American State Department, in response to frantic Japanese protests, threatened to deprive Chennault of his citizenship. Unreplaced casualties, however, steadily reduced this tiny Chinese air force until, in early 1941, the cities of China were providing defenseless bombing ranges for the hordes of smug Jap bombers.

During these long months of un-opposed terror, Chennault was compiling an unprecedented mass of intelligence on Jap air tactics, and preparing sound, far-into-the-future plans for a counteroffensive against Japan. Huge quantities of gasoline, bombs and ammunition were stored away near eastern airfields. In exact, minute detail all of the more than 200 Jap-held air bases in China were photographed and studied. Time was not wasted.

Until early 1941, all of Chennault's efforts to solicit material aid from the United States had been fruitless; all of his warnings concerning the inev-itability of a war with Japan had been scoffed at and ignored. When the United States finally realized the vital importance to itself of keeping open the Burma Road, Chennault acted quickly. He came to the United States with an urgent bid for planes and experienced pilots. With the help of Secretary of the Treasury, Henry Morgenthau, Jr., and the cooperation of Sweden, he was allotted 100 P-40B's which had been rejected by England and consigned to Sweden.

One hundred planes with no pilots to man them were as good as no planes at all. The Army, Navy and Marines had pilots — just about the only pilots experienced and well trained enough to suit Chennault's plans — but the Army, Navy and Marines were in no way willing to relinquish the pilots, all of whom were desperately needed to form the nucleus of their own rapidly expanding air forces.

By this time, Chennault, through Secretary Morgenthau and Presidential-adviser Thomas Corcoran, had reached the ear of President Franklin D. Roosevelt, the highest authority in the land. Shortly thereafter the plans for the AVG were approved and Chennault with his aides visited the various air bases of the three services. On the whole, Chennault's appeal was unemotional and rational, but through his measured words gleamed the exciting story of China's struggle to build, to develop and to maintain its only lifeline of supply — the Burma Road. With its scrawny planes and sparse numbers of pilots, so ineffectual as to belie the title of "Air Force," China was unable to protect the shipments of supplies and ammunition — without which its ten-year battle of desperation against the Japs would surely be lost.

The American pilots were not being asked to sacrifice their present comforts, safety and comparatively secure futures just for the love of China however. An attractive scale of pay was offered them: squadron leaders, $750 per month; flight leaders, $650 per month; wingmen, $600 per month. To this was added an unofficial $500 bonus for every Japanese plane destroyed. Hard-bitten Chennault had had an overly bitter dose of inexperienced, maltrained would-be defenders of China back in 1937. He wanted no more amateurs; he was after professional air soldiers, trained men who could pit themselves tellingly against a numerically and qualitatively superior enemy.

These pilots were to be released from the Army, Navy and Marine Corps to serve as civilians, "to manufacture, service and operate airplanes in Asia." The whole proposition involved delicate diplomatic problems, for we were still at peace with Japan. Thus the $500 bonus for each destroyed enemy plane had to remain unofficial.

The pilots themselves were naturally attracted by the promise of adventure and plenty of money. David "Tex" Hill, one of the charter members recruited from the Navy and later a full U.S. Army colonel, sums up the reasons that prompted most of them them to join: "At that time, it was a well-known fact in the Navy that war with Japan was imminent; we thought it would be a good idea to get in on the ground floor, and we decided that it would be a good chance to have a bit of adventure and also to make ourselves a little money."

In the early summer heat of 1941, the AVG left San Francisco. One hundred pilots and 200 ground crewmen were headed for the insufferable, steaming heat of Burma where Chennault had decided to train his pilots before sending them into China. The membership of the AVG was never greater than 250, but each man, pilot or ground personnel, was a specialist in his particular field.

Four long months these men spent at the feet of Chennault soaking up the tactics of aerial warfare. Some 20 of them quit, disgusted with the inactivity and the unlivable climate. Those who remained trained day after day until they, too, began to wonder whether it was worth the effort. Then in December, quickly and with infinite surprise, two squadrons moved to Kunming. The prep-school days were finished.

Modeled after a typical Army Air Force Group, the AVG had been divided into three squadrons: "Adam and Eve," "Panda Bear," and "Hell's Angels." The third squadron, "Hell's Angels," commanded by Arvid Olsen, remained at Rangoon while the first and second squadrons, commanded by Robert J. Sandell and Jack Newkirk, respectively, joyously left the miasmatic hell of Burma for Kunming, China.

Three days after their initial encounter with the flyers of the AVG's Panda Bear and Adam and Eve squadrons in China, the Imperial Jap airmen struck again — this time at Rangoon where Arvid Olsen's Hell's Angels were based. Coming in without any warning, the first wave of 18 Jap bombers caught the AVG on the ground, but before the Jap bombs had struck, a dozen Flying Tigers were in the air to meet the second wave of 30 bombers. The Japs had learned their lesson well; they were at 20,000 feet and were escorted by 20 fighters. Former Marine pilot Ken Jernstedt from Oregon raked his fire into a Jap bomber and saw a vibrating sheet of exploding flame envelope it. Following directly on Jernstedt's tail was Hank Gilbert of Wyoming, pumping his shells into two Jap bombers, feeling the exulting sweet uplift of long-awaited battle. Racking his P-40 up on one wing, he turned to attack again, but his plane never completed its second attack. To the exploding hell from a Jap turret, the AVG lost its first pilot.

Charlie Older, an ex-Navy pilot, bore down on the first Jap bomber to cross his sights; nearer and nearer he drew, his guns spitting lead into its length and breadth, unwilling to draw away until at last he saw it turn into a huge ball of flame. Vomiting its molten cargo of bombs and ammunition in all directions, it exacted its final revenge by splattering part of its flaming wreckage into the path of the P-40 piloted by Neil Martin, the second AVG pilot to die in the service of China.

Shortly thereafter, Robert Smith drew his first blood; Charlie Older sent another bomber spinning earthward. Paul Greene, from California, happily attacking his first bomber, saw a steady line of tracers inch along his wing; he turned in a steep dive with two Jap pursuits on his tail, each pouring their vengeance into his ship, until there was no recourse open to Greene but to hit the silk. Floating earthward, Greene was still pursued by the relentless Japs. Only by frantic side-slipping was he able to prevent them from turning his parachute into a sieve.

The Japs had come prepared for opposition, but they had not expected the furious onslaught of reckless, terrifying firepower that they received. They had been thwarted in their attempt to drop all of their bombs on the target, and they turned tail and headed for home.

The primary aerial battle over the polyglot city of Rangoon was in essence a decisive victory for the AVG. They had accounted for six Jap bombers and four fighters, losing three of their own planes and two pilots. But they had not completely prevented the bombing of Rangoon; indeed, the first enemy wave had devastated the city.

43

However, one of Chennault's points in his theory of tactical air warfare had been borne out. Repeatedly he had stressed the necessity, in the absence of numerical and qualitative superiority, of using to the last stretch of possibility every advantage which the P-40 held over the Jap aircraft. One of these advantages was its comparatively heavy armor plate.

Unlike the thinly clad Jap Zero, the P-40 was well protected with this armor plate, and after this first bloody battle the AVG pilots saw on their ships the scars and indentations of Jap bullets, frustrated by the protecting armor. There were no such marks on Jap planes similarly hit; they simply exploded.

Christmas Day of 1941 was a joyless day of lonely waiting for the Hell's Angels Squadron at Rangoon. Radio Tokyo had long promised a Christmas visitation, and it was not until the enemy force of 60 bombers and 20 fighters was but ten miles from the field that the AVG received an alert. Frantically scrambling for altitude, the Flying Tigers fought off the escorting Japanese fighters and dived in for the kill. Hitting the Japanese bombers with .50-caliber hail, the Tigers scattered them, knocking down one after another. Then, out of nowhere, a new force of 20 additional bombers and eight fighters appeared. The sky was filled with a chaos of exploding, burning planes and screaming tracers. Short, dynamic, Duke Hedman, from South Dakota, rolled like a bowling ball down the alley of ripe Jap targets, hurtling confirmed destruction into three death-laden bombers in quick succession. Tearing upward for altitude again, he tacked on to three fighters, knocking each one out of the sky.

The sky battle dissolved into a complete rout of the Japanese. All told, the AVG accounted for more than 25 enemy aircraft that lonely Christmas Day.

During the next five months, the reputation of these men of the AVG grew to the proportion of legend. Men like "Scarsdale" Jack Newkirk, Tex Hill, Duke Hedman, Eddie Rector, and Bob Neale rose from obscurity to capture the worshipful imaginations of the Chinese and also of their own countrymen. Despite their pitifully inadequate equipment and supplies, they destroyed well over 500 enemy planes, killing at least 1,500 members of the Imperial Japanese Air Force; they strafed countless numbers of troops, supply lines, vehicles; they even bombed warships. And yet the importance of the AVG lay in another direction. These men, whom Madame Chiang affectionately called her "angels with and without wings," served an end more vital, more far-reaching than their glorious combat record against the enemy.

The AVG served as a proving ground for the tactics and theories of Chennault. With his adaptable, quick, logical mind, Chennault had easily recognized the impossibility of ac-

Flying Tiger pilots dash to their waiting P-40's as word of incoming Japanese bombers is received.

quiring sufficient force with which to meet the Japanese on equal grounds in China. He readily foresaw the long months ahead during which time the United States would be about to establish only a small air force in China and during which time that same inadequate air force might well be obliterated by the overwhelming numbers of Jap planes. Thoroughly familiar with the P-40's limitations and advantages, he drummed into his pilots' minds the rule that would keep them alive: "If you take the best characteristic of your plane and fight with it, never letting the enemy fight with the best characteristic of his plane, then you can lick him!"

Against all established protocol, Chennault insisted on a tight, two-plane fighting formation which doubled the firing power against the enemy and provided a tail protection for whichever of the two ships was leading the attack. The P-40 was a heavily armored ship, much more so than the light, unprotected Zero. As a result, the P-40 could take punishment which would destroy a Zero. Further, as a result of its weight, the P-40, in a dive, rapidly built up speed which left behind any pursuing enemy plane. It had self-sealing gas tanks which the Zeros did not have. On the other hand, the Zero was a highly maneuverable plane which could out-

45

climb and outturn the P-40. These two features gave the Japs a tremendous advantage in individual dogfights, for if a P-40, hot on the tail of a fleeing Zero, were to attempt to follow its prey in a turn, the Zero would turn in a much tighter circle and snap on to the tail of its erstwhile pursuer. Should a P-40 attempt to follow a Zero's climb, the P-40, speedily losing airspeed, would stall out and become a fluttering helpless target.

Bearing in mind these relative advantages and disadvantages, Chennault trained his men to use all of their advantages and avoid their disadvantages. "Altitude, altitude," he cried, "get above them; build up airspeed in a dive; strike fast, don't stay around to tangle with them; dive away; climb up above them and dive in again!"

Of the Japanese pilots, Chennault said: "They have been drilled for hundreds of hours in set tactics for each situation they may encounter. Japanese pilots fly by the book. Their pursuits always pull the same tricks. God help the American pilot who tries to fight them according to their plans."

The AVG pilots were schooled incessantly to recognize beforehand every possible move in the Jap pilots' book of situations. Skeptical as many of them were about the reliability of Chennault's unproved theories, each and every one of them came to regard the retired Army captain as the master tactician and air strategist that he was.

Under his stern guidance, these men, proving his tactics and theories as they did in their almost legendary victories over the Japanese, laid the foundation for the China Air Task Force. This subsequently became the 14th Air Force that completely broke the back of the Japanese Imperial Air Force in China.

With the possible exception of the A-bomb on Hiroshima, no single military action electrified America and its Allies as did President Roosevelt's announcement early in the war that American bombers, based in the fictional land of Shangri-la, had blasted Japanese cities. It came in the midst of a rapid succession of enemy military victories all over the Far East and it gave the world hope when there was despair. The tumble of bombs on Tokyo shattered the myth of Japanese invincibility here at home and in the minds of the Japanese people themselves.

The Tokyo Raid of April 18, 1942, was a bold and imaginative plan to hit industrial targets in the Japanese homeland with twin-engine B-25 medium-range bombers flown off an aircraft carrier. It took form in the minds of Admiral Ernest J. King and Gen. H. H. Arnold less than a month after Pearl Harbor. The objective was to damage Japan, both materially and psychologically, and in a small way begin to return, tit for tat, what the Japanese had profusely dished out at Pearl Harbor.

To select and train the crews and prepare the mission, General "Hap" Arnold called in one of his most versatile and skilled thinkers and flyers, Lt. Col. J. H. "Jimmy" Doolittle, that doughty early air pioneer.

Twenty-four crews were needed and 24 crews volunteered from the 17th Bombardment Group at Columbia, South Carolina, for an unknown "one-mission overseas tour" on a fifty-fifty chance they would not come back. These young American airmen, not long out of flying school, flew their B-25's, also from the 17th Group, to Eglin Field, Florida, in the latter part of February 1942. Here they began intense training under the wiry Doolittle, including short-distance takeoffs. All pilots soon qualified in 500-600-foot takeoffs in fully loaded B-25's at 70-80 mph (normal take-off speed for a loaded B-25 was 105-110 mph). Some even made it in 300 feet. Other parts of their training included formation flying, gunnery practice, low-level bombing, navigation, fuel consumption tests, and quick ground refueling under enemy attack. All these things were performed under conditions that simulated a highly secret mission which the flyers themselves knew nothing about.

Since the famed Norden bombsight was of little use at low level, Capt. C. R. Greening, one of the pilots, designed and built a low-level device with materials costing about fifteen cents per bombsight. It worked magnificently.

The Eglin training was completed on March 25 and crews, with their airplanes, left for Sacramento, California, for final flight training up and down the valley, the specific mission yet unknown to all but a very few of the group leaders.

The Tokyo Raid is one of the best known war epics in American history, the subject of frequent high dramatization in the printed word and on the screen. Here, for the record, in a simple, matter-of-fact way, bereft of the glittering dramatics of the professional pen, is an earthy account by one of the Tokyo Raiders himself.

The Tokyo Raid—An Avenging Call

Col. Jack A. Sims, USAF

ON MARCH 31–April 1, 1942, 16 out of the original 24 airplanes were loaded aboard the carrier *Hornet* at Alameda Naval Air Station. That night the flattop moved out into San Francisco Bay and anchored. The Navy crew and the AAF complement were permitted a one-night shore leave.

In the early morning hours of the 6th, the task force moved out to sea. The weather was foggy with visibility at 1,000 yards. Air coverage was provided by the Western Sea Frontier until late afternoon.

The crew of the *Hornet* knew nothing of the mission of the bombers until the first day out. Late in the afternoon it was announced to all vessels of the task force by semaphore and loudspeaker. Cheers went up from every section of the ship and morale reached a new high. From that time on, the *Hornet*'s crew did everything they possibly could to help us prepare for the mission. Lectures on Japan and the Japanese were given, as was infor-

mation on the Chinese people and what could be expected of them. We attended courses on identification and destination, on hygiene and sanitation in China, on first aid and celestial navigation. Most important, we got the latest information on weather en route to the target area.

Because any one of a dozen things could go wrong, numerous alternate plans were devised for almost any eventuality. If, for example, takeoff was forced by enemy action too soon for the planes to reach Tokyo, we would fly either to Hawaii or Midway, whichever was the closest. If the task force was sighted or attacked beyond the point of no return, all aircraft would proceed to accomplish the planned mission.

Insofar as possible we were given choice of targets in Japan. Many hours were spent by each crew studying target information and looking at pictures to become as familiar as possible with the method under which attacks were to be carried out. Repeated bat-

48

tle station drills were conducted in which we always manned our aircraft on the flight deck.

Six days after the *Hornet* was at sea, the naval operation plan was issued. The entire fleet was to be known as Task Force 16, under the command of Vice Admiral Halsey whose flagship was the aircraft carrier *Enterprise*. Capt. Marc Mitscher was skipper of the *Hornet*. In addition to the carriers *Enterprise* and *Hornet*, the force consisted of four cruisers, seven destroyers, two submarines and two tankers. Rendezvous of Task Force 16 was to take place at a predetermined position at 0600, April 13, 1942, at which time the force was to proceed to a point approximately 400 miles east of Tokyo where bombers would be launched for attack. En route, Japanese radio stations were continuously monitored to determine whether or not they were suspicious, and to obtain information that might be useful in carrying out the mission. Surface speeds were frequently reduced because of heavy seas and high winds. Air patrols from the *Enterprise* were maintained whenever weather permitted, and extended out

Before the war, good-friendship medals had been presented to certain American citizens by the Japanese government. Here, in a ceremony on the *Hornet's* flight deck prior to takeoff, Lt. Col. Jimmy Doolittle wires medals to bombs slated to fall on Tokyo — for return to their original owners.

to 200 miles on each bow. Surface warning submarines, the *Trout* and the *Thresher*, occupied prescribed patrol stations in order to report any information that might threaten Task Force 16. The Navy's operational plan was magnificent. They were taking no chances.

ENEMY SHIPS SPOTTED: On April 16 refueling of the combat vessels was attempted but heavy seas forced abandonment of the operation until the next day. It was then accomplished successfully, but hardly completed when the wind rose to gale force. One man washed overboard from the tanker *Cimarron* . . . but was recovered by an escorting destroyer a short time later.

Early on the morning of April 18, two enemy vessels were picked up on radar and the task force changed course to avoid contact. The night before we were given our final briefing and a last offer was made to those who might wish to withdraw, but again no takers. The briefing instructions included three warnings: under no conditions go to Vladivostok in Russian Siberia; nonmilitary targets, including the Temple of Heaven, would not be bombed; and finally this would be the last briefing before takeoff. H hour was understood to be on the evening of April 19 unless the task force was intercepted or discovered by Japanese air- or sea-craft. If any such intercept happened we would immediately take off. The original plan, with takeoff on

the evening of April 19, would place us over targets in Japan at midnight with arrival in China at daybreak.

As fate would have it, the contingent plan was destined to go into effect. There had been two radar intercepts of Jap surface vessels since the *Hornet* left San Francisco. When a third contact was made the day before our scheduled takeoff, Admiral Halsey decided to launch the B-25's. The warning came to us over the loudspeaker system of the *Hornet* at approximately 0740, April 18 in this manner: "Army pilots, man your battle stations for takeoff."

At the same time the cruisers' batteries opened fire on the enemy craft, three and one-half miles to the left of the task force. The cruiser *Nashville* obliterated the Japanese craft and then dashed off in the direction of the kill to make sure.

Later developments indicated the enemy vessel had made a report to Japan on the task force and its course. The report had been received and confirmation of it requested. By the time Tokyo asked for confirmation, however, the Jap patrol boat had been sunk by the *Nashville*. Hearing no more from the patrol boat, the Japanese government chose to ignore the message until the bombs started hitting the target. By that time it was too late.

WE TAKE BATTLE STATIONS: At the sound of the *Hornet's* loudspeaker, we all rushed to battle stations (our aircraft) and were packed and ready to go. We had done this before and many of us thought it was another dry run in spite of the gunfire. When we learned it was the real thing, excitement increased. The carrier. *Enterprise* could be heard shouting instructions over her powerful loudspeaker on deck, directing the *Hornet* to launch the bombers immediately.

The position of the *Hornet* at this time was 823 miles from Tokyo — over 400 miles farther out from our destination than available fuel would allow us to fly. Maximum possible flying time would be exceeded. The weather was bad in the vicinity of the carrier and most disturbing was a head wind of 24 knots that could be expected all of the way to Japan. Under these conditions, if they indeed did prevail, we could never make China and we all knew it. We were heading into a great experience and we had no illusions about it.

The first B-25, piloted by Lt. Col. Doolittle, left the *Hornet*'s flight deck at 0820, ship time. The last one was launched at 0919. The average interval for the takeoffs was 3.9 minutes. The sea was rough as the *Hornet* sped into the wind at 27 knots.

A set of wheel markers were placed on the deck approximately 450 feet from the bow. These markers were composed of cork and sand to serve the purpose of preventing the wheels of the bombers from slipping on the wet deck during the engine run-up. Navy deckmen followed each bomber with a set of wheel chocks in order to prevent backslide that might be caused by the pitch of the ship.

To launch the aircraft, the *Hornet* came up with the fastest speed it attained during the entire trip. This gave us an additional margin of take-off speed. The signalman at the chocks gauged the waves to put the rolling B-25 at the bow just as the carrier surged up on the crest. On signal, each pilot pushed throttles to full power, held his brakes, with flaps full down, and awaited the flag. At the signal from the flagman, the pilot released his brakes and shot forward. Few aircraft had any major difficulty in getting off. However, one pilot forgot to put his flaps down. Luckily he was able to make a successful takeoff even though his B-25 dipped very low to the water off the end of the flight deck. Another aircraft slid backward on the wet deck while taxiing into position. It hit a sailor who lost his arm as a result. Each plane, after takeoff, circled the carrier and flew directly back over the deck to read the course the carrier displayed on a large card on the island.

All pilots had been given selected objectives consisting of steelworks, oil refineries, oil tank farms, ammunition dumps and factories, dockyards, airplane factories and supply areas. They were also given secondary targets in case it was impossible to reach the primary targets. In almost every case the primary target was bombed. The damage done far exceeded the most

Lt. Col. Doolittle takes off in the first plane of the Tokyo attack force. At this point, the *Hornet* was more than 400 miles farther out from the target than safe takeoff distance would allow.

optimistic expectations. The high degree of damage resulted from the highly inflammable nature of Japanese buildings, the low altitude from which bombing was done, the perfectly clear weather over the targets and the careful and continuous study of charts and target areas. Descriptions of the bombing results are found in the following actual crew reports:

"Bombing done from 900 feet. Debris flew higher than the plane . . ."

"All targets were considered hit. A chemical works burst into flames. Military barracks were machine-gunned during withdrawal . . ."

"Smoke column from target observed billowing to several thousand feet, at least 50 miles behind us. Three patrol boats were attacked with machine-gun fire near mouth of Tokyo Bay. One left burning . . ."

"Bombed large warehouse, railroad siding and oil refinery in Yokohama dock area. Sunk one weather boat 100

52

miles east of Japan with machine-gun fire . . ."

"Hit building area, naval ships and docks in Yokosuka naval base area. One ship was hit in dry dock and seen to fall on its side; another was left burning while apparently refueling, and a giant crane collapsed . . ."

"Over 30 miles from target a column of smoke more than 5,000 feet high could be seen . . ."

The flights were spread over a large area in order to provide the greatest possible coverage, thereby creating the impression that a large number of airplanes were involved. This also aided in diluting enemy ground fire and air opposition. One flight covered the northern part of Tokyo, another the central part and a third flight the southern part of the city. A fourth flight covered Kanagewa, Yokohama and the Yokosuka navy yard. A fifth flight of three B-25's proceeded to the vicinity of Nagoya where the flight broke up and one plane headed to Nagoya, another to Osaka and the third to the ancient, historic city of Kobe.

Prior to takeoff, the best Army and Navy intelligence informed us there were some 500 combat planes in Japan with most of them concentrated in the Tokyo Bay area. The comparatively

Dramatic moment aboard the *Hornet*. With his throttle wide open, the pilot is literally standing on the brakes, waiting for the "go" signal. Navy hands crouch near edge of flight deck.

few fighters encountered on the raid indicated Japanese home defense had been reduced in the interest of making the maximum number of planes available to active combat theaters. The pilots of home defense planes appeared to be inexperienced. In some cases they actually did not attack, and in others failed to drive home the attack. In no case did a Japanese pilot try to ram one of the B-25's, even though the economy of such a course would appear sound from the Japanese point of view as occurred later on in the war.

The fire of the Japanese pilots who actually attacked the B-25's was very inaccurate. In some cases the machine-gun bullets bounced off the wings, without penetrating them. The same effect was observed when a train upon which some of the crew members were riding in China was machine-gunned by Japanese planes. One of the projectiles which had bounced off the top of the train was recovered. It had no rifling marks and was apparently fired from about a .25-caliber smooth-bore gun.

The antiaircraft defense over Japan was active, but inaccurate also. All bursts were black and small. Several

Proof that the Tokyo Raid was not a mere publicity stunt or morale-building mission. Photo shows a pinpoint bomb hit on a cluster of Japanese army barracks in the Tokyo outskirts. All crews were assigned military targets and did not scatter bombs at random in populated areas as the Japanese accused them of doing.

of the B-25's were struck by fragments but none of them was damaged to an extent that impaired their mission.

A few barrage balloons were seen, particularly in the Tokyo Bay area. These were flying at about 3,000 feet altitude, but were not in sufficient numbers to impede the bombing. Jap ack-ack shot down several of their own balloons.

Apparently home defense had received secondary attention to efficient operation in the war theaters. In spite of at least one radio message Tokyo received prior to our takeoff, the Japanese were unprepared for the attack. They didn't think it could happen.

As luck would have it we encountered favorable weather conditions over the target, and favorable tail winds from target to China, instead of expected head winds. This added boost was enough to allow the B-25's to reach the China coast on their limited fuel supply and precluded ditching in the China Sea — which we had all expected when our takeoff from the *Hornet* was made 400 miles farther out than planned. However, a storm center had developed over China in the preplanned landing areas and it prevented any of the planes from finding their destination.

As things happened, the takeoff occurred ten hours early and 400 miles farther away from Japan than planned because of contact with enemy surface vessels. In addition, the takeoff was made on April 18 instead of April 19. In view of the early launching of the mission it was requested that, if possible, the Chinese government at Chungking be advised shortly after takeoff. If not, it was felt that Chungking might learn of the bombing from the Japanese radio and establish, prematurely, the ground assistance requested prior to departure from San Francisco. Actually Chungking did learn of the coming bombers but the airplane dispatched to the preplanned airfield in the Chuchow area crashed en route, killing all aboard. As a result of this, no radio homing facilities were provided in the Chuchow area. Neither were light beacons or landing flares. When the B-25's were heard over the China coast, an air-raid warning alarm was sounded, and all lights were turned off. This, together with the very unfavorable flying weather over the mountainous China coast, made any kind of a safe landing at destination impossible. Thus, all planes either crash-landed in the water near the coast or the crews bailed out.

From here on, the stories of the individual crew members — 80 in all — would fill a volume. Some were harrowing, some humorous, several tragic, and certainly all of them varied. Within a few days after that night in which all aircraft were lost, crew members began being picked up by friendly Chinese guerrillas and soon straggled into the Chuchow area, where others were waiting to withdraw to Chungking. Here the stories of the grim toll began to unfold.

One enlisted crew member had been

found dead as a result of an unsuccessful parachute jump. One crew crash-landed in the Nanchang area; three of the members were captured by the Japanese while the other two were believed to have been drowned in Poyang Lake. Of the three that were captured, one was executed, one died of mistreatment and malnutrition in prison, and the third spent the rest of the war in a Japanese prisoner-of-war camp in solitary confinement.

Another aircraft attempted a landing on a coastal beach in rain and fog. The wheels hit the water and wrecked the plane. All crew members with the exception of one, were seriously hurt. Medical aid was reached with the help of Chinese guerrilla forces after three days. Lt. T. R. White, the only medical man on the raid, crash-landed in the water in the same vicinity and was taken to the injured crew members. He was forced to amputate the pilot's leg because of infection.

Another aircraft, owing to extremely high gasoline consumption and complete failure of the top gun turret (which left them defenseless), proceeded to land 40 miles north of Vladivostok, Russia. All crew members were safe but interned by the Russians and sent to Penza, 350 miles southeast of Moscow. Another crew landed on the coast south of Hanchung and was captured by soldiers of the puppet government. The pilot and the bombardier were executed by the Japanese. The remainder of the crew survived 40 months of confinement in prison camps. Attempts to ransom those who had been taken prisoner were futile.

One of the pilots, who weighed 245 pounds and stood 6 feet 7 inches, possessed a fine portable phonograph as well as two .45-caliber pistols and a 24-35 carbine rifle, all of which he took with him in his B-25. When the time came for him to bail out, he strapped on both pistols, took the carbine in one hand and the phonograph in the other, and jumped. When he landed all he had was the handle of the phonograph in his hand.

One crewman accidentally pulled the rip cord to his parachute while in the nose of the aircraft. He calmly crawled back to the navigator's table and repacked it, finishing the job just as the engines sputtered out of gas. The job was a bit haphazard, but the chute worked.

Strike Back: Lae, Salamaua, and the Coral Sea

Maj. James F. Sunderman

WITHIN a month after Japanese forces overran the Philippines, they engulfed the Netherlands East Indies, pushed southeast to occupy the key base at Rabaul, on New Britain Island, a short distance northeast of New Guinea.

On the night of March 7-8 the Japanese moved into Lae and Salamaua, two sites on the north coast of New Guinea proper. This placed the enemy less than 200 air miles from Port Moresby, key Allied base of New Guinea's southern coast, and the jumping-off place for Australia. The peril and squeeze on the great continent "down under" was now obvious. Indeed, Jap bombers had already heavily plastered Darwin from their East Indies bases. Japanese conquest of New Guinea would eliminate the last barrier to Australia. The Japanese had to be stopped in New Guinea.

American air strikes on Rabaul, Lae and Salamaua began immediately with a small token force of 12 B-17's based on Australia. They were largely ineffective because of violent weather, mechanical difficulties and strong enemy resistance. Meanwhile a U.S. Navy single carrier task force, composed of the *Lexington* and attendant ships, secretly approached Rabaul from the northeast for a surprise attack.

While still 400 miles from Rabaul, this force was spotted by a Japanese flying boat and attacked by nine enemy twin-engine bombers off Bougainville. In the ensuing conflict, Lt. Edward "Butch" O'Hare shot down five of the bombers in one mission, a remarkable and historic feat. With the cat now out of the bag, Admiral Sherman, Task Force Commander, turned his fleet southeast, sailed around the Solomon Islands, rendezvoused with another single-carrier force (the *Yorktown*) north of New Caledonia and the combined two-carrier task force steamed toward the southern coast of New Guinea. The objective was to strike Lae and Salamaua from the south, across the towering Owen Stanley Mountains, the least likely quarter from which the enemy would expect Navy planes to come.

Quietly the force slipped into the waters of the Papuan Gulf near Port Moresby and on the morning of March 10, 1942, the two carriers launched 104 fighters and dive bombers which

57

Hangar and quarters at Lae, New Guinea, were devastated in swift air attack. "Betty" bomber in foreground and "Oscar" and "Zeke" fighters nearby were left in various stages of destruction.

The Navy and Air Force coordinated attack left the Japanese newly acquired base at Salamaua in ruins.

Lt. Edward "Butch" O'Hara in the cockpit of his carrier fighter. Off Bougainville, just before the attack on Lae and Salamaua, O'Hara shot down five Japanese bombers in one mission.

headed toward a pass in the towering 16,000-ft. Owen Stanley Mountains. On the other side of the mountains across the island at Salamaua, unsuspecting Japanese were hustling troop reinforcements and supplies ashore. The fighters, led by Lt. Comdr. Jimmy Thach of the *Lexington* units, slipped through the Owen Stanley Pass and began their descent in a long, fast dive. From afar they could see the shipping anchored in the harbor at Salamaua disgorging troops and supplies. As they drew near — fighters and torpedo planes in the van — the Japanese bases buzzed like a stirred-up anthill. The enemy had heard the distant roar of

the big formation and frantically scrambled to set up a defense.

The torpedo planes went after the warships and transports in the harbor, followed by the dive bombers in systematic combat rhythm. Meanwhile, fighters took care of the little air opposition and began working the place over in low-level strafing passes.

Simultaneously a portion of the attacking force hit Lae in much the same vicious style.

The sneak attack swept across the two Japanese bases like a tornado. It ended abruptly much as it had begun, and when the last plane gathered into the returning formation, losses were

This never-before-published photo shows the proud carrier *Lexington* being shattered by a tremendous explosion during the Battle of the Coral Sea, May, 1942. Camera catches a plane in mid-air being thrown off the flight deck by the force.

counted. Only one Navy fighter was gone. It had been seen landing wheels up in the waters of Salamaua harbor. Two Japanese seaplanes, which had managed to get off during the attack, had been shot down.

The victorious formation swung back across the plains of New Guinea, headed up into the pass of the Owen Stanley Mountains, then down to the Papuan Gulf on the other side and onto the decks of their waiting flat-tops, *Lexington* and *Yorktown*.

In terms of overall Japanese war effort, the damage inflicted at Salamaua and Lae had been small. But the Japanese had been stung in a swift hit-and-run combat strike they had not expected. It was a sign from the sky that their unopposed conquest was quickly running out.

Eight B-17's from Australia followed

up the carrier raid on Salamaua, damaging one transport. Crews reported four ships burning in the harbor, two sinking and a fifth beached. It had been a successful, combined AAF-Navy air strike, the first of many like it during the war.

Despite continued Air Force attacks on Lae, Salamaua and Rabaul, the Japanese became firmly entrenched on the northeast New Guinea coast and began plans for the capture of Port Moresby on the other side of the island. Their tactics were to make an end run by sea around the tip of New Guinea rather than push overland.

And so it was that in early May, 1942, the *Yorktown* and the *Lexington* carrier task force swept back into the Coral Sea to deal with a strong Japanese invasion force, reported by AAF reconnaissance planes to be headed for an amphibious assault on Port Moresby. In a dramatic, historic engagement which lasted several days from first contact, the U.S. Navy fighter and dive bomber pilots sank the Japanese escort carrier *Shoho* and severely damaged *Shokaku*, newest of the Jap carrier fleet. Like a whipped dog, the enemy amphibious force turned and headed back from whence it came. The price of victory was the U.S. carrier *Lexington*, fanatically at-

On the order "Abandon Ship," American pilots and seamen stream down the sides of the *Lexington*.

tacked by enemy torpedo planes and bombers. Severely damaged and fire-gutted, the proud "Lex" remained afloat and had to be sunk by the guns of one of our own destroyers.

This, the "Battle of the Coral Sea," was the first naval engagement in history in which opposing ships never fired a shot at each other! It was fought on both sides by air action entirely and it set the pattern for naval carrier warfare throughout the rest of the war.

The victory of the Coral Sea saved Port Moresby from Japanese occupation. It lightened the pressure on Australia and marked the beginning of the turning of the Japanese tide of conquest.

Marianas Islands. Two mechanics of a 7th AAF fighter base, who have helped build new planes from scrap parts in this aircraft graveyard, look up from their work to see these Thunderbolts returning from a successful mission against a Japanese base.

PART TWO

THE ROAD BACK

"God in your guts, good men at your back,
Wings that stay on — and Tally Ho."
— GILL ROBB WILSON

A Navy scout plane looks down on a sight familiar to all American airmen in the Pacific. While air-and-sea bombardment plasters the island of Anguar (right), troop-laden landing craft head for beaches.

A "Kenney cocktail" exploding in flaming tentacles of white phosphorus over Lakunai airfield, Rabaul. An ingenious adaptation of the incendiary bomb, the "cocktail" could be set either to burst in the air or on impact.

Introduction

THE FIRST six months of the war was largely a Japanese show. Retreating Americans, Australians and Dutch mounted a few hit-and-run strikes, but these were small and ineffective blows. One by one, all bases north of Australia — with the exception of Port Moresby, Milne Bay and Merauke — were abandoned as the Oriental tide spread like oil on water from the Philippines south into the Dutch East Indies, the Solomon Islands, New Guinea and across the Central Pacific.

It was in Australia that the major air buildup for the road back began and by a stroke of fortune it got under way almost immediately after Pearl Harbor. On December 7, 1941, word of Pearl Harbor was flashed to a convoy of eight American troop transports and miscellaneous supply ships, plowing through the high seas bound for the Philippines. The convoy was radioed to change course for Brisbane, Australia, and on December 22, after a zigzag course weaving through the Pacific, it unloaded there its precious cargo of about 70 P-40 fighters and A-20 attack bombers, along with 2,000 airmen (48 pilots) and a variety of supplies. To these aircraft were added the handful of B-17's and aircrews who flew out of the Philippines, forming a small offensive force before the year was out.

Combined with remnants of the Dutch (flying obsolete B-10's) and the Royal Australian Air Force, these men and aircraft ranged north to Lae and Salamaua in New Guinea, Rabaul on New Britain Island and points in the Dutch East Indies. The missions were feeble pokings at best, but they helped keep an eye on the advancing Japanese.

Meanwhile ferry routes were set up from the United States through North Africa and India to Australia and from San Francisco through Hawaii, the Fiji Islands, New Zealand and New Caledonia. In early 1942, B-24's, B-25's, B-26's and C-47's began to arrive in Australia at the rate of three or four a day at first, while fighters had to make the long trip on aircraft carriers or lashed to the decks of ocean freighters. Never were large numbers allocated to the Pacific, however, since events and priority of the European war took first place. It was a situation that would plague the air forces in the Pacific throughout the first two years of the war.

Within six months after Pearl Harbor the organization of American air power in the Pacific began to take shape in a gigantic ring around the periphery of Japanese conquest as men, aircraft and units poured out of U.S. training bases and onto airstrips newly scraped from the primitive soils of strange weird-sounding islands. The buildup, once it began, enlarged like a rolling ball of wet snow, for behind it was a determined nation with unlimited resources.*

The main air unit in the Southwest Pacific was the 5th Air Force, redesignated from the prewar Far East Air Force in mid-1942. It was made up of the aggregate of American units, personnel and equipment in Australia. General George C. Kenney was appointed commander. It was the 5th which planted itself between the advancing Japanese and Australia and stole the offensive from the enemy over New Guinea. Led by the astute Kenney, the 5th was the maker of combat air commanders such as Ennis Whitehead, Paul B. "Squeeze" Wurtsmith, Frederic H. Smith, Roger Ramey and "Big Jim" Davies. It was the breeder of fighter heroes and

* EDITOR'S NOTE: In January of 1942, American air forces had 8 combat air groups (3 heavy, 5 fighter) facing Japan. By January 1943 it had grown to 23¾ groups (6¾ heavy bomb, 4¾ medium bomb, 9¾ fighter, 2 troop carrier, ½ reconnaissance); in January 1944 the figure rose to 42 (10½ heavy bomb, 7½ medium bomb, 15 fighter, 6 troop carrier, 3 recon); in January 1945 it had reached a high of 69 groups (12 very heavy bomb, 11½ heavy bomb, 9½ medium bomb, 19 fighter, 13 troop carrier, 4 reconnaissance); and at war's end in August 1945 the peak figure reached 86 groups (23 very heavy bomb, 13 heavy bomb, 9 medium bomb, 23 fighter, 14 troop carrier, 4 reconnaissance). In addition there were 65 special squadrons, mainly recon and night fighter. Generally speaking each group had 3 or 4 squadrons and group aircraft strength was as follows: 45 very heavy bomb, 72 heavy bomb, 96 medium bomb; 111-126 fighter; 80-110 troop carrier; 125 combat cargo; 27 per recon squadron; 19 per combat mapping squadron.

among the 147 5th Air Force aces were top scorers like Dick Bong (40 kills), Tommy McGuire (38 kills), Charlie MacDonald (27 kills), and Maj. William Shomo who shot down seven enemy planes in a single action. From five miles up to treetop level, the versatile and aggressive 5th unpacked a bag of surprises that caught the Japanese off-balance and reeled him back with weapons such as the beefed-up B-25, the parachute bomb, the "Kenny cocktail" phosphorus bomb, and techniques like skip-bombing and on-the-deck attack which swept scythe-like from the Darwin–Port Moresby area across the Owen Stanley Mountains of New Guinea to Nadzab and up to Lae, Wewak, Hollandia, Biak, Morotai to Leyte, Mindoro and Luzon in the Philippines.

The strong right arm of the 5th in the lower South Pacific was the 13th Air Force, organized in January 1943 in New Caledonia. Called the "Jungle Air Force," for the tropical jungle was its home during the entire war, this small, hard-hitting unit moved up into Guadalcanal to work with the Marines. Then under the overall command of Admiral Nimitz's Pacific Ocean air forces, it joined marine and naval air in the campaign for the Solomon Islands, New Georgia, Bougainville and Rabaul, while its B-24 heavies ranged out to strike faraway targets in the Carolines and Marshalls on 1400-1800-mile round-trip missions to enemy bastions like Truk,

Yap and Palau. When the 13th arrived in the New Guinea area, it joined its efforts with the 5th in the air offensive back to the Philippines. It was the P-38's and B-24's of the 5th and 13th which neutralized the vital oil-producing center at Balikpapan and supported the invasion of Palawan and Borneo. The 13th's roster of war personalities included its commander, Brig. Gen. Nathan F. Twining (later Chief of Staff USAF and Chairman, Joint Chiefs of Staff) , Brig. Gen. Hubert Harmon (first Air Force Academy Superintendent) and among its 29 aces were Bob Westbrook (20 victories) and Tom Lamphier who shot down Admiral Yamamoto.

Third of the major air forces was the 7th, created out of the Hawaiian Air Force of Pearl Harbor days and committed to the island-hopping campaign across the Central Pacific. It was the 7th that shared with the Navy in the historic Battle of Midway (turning point of the war in June 1942), struck the Jap strongholds in the Gilbert and Marshall Islands, reduced the bastion of Truk and Yap, and moved on into the Marianas and the Philippines. The 7th generated few aces since most of its work was long-range bombardment of pinpoint islands always beyond the horizon. One of its commanders, Brig. Gen. Thomas D. White, later became Chief of Staff, USAF.

By 1944 these three air forces had

The Japanese aircraft carrier *Agaki* makes desperate maneuvers to miss the falling bombs from B-17's during the Battle of Midway on June 4, 1942.

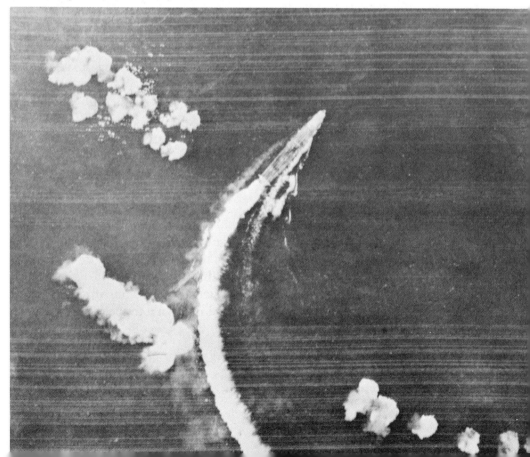

driven across the Pacific to the Philippines and there were eventually combined into the Far East Air Force under Gen. George C. Kenney to prepare for the final assault on Japan. It was a mighty air organization.

In the far north, flying out of Alaskan and Aleutian bases, the 11th Air Force experienced more bad weather than Japanese opposition. Against the most rigorous hardships of weather, the bomber and fighter crews of the 11th struck the Japanese entrenched on Kiska until they left that rocky island, supported the recapture of Attu and went on to hammer targets in the Kurile Islands — the approaches to the Japanese mainland. Throughout the war the 11th stood guard on the northern approaches to the North American continent, and never were the Japanese a serious threat in that quarter of the combat world.

Confronting Japan in Asia were two China-Burma-India Theater (CBI) air forces whose job was a holding action — to pin down and prevent a major Japanese advance on the mainland. Primary work of the India-based 10th Air Force was the destruction of enemy communications and supplies, disruption of rail, road and water transport systems, and the transportation of troops, guerrillas, and fifth column agents behind enemy lines.

Copartner of the 10th in the Orient was the China-based 14th Air Force which evolved from the AVG. Small, inadequately equipped and supplied, but brilliantly led by Gen. Claire Chennault, the 14th kept the overwhelmingly superior enemy at bay for three long years, helping to prevent the collapse of the Chiang Kai-shek government and the Japanese overland thrust to interior China.

Together the CBI air forces produced 123 aces, top among whom were John C. "Pappy" Herbst with 23 victories, John Hampshire with 17, Bruce Holloway with 13 and Ed McComas and Robert L. Scott with 14 each.

Key to the support of the combat operations in this area was the China-India Wing of the global Air Transport Command. This was the combat cargo unit, under Brig. Gen. William H. Tunner, which unveiled a miracle in war logistics by airlifting over the "Hump" — the rugged Himalayan Mountains between India and Yunnan Province in China — all the materials of war needed by the 14th Air Force after the Burma Road was cut by the Japanese in 1942. By day and by night, over the perilous roof of the world, C-47's, C-46's, C-54's, and C-87's shuttled their precious cargoes of a thousand things from sulfa pills and powdered eggs to ammo, gasoline and mules.

The five major land-based air forces which helped carve the road back were made up of essentially the same type combat units and aircraft — heavy and medium bombardment, fighter, troop carrier, and reconnaissance. Their mission was not to specialize in any one phase of strategic or tactical air war like their European counterparts. But specialize they did in both. The nature of the theater and of the enemy, the distances involved and the job to be done required their mastery of all combat tactics. By and large the aircraft they had were the same. Mainstay in the heavy bomber category was the four-engine B-24 "Liberator," which eventually replaced most B-17's in the Pacific area. The main medium bomber of Pacific combat was the twin-engine B-25 "Mitchell"; others included the A-20 "Boston" and A-26 "Invader" light attack bombers, and the B-26 "Marauder." When the war began two types of fighters, the P-39 "Aircobra" and P-40 "Warhawk," were available in substantial num-

bers. By December 1942 the twin-engine, twin-boomed P-38 "Lightning" began to replace the P-40's and went on to become the major Jap killer. In 1943 the P-47 "Thunderbolt" appeared and during the last year of the war the superior long-range P-51 "Mustang" outclassed everything it flew with or against.

Transport workhorses of all air forces included the beloved, dependable twin-engine C-47 "Skytrain" (Gooney Bird) for short-haul duty. By 1944 the twin-engine C-46 "Commando" was introduced into Troop Carrier Groups in all theaters. It extended the radius of theater transport and allowed larger cargoes. Long-range workhorses primarily used by the Air Transport Command on trans-

With engine dead and on fire, a gaping hole in the right wing, this P-38 Lightning fighter is limping back to Saipan after a strike on Japanese-held Iwo Jima.

The Republic P-47 Thunderbolt was a versatile, all-around fighter bomber that came into Pacific service in 1944.

oceanic flights, but found in limited quantities in numbered air force units, were the four-engine C-54 "Skymasters" and the cargo-converted B-24 bomber, designated the C-87.

Special kudos are due the men of Troop Carrier. Theirs was the unenviable task of supporting the fast-moving combat air offensive by flying their cargo-laden C-47's and C-46's unarmed through combat zones over measureless miles of open ocean, in and out of crude airstrips surrounded by impenetrable jungles, and through sudden, violent tropical thunderstorms and fronts. Troop Carrier pilots kept the war moving forward, and they got no glory for it.

Water-based air power partners in the Pacific were Navy carrier task groups and forces under the direction of Admiral Chester Nimitz, Commander of the Pacific Ocean areas.

These surface ship forces, built around aircraft carriers, were formed and re-formed into numbered units to meet whatever specific task lay ahead. Led by distinguished naval air commanders like F. J. Fletcher (Task Force 17), R. A. Spruance (Task Force 16), Marc A. Mitscher (Task Force 58 and First Fast Carrier Task Force), C. A. Pownall (Task Force 15 and 50), W. F. "Bull" Halsey (Task Force 8 and 16), F. C. Sherman, A. W. Radford and J. S. McCain (Second Fast Carrier Task Force) and a dozen more brilliant combat leaders, mobile air-strike fleets swept from the bleak Aleutians through the Gilbert, Marshall, Caroline and Marianas islands, to the tangled shores of the Solomon Islands, Bougainville, New Britain, New Guinea, the East Indies and up to the Philippines, supporting all major military offensives. To the task forces were added shore-based Navy patrol wings and bombing squadrons.

Small but tough brothers of the Navy air forces were Marine air squadrons. Tied largely to Marine ground divisions, these fighter and fighter-bomber units island-hopped through the Central and South Pacific wherever the marines set foot ashore to root out the enemy. Theirs was some of the worst, bitterest infighting of the war — meeting the enemy in the air and laying down firepower on the ground in support of their fellow marines.

Naval carrier and land-based marine pilots contributed their share to taking out the enemy. Leading the roster of 330 naval aces was David S. McCampbell with 34 victories, Cecil Harris with 24, Eugene Valencia with 23. Top three marines on the list of 120 leatherneck aces were "Pappy" Boyington with 28, Joseph Foss with 26 and Robert M. Hansen with 25. Together naval and marine pilots destroyed more than 12,000 Japanese planes at a loss of only 922 of their own. In addition they sent to the bottom of the Pacific 161 Japanese warships, 447 merchantmen, totaling 2,250,000 tons — a creditable record indeed.

Chief among the naval combat aircraft were the SB2C "Helldiver" which replaced the SBD "Dauntless" on carriers in 1943 — both were dive bombers; the TBM-TBF "Avenger" which re-

Seamen gunners watch intently as a graceful but potent F4U Corsair leaves a carrier deck for a combat mission.

placed the TBD "Devastator" in 1942; the F4F "Wildcat," carrier-and-land-based fighter of Pearl Harbor vintage, Wake and Guadalcanal; the graceful, beautiful but deadly F4U "Corsair," fighter-fighter bomber; and the F6F "Hellcat," one of the outstanding, most potent fighter planes of the entire war. It became the nemesis of Japanese military aviation and superseded the F4F "Wildcat" in 1943.

All-around patrol bomber was the twin-engine PBY "Catalina" with the big parasol wing. This ungainly craft rescued many downed aircrews and was the workhorse of naval air in the Pacific. The four-engine B-24 "Liberator" in Navy Blue, the PBY4Y-1 performed long-range, shore-based patrol and bombing tasks, along with its smaller colleague the PV-1 twin-engine "Ventura." Big boy was the PBM "Mariner," a seaplane.

The two principal Marine aircraft were the F4U "Corsair" and SBC "Dauntless" though later in the war some squadrons flew TBM "Avengers" and F6F "Hellcats." Most leatherneck air combat was from land-based strips; however, in the closing days a few Marine units operated from carriers.

Small numbers of Royal Australian and Royal New Zealand planes and crews contributed measurably to the offensive but mainly kept bypassed Japanese garrisons neutralized. The Royal Netherlands East Indies Air Force, which fled to Australia in the early part of the war, came back to hit the Japanese in the East Indies. In the far north the Royal Canadian Air Force joined 11th Air Force operations guarding the icebox door to North America, while the Mexican Air Force entered combat in the Philippines during the last three months of the war. For the most part the Allied air forces in the Pacific flew American combat aircraft.

This, then, was the organization of air power in the Pacific and the Far East — a mighty, deadly array of combat air weapons and crews which within one year began to rise out of the ashes and debris of Pearl Harbor and Clark Field to draw a ring around Japanese Pacific conquest. By January 1943 this ring began to close.

It was a combination of many things that made this rapid buildup possible — the miracle of American production line manufacture of aircraft,* the mass training of pilots and technical service personnel, the rapid or-

* EDITOR's NOTE: Between July 1, 1940 and August 31, 1945 American aircraft industry produced 174,768 combat planes of the 18 major types used by the Army Air Forces and the Navy-Marines in all theaters, Pacific and Europe. This was 86 percent of the total combat aircraft production of 201,687. In addition, 1,089 C-54's, 3,144 C-46's, and 10,245 C-47's were among the 23,929 transports produced for U.S. and Allied Nations. Total U.S. military aircraft production between July 1, 1940 and August 31, 1945 was nearly 300,000. From 6,500 in 1940 it skyrocketed to a high peak of 96,000 in 1944. In engines the increase jumped from 6,000 in 1940 to 256,912 in 1944, for a total of 802,161 engines and 807,424 propellers. Total cost of the entire military aircraft production for the war, including spare parts, was $45 billion.

ganization and deployment to the Pacific bases of land-based aircraft and the appearance of new aircraft carriers. By the end of 1943 the Navy air arm had added 48 new carriers and a year later the number had doubled with the majority assigned to Pacific waters. The growth of land-based air units was phenomenal. Between paper organizations and combat-ready outfits lay an accelerated training program that reflected the greatest American effort in its history.

From a near-zero number of Pacific-based combat planes in January 1942, American air forces grew to over 3,500 first-line combat aircraft in January 1943, and a year later the figure stood well over 12,000. By January 1945 it topped the 18,000 mark by a healthy margin.

In comparison, at the time of Pearl Harbor, first-line Japanese combat aircraft strength was nearly 3,500. So great were Japanese combat losses that at no time during the entire war did Japanese air strength on the far-flung fronts measure beyond 4,100 combat aircraft, and this despite her mass production turnout of warplanes.*

* EDITOR'S NOTE: Japanese air power was geared for a quick offensive war, not a long drawn-out defensive war of attrition. As American production rose, Japanese dropped. American air and sea forces so effectively sealed off Japan's sea-lanes, cutting imports of raw materials and causing paralysis of lines of sea communications, that during the last four months of 1944 Japan's aircraft industry turned out only 11,698 aircraft of all types. With the beginning of the B-29 heavy offensive in 1945 it dropped to 10,778 during the first six months, and almost completely stopped, except for a dribble, after July 1945.

Here, in cold statistics, lies the big story of the Pacific air war — the destruction of around 28,000 Japanese* first-line combat planes in the air and on the ground — an attrition rate beyond the aircraft replacement and crew training capability of the Empire. Add to that the B-29 strategic offensive which put the *coup de grace* to aircraft manufacture in 1945.

Without control of the air, Japanese land and sea forces could not survive the offensive — from land, sea and air — thrown against them.

This, then, is the reason why in a short six months after Pearl Harbor the wheels of Japanese conquest began to grind to a stop and by January 1943 had slipped into reverse gear.

There were many events which marked the end of the line for Japanese advances and the beginning of the Road Back for the Allies. But the first big one was the "Battle of Midway," June 2-6, 1942. Here the U.S. Navy Task Forces 16 and 17, under Admirals Fletcher and Spruance, assisted by Midway-based Marine aircraft and 7th Air Force B-17's, intercepted a powerful four-carrier mobile force (the Japanese First Fleet) heading toward Midway Island. In a surprise air attack, four Japanese aircraft carriers were destroyed along with a cruiser and 275 Jap planes. Forty U.S. shore-based and 92 U.S. carrier planes were lost, as was a destroyer and the carrier

* EDITOR'S NOTE: U.S. aircraft losses on combat missions against Japan in the Pacific totaled 5,510.

Yorktown. But it was a decisive victory for U.S. air power and the turning point of the war. Stopped in the Central Pacific, the Japanese next turned toward Guadalcanal in the south where they made one of their most determined, desperate efforts of the war.

In August, 1942, U.S. Marines poured ashore at Guadalcanal, anchor bastion of the Japanese in the South Pacific. Here the marines began a bitter, bloody six-month campaign for that island. By February of 1943 Guadalcanal was secured and the Japanese thrust into the South Pacific, aimed at outflanking Australia, had been reversed. With their anchor position gone, the retreat began.

Meanwhile, by fall of 1942, the 5th Air Force had gained control of the air over New Guinea and helped turn back a Japanese land push to capture Port Moresby by flying a 20,000-man Allied Army across the Owen Stanley Mountains where the decisive, fiercely fought "Gona-Sanananda Battle" put an end to Japanese plans for New Guinea. Six months later, when the Japs were to try again, their invasion convoys were spotted in the Bismarck Sea north of New Britain Island. Throwing everything it had at this amphibious fleet, 5th Air Force B-17's, B-25's, A-20's, P-38's, P-40's, and Australian Beauforts and Beaufighters sank 20 ships. Only one Japanese destroyer escaped. The "Battle of the Bismarck Sea" was a decisive victory for land-based air forces.

The Road Back had begun. What had taken the Japanese six months to capture, would take the Allies more than two years to get back. Such was the ferocity and the tenacity of the enemy in retreat, an enemy who did not know the word surrender.

Into the islands and jungles of the Pacific, American airmen brought their fighters, bombers and transports to meet the flood of Japanese conquest and turn it back. And they found here a nightmarish never-never land. There was no precedent for fighting a war in it.

The Setting—Into a Strange, Weird World

Capt. Donald Hough and Capt. Elliott Arnold

WHEN WE brought airplanes into the sweating jungle islands of the Pacific we stepped back thousands of years.

We brought the latest aircraft, the most modern mechanical flying wonders from the most mechanical-minded country in the world, equipped them with trained, expert technicians both on the ground and in the air, and then dumped everything into a primitive

Life was lived in a jungle nightmare in the Pacific War. Often, the nearest thing to cities were groupings of grass shacks such as this one southwest of Hollandia, New Guinea. Three American crash victims were awaiting rescue here.

green sea of trees where a canoe's outrigger was a device of marvelous ingenuity.

To the jungle archipelago, to the swampy, unmarked, unroaded, unbroken land of cannibals, headhunters and savages who regarded poisoned arrows as the latest tricky implements of war, we brought P-38's, P-47's, B-25's, B-17's and B-24's.

Next to a witch doctor's hut, still stinking from the greasy brews concocted with screeching incantations to native gods, still decorated with the shriveled heads and the rib bones of slain enemies, we set up repair shops and communication depots, antiaircraft batteries and radar installations.

This, from the beginning, was the difference between the war against the Japanese in the Southwest Pacific and any war we were fighting or ever had fought anywhere else — the country itself, its whole unbearable strangeness and unfamiliarity, its sense of entire removal from anything we had ever known. The country itself had to be met, figured out, overcome, and only after that could we turn our attention to a tough, savage enemy who already was there, who already was entrenched and protected within it.

Somehow airplanes belong over Europe, because Europe is modern. It knows of airplanes and trucks and radio and radar and tanks. Europe is a continent of cities. It is fitting to use airplanes to fight over Europe. There is a sameness in time.

Fighting with airplanes in the Southwest Pacific was an anachronism greater than that of the Yankee who invaded King Arthur's court with a firearm. It would have been closer in time and understanding and relative civilizations if suddenly we had found ourselves fighting over medieval Europe or in the French and Indian wars or with Cortez and the Aztecs.

The Pacific to us was ancient beyond understanding.

Even in the primitive sections of North Africa where we first went to fight in enemy-held land there were some points of identification. There were people who were distant from us but who were close and understandable compared with the cannibal in New Guinea.

There were cities in North Africa. There were roads, docks, piers, bridges, stone buildings, stores.

In the Southwest Pacific there was nothing. There were but a few collections of grass buildings here and there from Australia to the Philippines. There was nothing we could call a town. Only one or two places we would dignify with the name village.

There was not a single dock, a single wharf, a single pier, capable of large-scale unloading of war material. We could not use the scrubby little ports the enemy used because he unloaded from barges that never had to cross an ocean and could beach anywhere; or else, when he came in larger boats, he frequently tied his supplies in rubber envelopes, dumped them into the water, and floated them into shore.

He could do this because his supplies were lighter and scantier than ours. He lost a large proportion of them, but he could afford that too.

Where, occasionally, he had a decent harbor, in Rabaul, for instance, he also had too many men there to make it worth our while to put him out. We bypassed and contented ourselves with the lesser places. We had to work harder with those places but we saved our men and we left great numbers of his men behind us to wither on the vine.

We could not use the paths the enemy cut in the jungle because he carried his meager supplies on his back, or by native carrier, or by mule pack, and never needed a road that would accommodate heavy trucks and tanks in wet weather.

We could not use the primitive bridges he built because they were intended to support men, or light wagons, and not heavy vehicles.

There was nothing there for us when we arrived but the jungle.

The impact of the jungle was in many ways greater than the impact of the enemy. We fought trees and swamps and mountains and disease and strange flying things and insects and crazy noises more than we ever fought the Japs.

It bred a strange feeling in our men. There was no escape in surroundings.

5th Air Force carrier planes, landing on forward New Guinea strip areas with supplies, always drew curious throngs of near-naked, guttural-voiced natives.

There was no Algiers to visit, no Cairo, not even the dirty, twisted streets of a Constantine.

After a while, fighting in Italy or France, men came to cities. They found places where people spoke to them, where people were glad to see them, where people made a fuss over them and cheered and gave them a glass of wine. They were made to feel good, and they could laugh, and pictures were taken of them, and some of the ennui and exhaustion and filth and deadliness of war could be wiped away for a little while.

There was nothing of this in the Pacific. From the time that our fighting men left Australia until the time they arrived in the Philippines, more than two years later, they lived in a jungle nightmare, a poisonous, lush, terrible summation of all the unknowns, all the terrors. There were no cities, only grass shacks; and when some of the men finally got to the Philippines they looked at a two-story stucco house with unbelieving eyes. There were no welcoming natives, nobody who ever felt he had been liberated, no girls to cling to jeeps, no cheers, no waving flags.

Just painful, exhausting creeping through the jungle, where this year's fighting seemed the same as last year's and where the distances were so great, the end never seemed in sight.

There was nothing of a life outside of the life the men brought with them. Inside their camps was a semblance of America — two feet from the last tent in the line was the jungle.

There was nothing to absorb the shock of war. The men had to absorb the shocks among themselves, as though floating in space alone, for months and months, until the months became years. The men were pushed together in a way that few of our soldiers anywhere else were pushed together. Each little bit of America that was clawed out of the jungle was clawed out personally, by machine and by hand, and with effort and desperate need. Need, because without the reminders, you might think that this was life, that Kansas City and Idaho and Texas and New York and Maine and Georgia and California were just delirious dreams caused by malaria and jungle heat and dengue.

The jungle closed in again the moment you turned your back, the way water closes in around stones on shore when the tide rises. And that was more than just a mental hazard. It was not only that you might begin to think strange things — an airplane might fall into the jungle right under your eyes, a huge Fortress, for instance, and in a day the jungle would swallow it up silently, and in two days the green thickness would enclose it so that you might fly a hundred feet above it, looking for it, and not see it.

The enemy counted on the jungle when he started out on world conquest. He figured the jungle and the weather would beat us as they had beaten other men into lethargy and insanity for hundreds of years. He figured out that what little was left of us when nature got finished, he could handle easily. Besides, we were supposed to be flabby, anyway. Remember the jitterbugs and the loafers who used to stand on street corners?

That concept was the enemy's gigantic error of the war, and because this concept was in error, the war did not go the way he planned it. So sure was he, his men were never trained in retreat. So sure was he, he had no backlog of technicians and mechanics to replace those specialists we left stranded behind us in our leapfrogging to the Philippines.

Our failure to fight his war, the war he planned, was one of the chief reasons he lost the war, and lost it long before the end of the final battle.

Yards from where the jungles came down to meet the strip, armament experts attached tail fins to the aerial bombs just before they were loaded for delivery to Japanese targets.

Heady with easy victory from Pearl Harbor to the Asian mainland, the Nipponese air, sea, and land forces plunged headlong into the Southwest Pacific. Here they met an airman whose small, pudgy frame belied the master air tactician that he was, and they were stopped.

Maj. Gen. George C. Kenney had one basic strategy: "to take out the Jap air strength until we owned the air . . ." — and he did just that with an array of tactical air surprises and weapon innovations which sent the Japanese reeling backward. Kenney arrived in the Southwest Pacific in the summer of 1942 as a troubleshooter from Headquarters Air Force in Washington, and he organized the small, badly demoralized, ill-equipped American air units in Australia and New Guinea into a potent, fighting outfit called the 5th Air Force.

The 5th's bomber, fighter and troop carrier pilots did more than stop the Japanese in the air at the gates of Australia. With only a small number of new aircraft and pilot replacements, they took the offensive, cleared the skies over New Guinea and drove the enemy back from whence he came. Not only did this jungle air force defeat the Japanese in the air, but it also reaped a grim toll of their shipping and ground forces, paving the way for General MacArthur's island-hopping drive north to the Philippines.

Here, by Kenney's own intelligence chief, is a broad-brush campaign analysis of how the 5th Air Force helped build the main road back to Tokyo.

Southwest Pacific Boomerang

Col. B. B. Cain

"WE WILL come back and make the Japs pay a hundredfold in death and destruction."

That was the grim pledge made by a handful of survivors of the puny U.S. Far Eastern Air Force that was all but wiped out in the Philippines.

Recapture of the Philippines to the American mind was almost an end in itself, a matter of national honor.

PHASE I — THE JAPANESE THRUST

At the beginning of the war the Japanese military machine was an almost perfect offensive unit. For years the Jap had been trained in offense. His whole movement was based on advance or die, and inasmuch as he had been convinced by these teachings that death meant a beautiful afterlife, he was quite ready to die.

The speed of his advance after Pearl Harbor becomes almost breathless when one realizes that Manila fell on January 2, 1942, and that 18 days later he was softening up Rabaul, in New Britain. Rabaul fell three days later and became the Jap's principal forward supply depot. During the next month the Japanese steamroller overran Borneo, Timor in the Dutch East Indies, and Singapore; the rest of New Britain came into Jap possession, and from bases captured at Lae and Salamaua along the east coast of New Guinea the Jap was bombing Port Moresby and threatening Australia itself.

Early in March the Japs rocketed into Java on one side and occupied Bougainville in the Solomons on the other. Their tactics and strategy were superb: bold leaps, terrific shock. Meeting more opposition than anticipated at any one spot, they would bypass it and take another, finally surround the point of stubborn resistance and strangle it into submission. A large, first-class merchant marine easily supplied, garrisoned and assisted in consolidating newly captured territory.

The ease with which the Japanese merchant marine plied protected shipping lanes, entirely covered by land-based aircraft, backfired, as it made unnecessary the development of an air transport system. Instead, the entire Japanese aircraft industry was devoted to combat airplane production. With such a rapid advance, anything but light maintenance was impossible, but the resulting wastage was offset by a continuous flow of new aircraft.

In the spring of 1942, with the Australian continent as an objective, the Jap met a stubborn point of resistance that he could not afford to bypass — Port Moresby. Typical Japanese "Plan A," which had worked like magic up to this point, was put into effect for its capture. An air-covered, amphibious action supported by strong naval forces set out with the intention of sailing through China Strait around the southeast coast of New Guinea and taking Port Moresby by surprise.

For the first time, however, the formula failed to work. Instead of a smooth victory the enemy met a serious defeat in the Battle of the Coral Sea which was fought May 4-8, 1942. The score: 11 Japanese vessels sunk to one of ours. A month later, June 4-6, the Battle of Midway demonstrated forcibly to the Jap that naval forces cannot operate successfully within range of opposing land-based aircraft. This second setback to his shock power caused a serious scratching of the Nipponese head. He had lost 20 ships and 275 airplanes to our loss of a destroyer and a carrier. That wasn't according to the imperial plan. More than ever he realized that he must speed up his advance and completely cut off Australia from supplies by the occupation of Fiji and New Caledonia. Pressing this policy he captured Ysabel, Choiseul and Guadal-

Packed with ships, the circular harbor at Rabaul, New Britain, presented a lush target for incoming American pilots. Rabaul was a major Japanese stronghold.

canal in July. About the same time the Allied Air Forces were beginning to get some airplanes and the first phase of the war in the Southwest Pacific was drawing to a close.

PHASE II — ALLIES STRIKE BACK

The second phase actually began on August 7, 1942, with the successful landings of U. S. Marines at Tulagi and Lunga. The Japanese advance in the Solomons was halted. Supplies were coming through to Australia. General Kenney's air forces were becoming an air power for the enemy to reckon with as they struck heavy blows at Rabaul in New Britain and Jap-held Lae-Salamaua in New Guinea.

It became more and more evident that Port Moresby must be denied to the Allies if the Japanese were to continue their operations in the Bismarcks and Solomons. They landed forces on the east coast of New Guinea

82

at Buna and Gona on July 22, with a bold plan to march over the mountains and actually capture Port Moresby purely by land operations. By the middle of August, the Japs were well on the way and almost before we were aware of it they had seized a gap in the Owen Stanley Range near Kokoda. Backing up this operation, Japanese troops also landed on Milne Bay, our only base on the north side of the mountains. Fortunately this latter operation which, if successful, would have had a serious effect on our ability to hold Port Moresby, was repulsed on September 7 after some of the most difficult fighting in New Guinea. In the defense of Port Moresby, General Kenney concentrated his air power against Japanese supply lines from Buna to Kokoda. This factor, together with the new idea of Army Support Aviation, namely giving the Army the whole Air Force if it needed help, and backed by the magnificent fighting of Australian troops in the Owen Stanleys, stopped the Japanese advance on September 17. In fact, the enemy was turned back at a point so close to Moresby that the noise of our airplanes warming up on the strip disturbed the sleep of Japanese soldiers.

In adapting themselves to this second phase of the war, which threw them from offensive to defensive warfare, the confusion of the Japanese was evident. No provision had been made in the Jap code, his plan or his command for defense. The best pos-sible outcome of the war for him appeared to be the construction of air bases protected by strong defenses behind which he could hold out long enough to exhaust the patience of the Allies. Japanese engineers were impressed to work like beavers building these bases. Japanese logistics followed the German pattern, except that after devising a plan which carried full proof of success on paper, it was never revised no matter how utterly it failed to work in practice. This failing proved to be an impetus to Allied recovery.

Deficiencies in Japanese supply began to tell, and to further those deficiencies, General Kenney concentrated on shipping targets. Skip-bombing was developed and rehearsals began for the big air show that he knew was coming when a large enemy convoy or concentration of shipping could be attacked with our full available strength. Rabaul was at that time of great importance, since General Kenney was using it as a trap. Its harbor and airfields could always be depended upon to furnish lucrative targets of enemy shipping and aircraft.

Air facilities had been our number one priority target from the beginning, since the process of gaining and holding air superiority demanded constant attack on enemy air installations and aircraft. During the second half of 1942, however, our position was such that General Kenney was able to devote considerable attention to the second priority target, Japanese shipping, which was appreciably depleted by the middle of November.

Food, medicine and supplies were becoming critically short for the enemy through these constant attacks on his shipping. The Japanese had occupied Alexishafen, Madang and Wewak [in New Guinea] and made desperate attempts to strengthen their line across the north of New Guinea. One such attempt to reinforce the Lae area resulted in the Battle of the Bismarck Sea, on March 1-4, 1943, and the complete destruction of an entire Japanese convoy.

The Battle of the Bismarck Sea was the first real test of the much practiced low-level attacks against shipping, and was unquestioned proof of the effectiveness and economy of this type of attack. Again in April, 1943, a heavy bombardment attack against Kavieng resulted in two enemy warships being sunk, three damaged, and three merchantmen badly damaged.

Our own shipping lanes to the east coast of New Guinea were far from safe, but General Kenney took the bull by the horns and, using his troop carrier command, started flying everything in from goods to fully equipped troops. In order to get a base in the Buna area, he flew the airdrome, air force, bombs, garrison, gasoline and food across the mountains to Dobadura.

We were now getting the upper hand, but the Japanese still had some will to fight in the air. In the middle of April, 1943, the enemy raided Port Moresby with 100 airplanes, but the pressure was beginning to tell on the quality of his air force. An air attack on Guadalcanal in June cost the Japanese 94 out of 120 raiders; 22 out of 48 were destroyed at Darwin on the 21st, and 23 out of 36 were shot down over Lae on the 22nd. June also saw our forces move into Kiriwina and Woodlark, south of New Britain.

We were now on the advance and it became obvious to the Japanese that they would have to duplicate the now practically useless Rabaul elsewhere as a receiving and distributing point for supplies. Wewak was the logical alternative and construction was begun to convert it into a major installation; heavy concentrations of aircraft were being accumulated and maintained in the area. It was only natural that we, in turn, should look about for a desirable location on which to build a base from which we could bomb the Wewak area. Our choice was Marilnan, west by south of Lae and right in the enemy backyard. Here our engineers, after a perilous overland trek, constructed a C-47 landing strip under the noses of the Japs; again an airdrome and an air force were flown into a forward base. The move paid off on August 17 and 18 when we destroyed 200 Jap planes at Wewak. This attack marked a turning point that brought us into the third phase of the Pacific War.

PHASE III — THE JAP IN RETREAT

This third phase was the reduction

84

Wewak-bound Japanese freighter is skip-bombed and sunk by two 5th Air Force A-20's. Four splashes can be seen, two of the bombs having been dropped from the plane in front (which took the picture), and two by the plane just clearing the ship's mast.

of the Japanese from a position of defensive holding to positive retreat. It began on September 4-5, 1943, with the amphibious landing east of Lae and the paratroop operation at Nadzab. After that, strike followed strike in rapid succession. Salamaua was captured, and battered Lae became ours on September 16. The Kenney air thrust secured us an advance airdrome up the Markham Valley at Kaiapit on the 20th, followed shortly afterward by the capture of Gusap and Tumpu. An amphibious landing at Finschhafen on the 22nd completed the rout of the Japs on the Huon Peninsula.

During October Rabaul was being squeezed dry of air and shipping targets. A perfectly planned and executed bombing attack on October 12 netted three enemy destroyers, three large cargo vessels, 43 small cargo vessels, 70 harbor craft and 126 airplanes destroyed. Another attack, on November 2, permanently put Rabaul out of the running as a base of any importance to the Japs.

This bleeding white of the enemy air forces and shipping in the Southwest Pacific resulted in the enemy's inability to maintain sufficiently strong air power at any one of his far-flung mandate bases to jeopardize operations of our surface forces against him. Makin and Tarawa were occupied by us on November 21. The Australian 9th Division had pushed the Japanese up to Satelberg, and 1943 was closed with a successful landing at Cape Gloucester and the capture of a PT base at Arawe. New Year 1944 was celebrated one day late with a landing at Saidor, New Guinea.

Whereas the Allied air forces under General Kenney were functioning with deadly efficiency, the enemy's organization had become disrupted to the point of rendering his order of battle useless for tactical planning. A Japanese striking force of 100 planes had become comparable to the power of 25. The enemy was definitely in retreat.

Although Rabaul had been neutralized, it was still too strong for us to chance a frontal attack. As an alternative we captured Green Island to the east and cut off a possible avenue of escape. This move also cut off any chance of the Japanese forces escaping from Bougainville or other parts

A D-Day in the Southwest Pacific. B-25's en route to blast Rabaul cross high over an American invasion convoy headed for Green Island, which lies between Rabaul and Bougainville.

of the Solomons. Our next need was an air base from which we could strike at the enemy's New Guinea flank and completely bottle the Rabaul-Kavieng area. The Admiralty Islands were ideal for this purpose and would also give us a valuable base for deep reconnaissance to the north.

Our objectives, Manus and Los Negros in the Admiralties, were garrisoned by some 4,000 Japanese troops. On March 15 a reconnaissance party in force, consisting of a few hundred rifles of the 1st Cavalry Division, landed at Los Negros. General MacArthur was unexpectedly on the scene and went ashore with the troops. He surveyed the situation and ordered the troops to remain in occupation. Thus Momote airdrome was captured and our perimeter was reinforced just ahead of Japanese reinforcements. This was perhaps the most important operation ever conducted in this theater.

With air coverage available from Momote we were in a favorable position to begin leap-frogging operations in New Guinea. It was no longer necessary to attempt a landing east of the Japanese stronghold at Wewak. Instead a bold stroke was planned to bypass this heavily defended section and land at Hollandia, to the west. On March 29 and 30, heavy bombers covered Hollandia with a perfectly planned attack, destroying a considerable part of the Japanese army air forces in New Guinea. On the following day, fighter-covered strafers followed up and completely wrecked enemy air facilities in the area, burnt out Hollandia and destroyed fuel, maintenance and supply dumps. During these attacks more than 400 enemy airplanes were accounted for, and there is evidence that the Japanese air command in the area was relieved in disgrace.

Hollandia, and Aitape to the east, were occupied without substantial resistance on April 22, cutting off the Japanese 18th Army concentrated mainly at Wewak and the Hansa Bay area* and giving us airfields which increased our heavy bombing range to a sweeping arc that included Soerabaja, Balikpapan, Davao and Saipan. The Halmaheras were open to attack and airdromes of the Vogelkop and Geelvink Bay areas came within range of our mediums.

The aerial blitz against the enemy's bases in the Wakde Islands began on May 6 and nearly 1,000 tons of bombs were dropped on the area from then until May 17 when Allied forces landed in the Toem sector on the Dutch New Guinea mainland opposite the islands. One island of the group was occupied, followed by

* EDITOR'S NOTE: This bypassed army of tens of thousands was left to wither and die in the rotten jungles of the Wewak area. Late in the war, with the front 1,000 miles away, this army, or what was left of it, was still there. Allied air and sea power prevented its resupply or evacuation. It was a typical example of the American bypassing technique employed in the Pacific War. Smaller groups of such "forgotten troops" held out for years after the war ended. Many just melded into the native population and became permanent residents of the area.

87

In three days of concentrated attack on the Hollandia airfield, 5th Air Force fighters and bombers destroyed 288 enemy planes.

others. With our seizure of air facilities in the Wakdes, the whole elaborate system of Jap airdromes in western Dutch New Guinea was in jeopardy. The most distant airfield at Jefman was only 490 miles away, easily within fighter range.

Meanwhile, although some enemy resistance still was being encountered at Wakde, General Kenney would not halt his schedule of aerial advance. Progressively heavy air attacks were being directed against Biak in a repeat performance of the deathblow at Hollandia.

With the stage set, the first act of the plan for Biak came on May 27 when Allied troops established beachheads on the island. Although the landings were made at little cost, stiffening enemy resistance indicated the Japs had a strong cast lined up back of the beaches to keep us from stealing the show. Japanese army and navy aircraft were rushed hurriedly to the scene and the number of fighters intercepting our attacks doubled. Thirteen enemy bombers, of which six were destroyed, bombed and strafed Allied ground positions. On June 2 there were 13 enemy bomber raids. We had a strong cast in the area, too, however, and 59 Jap planes were destroyed, with 15 probables.

Displaying a measure of his former daring, the enemy attempted to reinforce Biak on June 8. Two cruisers and five destroyers heading for the island were successfully attacked by ten B-25's north of Vogelkop. One destroyer was sunk, another was left in a sinking condition, a third was seen blazing furiously and a fourth also was set afire. Late that night, the remnants were observed bearing northwest.

General Kenney's technique of pressing one gain while paving the way for the next jump was evidenced by a bold Allied air attack against the Jefman-Samate area on June 16. Seventeen B-25's with fighter cover destroyed more than 50 enemy planes in combat and on the ground and sank several ships. Our fighters estimated that there had been between 85 and 90 Jap planes on the ground, waiting to intensify resistance at Biak. The plan was nipped in the bud and at Biak the end was in sight. During the week of June 24, all Biak airfields were occupied by the Allies, and to make things even more difficult for the Jap to supply and reinforce his battered garrisons, 5th Air Force search units were regularly knocking down enemy transport planes operating along the formerly safe routes between the Philippines and southern area.

Our persistent attacks in the enemy's backyard paid off on July 2 when an Allied amphibious force landed at Noemfoor, occupying Kamiri airstrip. Lack of air opposition could mean only that the enemy had at last conceded defeat in western Dutch New Guinea and had abandoned it as untenable.

July 27 saw the first of our medium and fighter units over the Halmaheras, when B-25's joined fighter-covered B-24's in an attack against airdromes in the islands. Thirty enemy planes were destroyed on the ground and 15 in the air against a loss of two planes for the attacking force. The major result of this attack was not the actual destruction of enemy aircraft but the fact that it forced the enemy to evacuate to the Philippines all of his air strength except that needed for immediate defense.

To the south, the final step in the retaking of New Guinea came on July 30 when an Allied amphibious force with strong air cover landed at Sansapor in the Vogelkop area. Thus, Manaokwari was added to the by-passed roster, leaving a Jap garrison of some 15,000 effectively cut off. Following this occupation, only token enemy air activity was encountered in the Halmaheras, and the islands became a happy hunting ground for Allied planes.

During August, our bombers pounded airfields and shipping in the islands virtually at will. Days went by without a single case of interference.

Ships and parked planes were destroyed in quantity with very few losses on our part.

This lack of opposition continued into mid-September, even over the southern Philippines where our bombs had begun to fall with regularity. Then on September 15, with almost monotonous repetition, an Allied amphibious force, preceded by air and naval bombardment, landed on Morotai in the northern Halmaheras without opposition. Not a single Japanese rose to question our dominance of the air.

Thus, Japanese tactics and strategy had become an almost unfathomable pattern of confused defense. With the hysteria of a man overturning furniture in the path of a pursuer around a locked room, the enemy had continued to throw reinforcing troops into our line of advance, knowing full well that they inevitably would become lost battalions, isolated and strangled.

In the early days of the Pacific air war, the Japanese pilot was a tough man in the air, well trained, well disciplined. Many had cut their eye-teeth on air combat in China prior to World War II.

There was no doubt that Japanese warlords sent their best pilots to the Southwest Pacific to meet the Americans. One of them was Saburo Sakai, ace supreme who finished the war with 64 enemy aircraft to his credit.

One of Saburo Sakai's greatest ordeals came on August 7, 1942. A strong American amphibious force, covered overhead by Navy and Marine car-rier-based fighters, was speeding toward the beaches of Guadalcanal to disgorge the 1st Marine Division and wrest that strategically located island from the enemy. Approaching from the horizon, sounding like a swarm of angry desynchronized hornets came a cluster of Rabaul-based Japanese bombers and Zero fighters.

Among these attackers was Saburo Sakai in his Zero fighter, and here is his account of tangling with a Navy flyer in a swirling dogfight above the beaches of Guadalcanal.

Saburo Sakai: King of Jap Aces

Saburo Sakai with Martin Caidin and Fred Saito

THIS WAS my first look at an American amphibious operation. It was almost unbelievable. I saw at least 70 ships pushing toward the beaches, a dozen destroyers cutting white swaths through the water around them. And there were other ships on the horizon, too far distant to make out in detail or to count.

Meanwhile the bombers swung slow-ly for their runs. Dead ahead of them small clouds drifted at 13,000 feet. To our right and above was the sun, its blinding glare blotting everything from view. I was uncomfortable; we would be unable to see any fighters

dropping from that angle. My fear was soon realized. Without warning six fighter planes emerged from that glare, almost as if they had suddenly appeared in the sky. A snap glance re-vealed that they were chubbier than the other American planes we had fought. They were painted olive green, and only the lower sides of the wings were white. Wildcats; the first Grumman F4F fighters I had seen.

The Wildcats ignored the Zeros, swooping down against the bombers. Our fighters raced ahead, many of them firing from beyond effective range, hoping to distract the enemy planes. The Wildcats plunged into the bomber formation, rolling together, and then disappeared in dives. Over the water just off Savo Island, the bombers released their missiles against a large convoy. I watched the bombs curving in their long drop. Abruptly geysers of water erupted from the sea, but the enemy shipping sailed on undisturbed.

It was obviously stupid to try to hit moving ships from four miles up! I could not understand the failure to use torpedoes, which had proven so effective in the past. Our entire mission had been wasted, thrown away in a few seconds of miserable bombing inaccuracy.

The bomber formation banked to the left and picked up speed for the return to Rabaul. We escorted them as far as Russell, beyond the enemy fighter patrols, and turned back for Guadalcanal. It was about 1:30 P.M. We swept over Lunga, the 18 Zeros poised for combat. Again bursting out of the blinding sun, Wildcats plunged against our planes. I was the only pilot who spotted the diving attack, and at once I hauled the fighter up in a steep climb, and the other planes followed me. Again the Wildcats scattered and dove in different directions. Their evasive tactics were puzzling, for nothing had been gained by either side. Apparently the Americans were not going to pick any fights today.

I turned back to check the positions of my wingmen. They were gone! Things weren't as obvious as they seemed; the enemy would fight, after all. I looked everywhere for Yonekawa and Hatori, but could not find them. Sasai's plane, the two blue stripes across its fuselage, regained formation, several other fighters moving up to

(Left) Japanese ace, Saburo Sakai, in military flight togs as he appeared during the heyday of his Pacific War combat. (Right) A decade after the war, in his shop in Tokyo, Saburo Sakai examines the flight helmet he wore during his combat days. Tattered white scarf about his neck is also a souvenir of combat.

position behind him. But not my wingmen.

Finally I saw them, about 1,500 feet below me. I gasped. A single Wildcat pursued three Zero fighters, firing in short bursts at the frantic Japanese planes. All four planes were in a wild dogfight, flying tight left spirals. The Zeros should have been able to take the lone Grumman without any trouble, but every time a Zero caught the Wildcat before its guns the enemy plane flipped away wildly and came out again on the tail of a Zero. I had never seen such flying before.

I banked my wings to signal Sasai and dove. The Wildcat was clinging grimly to the tail of a Zero, its tracers chewing up the wings and tail. In desperation I snapped out a burst. At once the Grumman snapped away in a roll to the right, chased around in a tight turn, and ended up in a climb straight at my own plane. Never had I seen an enemy plane move so quickly or so gracefully before; and every second his guns were moving closer to the belly of my fighter. I snap-rolled in an effort to throw him off. He would not be shaken. He was using my own favorite tactics, coming up from under.

I chopped the throttle back and the Zero shuddered as its speed fell. It worked; his timing off, the enemy pilot pulled back in a turn. I slammed the throttle forward again, rolling to the left. Three times I rolled the Zero, then dropped in a spin, and came out in a left vertical spiral. The Wildcat matched me turn for turn. Our left wings both pointed at a right angle to the sea below us, the right wings at the sky.

Neither of us could gain an advantage. We held to the spiral, tremendous G pressures pushing us down in our seats with every passing second. My heart pounded wildly, and my head felt as if it weighed a ton. A gray film seemed to be clouding over my eyes. I gritted my teeth; if the enemy pilot could take the punishment, so could I. The man who failed first and turned in any other direction to ease the pressure would be finished.

On the fifth spiral, the Wildcat skidded slightly. I had him, I thought. But the Grumman dropped its nose, gained speed, and the pilot again had his plane in full control. There was a terrific man behind that stick.

He made his error, however, in the next moment. Instead of swinging back to go into a sixth spiral, he fed power to the engine, broke away at an angle, and looped. That was the decisive split second. I went right after him, cutting inside the Grumman's arc, and came out on his tail. I had him. He kept flying loops, trying to narrow down the distance of each arc. Every time he went up and around I cut inside his arc and lessened the distance between our two planes. The Zero could outfly any fighter in the world in this kind of maneuver.

When I was only 50 yards away, the Wildcat broke out of his loop and astonished me by flying straight and level. At this distance I would not need the cannon; I pumped 200 rounds into the Grumman's cockpit, watching the bullets chewing up the thin metal skin and shattering the glass.

I could not believe what I saw — the Wildcat continued flying almost as if nothing had happened. A Zero which had taken that many bullets into its vital cockpit would have been a ball of fire by now. I could not understand it. I slammed the throttle forward and closed in to the American plane, just as the enemy fighter lost speed. In a moment I was ten yards ahead of the Wildcat, trying to slow down. I hunched my shoulders, prepared for the onslaught of his guns. I was trapped.

No bullets came. The Wildcat's guns remained silent. The entire situation was unbelievable. I dropped my speed until our planes were flying wing-to-wing formation. I opened my cockpit window and stared out. The Wildcat's cockpit canopy was already back, and I could see the pilot clearly. He was a big man, with a round face. He wore a light khaki uniform. He appeared to be middle-aged, not as young as I had expected.

For several seconds we flew along in our bizarre formation, our eyes meeting across the narrow space between the two planes. The Wildcat was a shambles. Bullet holes had cut the fuselage and wings up from one end to the other. The skin of the rudder was gone, and the metal ribs stuck out like a skeleton. Now I could understand his horizontal flight, and also why the pilot had not fired. Blood stained his right shoulder, and I saw the dark patch moving downward over his chest. It was incredible that his plane was still in the air.

But this was no way to kill a man! Not with him flying helplessly, wounded, his plane a wreck. I raised my left hand and shook my fist at him, shouting, uselessly, I knew, for him to fight instead of just flying along like a clay pigeon. The American looked startled; he raised his right hand weakly and waved.

I had never felt so strange before. I had killed many Americans in the air, but this was the first time a man had weakened in such a fashion directly before my eyes, and from wounds I had inflicted upon him. I honestly didn't know whether or not I should try and finish him off. Such thoughts were stupid, of course. Wounded or not, he was an enemy, and he had almost taken three of my own men a few minutes before. However, there was no reason to aim for the pilot again. I wanted the airplane, not the man.

I dropped back and came in again on his tail. Somehow the American called upon a reserve of strength and the Wildcat jerked upward into a loop. That was it. His nose started up. I aimed carefully at the engine, and barely touched the cannon trigger. A burst of flame and smoke exploded

94

outward from his engine. The Wildcat rolled and the pilot bailed out. Far below me, almost directly over the Guadalcanal coast, his parachute snapped open. The pilot did not grasp his shroud lines, but hung limply in his chute. The last I saw of him he was drifting in toward the beach.

Air Command, Cactus, was its code name. But on the map it was called Henderson Field, an airstrip on the lush tropical island of Guadalcanal. It was captured from the Japanese by the Marines in some of the most desperate and deadly infighting of the entire war.

Henderson Field was the key to victory or defeat in the battle for Guadalcanal and the Solomons, a base shared by the Navy, Marine and AAF flyers who moved in quickly to help ground forces take out the Japanese. After that it was as important for the enemy to destroy or recapture Henderson as it was for us to hold it. And so, in the first several months of Guadalcanal the enemy threw everything he had at the field and the handful of pilots there.

There were missions against the Japanese from daylight to dusk; and, after dark, throughout the night, enemy bombers homed over the airstrip spewing the runways, parking revetments and tent areas with destruction, robbing the exhausted flyers of the precious commodity, sleep, and taxing the very limits of their human endurance.

Here, in a vivid word picture, a Marine describes the life and times of his fellow flyers at Air Command, Cactus, in those bitter early days.

The Cactus Bumblebees

John A. DeChant

CACTUS was its code name . . .

"They lived right next to the field . . . in the middle of the bull's-eye . . . anything that offered camouflage or concealment . . . early flight pilots were up an hour before dawn . . . ate a slim breakfast or gulped coffee . . . bumped down to the field . . . warmed up their engines . . . and were ready to go at dawn . . . planes often had to be horsed out of revetments and onto the runway by tractors . . . tried to give the pilots three meals a day . . . sometimes though there wasn't enough food or time to eat it . . . only thing good about the chow was the hot coffee . . . rest was cold hash, spam, or sausage and those awful dehydrated spuds . . . often ate standing up . . . no mess hall . . only a tent . . . had to borrow their mess gear from ground troops . . . no liquor except what the Doc had . . . they were always tired . . . and weak . . . flew at high altitudes all day . . . sucking that oxygen increased pilot fatigue and made them groggy . . . the Doc kept stuffing them with vitamin pills to keep up their resistance. Sometimes the pilots got so hungry they would corral a mess sergeant and knock off one of the stray cattle out of no man's land . . . wasn't healthy but it meant rare beef.

"No PX's . . . no candy . . . no gum . . . smoked Jap cigarettes . . . not even any soap . . . mail came infrequently . . . no extra clothes . . . in a few weeks they looked like a ragged rebel army . . . they lived right on the ground . . . no flooring in tents . . . bunks just sank into the stinking, black mud . . . any gear or equipment they had was so moldy in a few weeks it wasn't fit to use . . . but it had to be . . .

"There was no entertainment . . . no radio . . . news came through Communications . . . they used to lie in foxholes at night and laugh at the broadcasts from San Francisco about how secure the place was . . . when they never knew if tomorrow would be their last day. They used to call themselves the Nameless Wonders . . . the communiques and news broadcasts always babbled about the Army this . . . or the Navy that . . . but when the Marines did it, they were seldom mentioned by name, but called 'our planes' or 'our fighters.' It made them a little bitter when they didn't get the credit . . . but 'what the hell' . . . they said, 'at least the Japs know we're here.'

"Pilots had never heard enemy shelling or bombing before . . . didn't know what to fear . . . they soon learned . . . too much strain and no sleep made their hands shake while smoking cigarettes . . . crouched in the foxholes . . . couldn't see what was coming over . . . couldn't fight back . . . a feeling of nervousness and bewilderment got them . . . pilots in the air knew only the sound of their own motors and chatter of their own guns . . . the whispering whistle of those bombs at night got under their skins . . . everyone strained his ear for the offbeat motors of Washing Machine Charlie or Louie the Louse when they came over at night . . . no lights to pick them out . . . no protection except foxholes . . . you feel yourself shrinking into the smallest possible space . . . and edging close to the other guy because he seemed to give you some protection . . . you could hear Charlie settle down on his bombing run . . . no one ever said a word . . . just shrank and waited . . . a very faint swish . . . as the bombs started down . . . just before they hit, everybody would holler 'here it comes' or some darn thing . . . then open their mouths to reduce the concussion in case it landed too close . . . then you'd

By day and by night, the Japanese made Guadalcanal's Henderson Field a holocaust. Shown here is a motley assemblage of Navy, Marine, and Army men patching up the bomb-pocked steel-matted runway just after a raid.

think . . . 'God, you better do me some good — right now!'

"Praying you did upstairs or down . . . and it was private . . . something quick . . . to make the other guy think you weren't afraid . . . but he knew better because he was . . . the pilots feared the shelling most . . . no warning . . . express train whine . . . harder to hide from . . . the more you took and the more you heard and the longer you were alive . . . gave you a smoky dread inside . . . like your luck was running out . . . and your number was getting close to the top . . . like the Irish sweepstakes drawing . . . you wonder if you won't win tonight . . . some guy always did . . . 'maybe this one is for me?' "

At September's end, those at Air Command, Cactus, felt a sort of be-numbed satisfaction that they had come off well in these early rounds. Three of the Marine fighter pilots had become the country's leading aces. They were Smith with 19 meatballs (tiny Rising Sun flags) on his plane, the gaunt Carl with 16, and Galer with 13. Medals of Honor were later awarded Smith and Galer for their scores and the expert audacity with which they led their squadrons. Carl twice received the Navy Cross.

The first overall tally (kept like all the early records, earnestly penciled on dirty sheets of scrap paper) showed 171 victories over the enemy air force by Henderson-based planes. VMF 223,

97

John Smith's Rainbow squadron, was credited with 93½ planes, of which 50½ were twin-engined bombers and 41 were Zero fighters, plus a Kawanishi four-motor flying boat and a twin-tailed, double-engined bomber of dubious lineage. Galer's VMF 224, with less combat time, had piled up six float planes, nine Zeros and 21½ Betty bombers. Navy's Fighting Five had accounted for 22 assorted kills and the AAF's 67th Pursuit, 4 Zeros.

These airmen in their blue ball caps, shoulder holsters, and filthy odd-lot flying gear looked and felt very unlike the giant killers that headlines called them. They were sick. Dysentery racked their bowels and stomachs. Malaria shivered and burned them. The tasteless, clammy food, Jap rice, and hardtack seemed only to nurture the gnawing of the hunger rat in their bellies. And sleep — sleep was a dream just beyond their fingertips. In their tired minds, behind their sunken eyes, they caressed the thought of a quiet night's sleep as if it were a lush treasure. But there was no break. The work and the weariness went on for those who flew and for the quiet, earnest men who kept them in the air . . .

A far cry from the headlines back home which pictured them as "knights of the air," these gaunt Marine flyers show the strain of incessant day and night combat. At center is Joe Foss, one of Marines' top aces.

98

There were those airmen also who didn't fly from the jungle-carved air-strips of the Southwest Pacific — the men on the ground who kept the planes in the air. They lived no easier life than those who flew, and shared fully the vicissitudes that made life a miserable entity.

Boldly exposed to the elements and the enemy alike, were the men who operated the airstrip control towers — at times shaky, makeshift elevated platforms that defied engineering principles and conspicuously reared themselves along the edge of the landing strip. Here, literally astride a keg of dynamite, was the nerve center of all flight operations, the primary target for enemy bombers and strafers.

For those of the Army Airways Communications System who manned these structures throughout the Pacific and whose voices went out from them into the endless days and nights, there was always comedy and humor to be found in adversity. And if the nimble, wisecracking jargon of Main Street, U.S.A., coupled with that of service talk, confused the listening Japanese, it meant home-sweet-home to returning American flyers.

Especially at Henderson Field, in the early touch-and-go days, was this so.

Henderson Tower

Capt. J. E. Roberts and S/Sgt. John R. Dunn

THE QUICK black of the tropic night settled down among the palm groves of Guadalcanal, and a great yellow bomber's moon rose out of the quiet sea, pouring its amber light along the runway of Henderson Field, down through the tops of the swaying palms, stealing up the crude, angular lines of the control tower.

Two young men, their figures vague and shadowy in the odd half-light, leaned over the railing which enclosed the platform of the tower and peered down from their perch, now into the dispersal areas, now over the runway, now out to sea. A field telephone jangled harshly. One of the men reached out, automatically without turning his head, and took the telephone.

"Henderson Tower."

A thin metallic warning crackled through the instrument.

"Bogies coming. Direction southeast. Stand by for Condition Red."

"Roger."

The tower operator who put down the phone was tall and stripped to the waist, and a blond fuzz struggled to form a beard on his face. He turned

99

The old Henderson Tower at left, target of Japanese strafing and bombing during the early days on Guadalcanal, stands in contrast to its successor being constructed after the battle lines moved south.

to his companion and, as though picking up an interrupted conversation, said:

"All right, Dogface, you can quit pining for Lamour. Tojo's little boys are coming over to play. On with the receiver, and let's keep posted on the Japs."

The other operator, small and dark, reached for his headset. A loudspeaker sputtered and through it came a distinct monotone:

"One Victor Two Three calling Henderson Field."

"Sold American!" the blond boy sang out as he grabbed a mike and flipped a switch. He went on in a monotone, "Henderson to One Victor Two Three. Go ahead."

"Search flight coming to you two minutes out. Request landing instructions, please."

"Come in and circle the field. You may have to go out again; Charlie is headed down the slot. Stand by and we'll give you the dope."

"Roger!"

He put the mike aside. The other boy turned to him and said, "These binocs don't help worth a darn in this light. Can't see a sign of the bogies yet."

"Can't see 'em?" shouted the blond one, snatching the binoculars from his companion's hand. "Who ya think you are? Superman? You couldn't see 'em in this light if they were right overhead. What's the matter with you? Buckin' for Section Eight?"

"It's the sweatin' them out gives me the jitters, I guess," the dark one said. "Just plain scares the hell out of me."

"You and me both. Those bombs whistlin' and crashin' around don't make like lullabies, son. A guy who says he doesn't get the shakes is a Grade-A snow artist."

The other laughed. "If every one of these raids takes a year off your life, brother, have a look at the walkin' dead."

"Yeah, those foxholes prayers of ours must be payin' off. Otherwise we'd be out of luck."

The loudspeaker broke in, blaring, "Bogies closing in fast from southeast. Two flights of three medium bombers each. Condition is red."

The blond, fuzzy-faced kid became all business. "Give 'em those lights," he said, jerking his head toward the field. "Hit the foxhole and leave the door open. I'll bring in this rubberneck flight and do a power dive right after you."

His companion looked at him, not moving. "Relax, junior," he said. "Let's both bring 'em in."

"OK, but you don't have to stay here on Condition Red, you know."

"Save it. Here go the lights."

The signal flare lifted and faded in the pale night, and with it came a raucous cacophony of old auto horns, gongs, clanging brake drums, and harsh voices. Over in the tent area, the lights went out as if turned off by a single switch.

Now the moon had the field to herself. The incoming search flight was overhead, its planes circling the landing strip.

On the ground, planes began warming up for the scheduled interception, their slipstreams churning clouds of dust.

By now the bogies were overdue.

In the tower, five speakers blared at top volume. The blond boy, his fingers clicking at switches, carried on a half dozen conversations, while his companion, pointing a directional-beam gun into the sky, signaled with green flashes to the planes coming in from the search flight.

From one speaker, "Bogies now orbiting. Direction south southeast."

Suddenly the noise quieted down in the tower, and then from below, new noises were added to the roaring of the planes — noises from the tent area where the men were shouting, gibing, catcalling, and whistling, like kids in a neighborhood movie on Saturday afternoon. Something like the kids, the men in the tent area were catcalling partly at the Japs, partly because their own movie had been called off for the raid.

The two tower operators were tense. The blond fingered the controls of the speakers, and the other played with the signal light. From time to time they grinned uneasily.

"You know," said the dark one, "this place really does have the old South Seas romantic atmosphere. At least in the moonlight it does. What a night to pitch a bit of woo. . . . Anything new on the bogies?"

"Nope. That flight of bombers we sent out early this evening is due back pretty soon or we could watch the little son-of-heaven's fireworks from the dugout."

"Yeah, from our nice, comfy little foxhole. Cozy like a sewer."

"Sewer? I've seen you whip in there, son, like it was Shangri-la. Oh, oh, there goes the searchlight over behind the mounted battery. Hear any motors?"

Soon they both could hear a peculiar, desynchronized motor sound — "Washing Machine Charlie." Then, as the noise seemed to be coming from directly overhead, six searchlights stabbed into the sky and converged on one plane high above.

"Let's see what the antiaircraft boys can do tonight," said the blond, looking up at the plane. "Last time they had Charlie hitchhiking to hell in nothing flat. Oh, oh. Sticks away! Hit the deck!"

As they dropped flat they could hear the shrieking whistle of the bombs, then a thudding roar as one struck, and boom, boom, as others hit. The bombs whistled and blasted, and each brief pause between sticks was filled in with echoes reverberating far out over the jungle.

The blond boy raised his head.

"You know what they remind me of? A big Douglas fir being felled. You hear that wind-splitting whish speed up as the branches whip through the air, and then — boom! She hits the ground. Timber-r-r-r!"

With a ba-*loom* that the men could feel press against them, a big one struck nearby. The tower seemed to lift, then it dropped and swayed and trembled. "Boy! That was close," said the blond, "but you see what I mean."

"Fir trees, he says. Those things sound to me just like a fast freight highballing over a crossing back home in Kansas. Listen and you'll get it — that kind of trembling roar."

Another bomb hit close by.

"Bing, bam! Thank you, ma'am! That last baby jarred my bridgework. You OK?"

"Roger. Let's take a look and see if he's using his good eye tonight."

They got up and looked from the platform over the moonlit field. "Set 'em up in the other alley," said one. "He didn't even hit the hospital area this time."

"Every time we get a bombing, I hope he lays an egg near our tent. We'd sure get a swell start on a new foxhole. Save us a lot of digging."

"Boy-oy, the ack-ack boys are hotter than a two-buck pistol tonight. Look at them bounce Charlie around. See him slip that one. Bet he got a fanny full of that burst."

"You ain't beating ya' gums, son. One more and Charlie will miss some geisha necking. If that hit's confirmed, it costs me just five bucks even. I bet that noisy AA corporal a fin that they wouldn't get a hit the next time they had a target. I won't even get to help drink up the fin. We won't get any beer around this place unless we make it."

A faint, imperative voice from a loudspeaker broke into their talk. "One Victor Four Three calling Henderson Tower. One Victor Four Three calling Henderson Tower. Go ahead, Henderson."

"Henderson calling One Victor Four Three. Henderson calling One Victor Four Three. You are S5, R5. Go ahead."

The light-haired kid listened awhile, and turned.

"Hey, quick, junior, alert the crash crew! Tell them to stand by for a crash landing on the strip. Get an ambulance there. Two unidentified planes, too, huh? A couple of Charlies pulling a sneak!"

The other operator dove to a phone while his companion went on talking with the men in the air.

"How much gas does your lowest plane have left?"

"Plenty. A couple of hours. How about landing instructions?"

"Hold everything. Circle the field until we identify the strangers. A P-38's going upstairs right now to look 'em over. Calling Four Victor Six Six. Calling Four Victor Six Six. Take off when ready, from the mountains to the sea."

From the P-38, "Roger, thank you."

The '38 roared down the strip, lifted and then zoomed upward, climbing almost vertically. The two men could see the strange planes, and the P-38 hanging on its props, rising toward them high in the moonlit sky. The boys listened to the pilot over the loudspeaker: "Four Victor Six Six calling Henderson. Two medium Jap bombers. And I'm right behind them. Closing in now. Here we go. Tallyho."

Other planes in the air came in over the loudspeaker. "Take 'em apart, boy! Teach the little rats to sneak in without a ticket!"

Other messages were received and the blond boy, answering one, said, "Plane with wounded, land on the strip. Mountains to the sea."

"Roger; wilco."

"Which one is it this time, *Gracie Allen* again?"

"Nope, *Butterfingers* this time. She's got no more landing gear than a bathtub."

Another plane cut in over the speaker, "Tell him to stick his feet out the bomb bay and run like the devil."

"Crash on the strip from the mountains to the sea. Good luck to you."

"Hate to do this. *Butterfingers* is gonna rip her Sunday panties. Embarrass the lady. Well, here we come."

Another speaker blared: "Six Peter One Two calling Henderson Tower."

"Henderson calling Six Peter One Two. Go ahead."

"Military transport coming in with general officers aboard. Request immediate landing instructions."

"Can ya' beat that?" the operator muttered, after flipping the turn-off switch on the microphone. "Those office boys bothering us at a time like this!"

He switched back in. "Sheer off and backtrack on your course a few minutes. Then come in again for instructions. Combat traffic over field."

"Roger," came the meek reply.

Both men leaned over the railing of the control tower and watched as the plane with the wounded hit the mat. As it touched the ground with the dirt spraying up alongside it like water around a speedboat, the ambulance, crash trucks, and jeeps roared across the runways. The propellers splintered into the air. The battered plane finally scraped to a halt, and before the emergency vehicles could reach it the crew members piled out.

"Guess this baby won't be a blazer, thank God! Call the ship and see what the score is."

The dark-haired operator plugged in on the command post party line, waited, then broke in: "What's the tale on those last two landings? Yeah? Swell!"

Another interruption: "Six Peter One Two calling Henderson Tower. On my way back to you. Have you landing instructions for us?"

"Come in and circle the field, but don't land until you get the green light." The boy at the transmitter turned to the other: "Guess we'd better get the rest of the technical unit in first. Let the brass hats wait."

"OK, I'll green light 'em. The strip is clear now. Tell 'em to land there."

Henderson Field in 1944, two years after the Americans and Japanese locked in combat for the swampy, jungle-ringed airstrip.

He took up the signal gun, pointed it at the leading plane of the flight coming in and flashed the green landing beam. The planes came in, almost nose to rudder.

The blond young man was still complaining about the generals. "Now we can green light the big shots. With this important stuff out of the way we can roll out the red carpet for 'em too. Too bad we don't have an eighty-piece band."

"Wonder how the Lightning is doing with the gate-crashing Charlies?"

"Don't worry about that baby. Those P-38's are bad news to anyone who has the bad luck to tangle with 'em. He'll make a good Jap out of a live Jap — wait and see. I'll call the message center and find out what they've heard."

On the phone, "Hello, Harry, any message from that '38?"

"On his way in. Just talked to the AA command post, and they say one of the bogies is down in the drink. The '38 got him in two bursts. No enemy craft now, so we're waiting for 'em to declare Condition Green. Wait up! Here it comes. OK. Condition Green!"

"Thanks, boy." The young man on the tower hung up, turned to his friend, and said, "Time for lights, bub. All clear."

He recharged his signal pistols, and, brandishing them like a cowboy star riding into town, he shot them into the air. This time the flares were green, and they were faint in the white moonlight. Lights began to wink all over the area.

In the tower the tension was over.

"Hey," yelled a man from the foot of the tower, "those frag bombs darn near chopped down this thing."

"Not frag bombs. The beavers did it." The dark young man tossed a canteen to his companion. "Here, have some horse medicine."

Tales of personal heroism from Southwest Pacific air combat are legion. No one place, one service, one unit held a monopoly on outstanding human performance, but certainly some of the most dramatic stories of it came out of Guadalcanal where the Japanese simply would not give up.

By day and by night the weary Marine, Navy and Air Force flyers at Henderson Field fought sustained attack from the air and the sea, while beyond the perimeter of the field the enemy hurled their shells at the airstrip and threatened to break through and overrun the field.

When a convoy of Japanese ships came down the "slot" to reinforce the island, the crucial moment had arrived for the weary and the sleepless. Everything with wings that could fly mustered and headed for the Jap troop transports, including Marine Maj. Jack Cram and his "Blue

Goose" — a bulky, slow-moving Catalina flying boat, never made for torpedo bombing, but this time jerry-rigged with a tin fish under each wing. Here is that epic story.

Maj. "Mad" Jack Cram and His Wild Blue Goose

John A. DeChant

It was late in the afternoon of October 14, 1942 when, in the weird light of coming dusk, a lumbering twin-motored PBY Catalina eased in over the shambles of Henderson Field. The daring, bloodshot eyes of the tired gun crews watched it barely clear the headless stumps that had been coconut trees. The plane spanked the end of the runway and then moved on furtively as if afraid to lose speed. Downfield, the Cat groaned painfully to the touch of a brake and hurried off the strip.

It was the Blue Goose, back from another ferry run to Espiritu, this time with two 2,000-pound torpedoes, one slung under each of its long, ungainly wings. The pilot was "Mad" Jack Cram, a wiry, eager major.

Before reporting in to the "Old Man," he got the word on the local havoc from bemoustached Maj. Joe Renner, an operations officer. Renner spoke with the clipped, haggard tension of a man who hadn't slept for 72 hours:

"They've got our backs molded into the wall. We've had a permanent Condition Red all day. No sirens now unless at least 15 Jap planes come in. The F4F's can't meet all the raids. We haven't enough gas or ammunition to send them up each time.

"What did you bring up this time? Torpedoes? What good are they now? Everyone of the TBF's got smashed up in the shelling last night. Good Lord, what a show that was! They must have had the whole fleet out there! It was like kicking a wounded guy in the groin time after time to see if he'd yell 'Uncle.'

"They frisked the place like a pickpocket. There were BB's out there in the channel with a flock of cruisers and destroyers in support. The insolent stinkers just stood off and plastered the place like they were in a free shooting gallery. Some of them walked searchlights up and down the shore, picking out the targets. The rest of them went over the place like a fine-toothed rake. If they ever try to break through what's left today . . . God help us, Jack . . . it'll be bad."

At dawn, activity along the front line remained sporadic, but ten miles up the coast a search plane found five enemy transports busily unloading troops protected by a heavy destroyer screen.

The runway at Henderson was rent and torn. There were 19 shell craters in the straightaway. Renner did the best he could, marking out a weird path for the pilots around the craters with flare pots.

He finally got one started at 0430 by running in front of the plane, flagging the pilot to the takeoff position. The first SBD crashed in the middle of the field.

Renner took the next pilot in his jeep and drove him carefully down the runway, pointing out each of the bad spots in turn by flashlight. Somehow, this SBD got off the deck, but the pilot was barely airborne when he found his wheels were frozen in place. He tried working the dive flaps. They were glued tight. Shell fragments had punctured his hydraulic system.

Quietly, the pilot turned and headed for the shadowy transports. He laboriously climbed the circle for altitude, then pushed over in his dive. The rushing air played queer tricks with no flaps and the wheels down. He corrected, jinked through the flak barrage from the destroyers, and jerked the release toggle for a direct hit on the first transport.

More lone SBD's followed, doing what damage they could.

An enemy photo plane appeared first, to make certain of the devastation at Henderson. What he saw must have convinced him, for on his third pass he came screaming down from 11,000 feet and flat-hatted across the airfield. Everyone within two miles cut loose at him. Even a heavy howitzer fired a few hopeful rounds. The plane crashed in flames at the edge of the strip.

At 0700, an umbrella of 30 Zeros took up station at 15,000 feet over the landing area. Geiger stopped the lone strikes and ordered all hands to prepare for a coordinated attack with all that was left.

Major Cram, who had been arguing for an attack in his PBY, was given permission to make a torpedo run on the transports under cover of the SBD mission. Of him, an officer at Geiger's command post later said:

"If ever I saw a man with sheer guts, it was Jack Cram. He knew it would probably be his last flight, but he jumped at the chance. As long as he had to, he was going out in a blaze of glory."

Renner did his coordination by jeep. The communications system had been obliterated the night before. Cram rode with him.

The Army fighter squadron promised to have four planes ready to fly. Maj. Duke Davis' squadron would furnish the balance of the fighter cover. (Davis' VMF 121 had arrived several days before.)

Col. Al Cooley said he could have 12 SBD's ready at 1010. On the way back to the Blue Goose, Renner told Cram, "This will be the most screwed-up show in history . . . but there's no other choice. If it works, miracles are still with us."

That a PBY had never before made a daylight torpedo attack or that he had no copilot didn't faze Cram. Neither did the fact that he knew little or nothing about using torpedoes. Before Renner dropped him off, he learned how to use them in a five-minute instruction course from a fighter pilot whose brother was a torpedo bomber pilot.

The Goose was first off. Cram nursed it into the air, climbing toward the rendezvous area for the eight fighters and 12 SBD's two miles east of Henderson and away from the Zeros. Behind him Duke Davis' Wildcats were airborne and the last of the SBD's was clawing for altitude. They had all taken off through an artillery barrage raking the field.

While they watched, the 30 Zeros on station were relieved by 30 more. The Japanese pilots seemed to watch incredulously this strange parade from Henderson, but they stayed on station over the convoy.

Then to the west at 9,000 feet the lurking SBD's exploded into action. The lead plane rolled over on its back, wings gleaming dull in the sunlight. As it whipped down on the transports, the mud-brown Zeros peeled off for the kill.

In the PBY, Cram hunched forward, then shoved the yoke to the fire

wall. The surprised Cat went over on its nose in an almost vertical dive toward the first transport, a mile away. Never built to go over 160, the Blue Goose hit 270 mph indicated in the dive. Cram fearfully watched the needle climb while the huge umbrella wings shrieked and groaned, flapping like an ancient crow's.

Afraid of what would happen, Cram hauled slowly back on the yoke. The Cat held together. He leveled out at 1,000 feet and went whistling past the first DD before they spotted him. Dead ahead, the Japs were living and dying like frantic ants as the bombs from the SBD's gutted their ships.

The Cat screamed past the first and second transports at 75 feet. Flak from the destroyers flailed the plane like a steel whip. It bucked and shuddered from the impact. At point-blank range, Cram lined upon the third transport, sighting off his bow. Holding the yoke steady with his left hand, he jerked the release toggle so viciously he almost tore it out of the instrument panel.

The first torpedo splatted in the water and bored into the hull of the transport. A second later he yanked the toggle and the second torpedo porpoised, then followed the first one into the side of the ship. Just as he pulled out of the run, flak from one of the destroyers sheared off the PBY's navigation hatch.

Five Zeros broke off from the dogfight and went after the flying boat. Cram started to pull up, saw the Zeros

(Above) Wiry, handsome Marine Major "Mad Jack" Cram received the Navy Cross for torpedo-bombing and sinking a Japanese transport with his Catalina flying boat. (Below) The slow, lumbering Catalina flying boat was used for just about everything. Maj. Jack Cram slung two torpedoes under the wings and made it into a dive bomber.

and stood the PBY on its left wing tip in a turn that headed him back to Henderson. As he passed his target transport, it was settling in the water.

The Zeros played tail chase, making pass after pass, in their eagerness to smash down the waddling Goose. Cram roller-coastered it up and down and back and forth to make it as poor a target as possible. The Zeros ventilated the plane conscientiously during the 12 miles back to the airfield. The Blue Goose barreled in over the tree stumps at the end of Henderson moving too fast to land and with one Zero still on its tail. It went on to Fighter One.

Lt. Roger Haberman was bringing his smoking F4F into the landing circle with his wheels down when he saw Cram's situation. Wheels still down, Haberman kept casually in his turn, wound up on the Zero's tail and shot it down. Cram pancaked somehow, he and his crew still intact and the Catalina everything else but.

He was awarded the Navy Cross for the attack.

Aerial combat performed in swirling graceful arcs of cotton-white contrails, magnificently etched high against the heavens — this picture of man's fight against man in the vastnesses of the sky perhaps best typifies war in the air.

In the Pacific there was this kind of war, too, but generally speaking the air war that rooted the enemy out of the protective jungle and hidden cove, from the bowellike cave and shallow coastal water was low-level attack. From the Solomons to New Guinea, from New Guinea up the island chain to the Philippines it was a treetop campaign for the men of the fighter-bombers, the lights and the mediums.

And when you landed back at your base with leaves and grass in the air scoop or branches in your wheel wells, or your undersurfaces pockmarked from exploding target debris, well, everyone knew where you'd been.

Down in and at 'Em

Capt. Donald Hough and Capt. Elliott Arnold

At Rabaul Harbor. The Mitchell bombers came down and spread out and swept the ship-crammed harbor, flying very low, no higher than the vessels they were attacking; they raked the decks and antiaircraft guns with a torrent of heavy machine-gun fire, then as they pulled up quickly they let the bombs go, skipping them on the water or flipping them into the sides of the ships. Then they were gone, and the ships sank slowly . . .

At Wewak. The Jap airstrip was packed with planes, concentrated there for a big strike at the Americans and ready to take off. The big .50-caliber bullets came in suddenly, like slanting hail, then the fast attacking bombers came in low behind their fire, like blackbirds in migration, swooping and fanning out over the reed-tips of a marsh; and with the machine guns now in drumlike thunder and the roar of the engines in swift crescendo there came the heavy crash of bombs as the planes melted away, as their own disintegrating metal sprayed the air around them and they fell apart . . . Then in the sudden silence the live Japs got up off the ground, pawing in shock; they scarcely had begun to understand what had happened when from the other direction came the ominous hail, and this time they saw the line of planes coming in like vicious darts over the tops of the jungle trees . . .

In the Bismarck Sea. The bombs from the high-flying bombers were falling and the Jap ships were maneuvering frantically, when from somewhere out of the waves planes came in swiftly and pulled up in a screaming lift over the ships; the bombs skipped once or twice on the water then crashed through the sides of the transports and the destroyers and exploded inside, and that was the death of a Jap convoy and of Jap hopes in eastern New Guinea . . .

At Buna. The jungle itself seemed to spew planes as the Americans came in around the trees, out of nowhere, in from the tops of the rain forest; and in the wake of these strafing planes there floated in the air a multitude of small white parachutes that had come from their bellies as spawn comes from great fish. It looked for a moment as though a field of cotton had sprung into the air above the heads of the Jap soldiers, but the Japs could see things swinging beneath the parachutes, then came the ripping crackle and roar of fragmentation bombs that tore the air and the jungle and the Japs apart . . .

That is low-level attack.

The story of this comes closer to being the story of our air campaign in the Southwest Pacific than any other phase of aircraft-use in that theater of war; it was the biggest military baby born in that neck of the woods, ranking beside the perfection of amphibious landing and attack throughout the Pacific in its effect upon the particular job at hand.

It is paradoxical in a way that, in such a region of great distances, long hauls, infinite emptiness and endless horizons, the air attack should largely be developed and carried on in terms of close contact and infighting — as near as air offense can come to hand-

Japanese gunners cringe in their dugouts (lower left) as a B-25 skims a few feet overhead in a bombing-strafing mission on the defenses at Rabaul.

On November 11, 1943, 5th Air Force B-25's swept into Rabaul Harbor at low level and turned the docks into a holocaust of fire and smoke. Fifteen ships were sunk and 11 damaged.

to-hand conflict. But that was the way it had to be done, because the targets were small, scattered, hidden with ground-hugging tenacity — jungle airstrips, coastal shipping by small creeping coastal vessels and shade-seeking barges; beachheads and little islands, shallow-water docks and handpower installations; cave-living Japs and isolated garrisons. The job had to be one of getting down to them; and just as the infantrymen and the marines on land had to do this in their sphere, so did air power have to develop its own technique and equipment for doing essentially the same thing.

In the end, the situation we had to meet — and which the Japs had counted on to beat us — we met in a manner as typically American as the Jap tactics were typically Japanese. Perhaps the Japs should have known what would happen, but they have a habit of knowing only what they hope will happen. True, they granted our capacity for turning out masses of mechanical products, but they were also sure that our civilization itself had become so mechanized that we were reduced by it to a nation of helpless polyps, at the mercy of our Turkish baths. Naturally, they had forgotten something. They had forgotten an American tradition, deeper than chromium plating, deeper than cellophane, deeper than the silver screens of the movies. The Japanese, who lean heavily on the interesting characteristics of their own ancestors, had forgotten that a scant generation ago we were fighting our last battles with the Indians, that not a great while before that the British had failed to solve our peculiar style; that we had conquered a continent, its distances and its barriers, in an infiltration such as the Japs in all their centuries never had known either in resourcefulness or speed.

And what was our air attack, in its ultimate development in this Southwest Pacific, but the cavalry charge at Gettysburg, the sweep of the Army troopers in Arizona and along the Rio Grande, the thunder of the cowboys on their way to rescue the heroine, the attacks of the Indians on the wagon trains, and of the bandits on the Wells-Fargo stage? . . . It was the stalk and the swift attack and the individual on his own in a country where improvisation and adaptability and ingenuity and aggressiveness were everybody's business — indeed were necessary for survival.

Lae, Salamaua, Rabaul, Buna, Hollandia, Guadalcanal, Ceram, Morotai. . . . What were these places? They were Tombstone, Rapid City, Flagstaff, Santa Fe, Dodge City, Carson City, Wounded Knee, the Little Big Horn. . . .

It was the thing the Japs had forgotten to remember.

One night in December, 1944, in the early days of our return to the Philippines, Gen. George C. Kenney, 5th Air Force Commander, dropped by to see his boss General MacArthur at the Price House near Tacloban strip, on Leyte. The Supreme Commander was reading a book — the life of General Robert E. Lee.

As Kenney entered, the General put down the volume. "George," he said, "I've been reading about a remarkable coincidence. When Stonewall Jackson was dying, the last words he said were, 'Tell A. P. Hill to bring up his infantry.' Years later when Lee died, his last words were, 'Hill, bring up the infantry.'"

He paused, lit his pipe, took a few puffs, and continued.

"If I should die today, or tomorrow, or any time, if you listen to my last words you'll hear me say, 'George, bring up the 5th Air Force.'"

Such was the confidence, respect, admiration and trust General MacArthur had in his wiry, tough, little air deputy, George C. Kenney, the man who organized scattered air units in Australia in the early days of the war into the 5th Air Force and drove the Japanese from the skies of the Southwest Pacific. This great airman, beloved and admired by all who served with him from the mechanic on the line to the top ranking officer in the theater, rightly earned the title "architect of air victory in the Southwest Pacific."

No one is more qualified to write intimate glimpses of the men and the events of that war. Here is a random selection.

Vignettes of New Guinea's Jungle Air War

Gen. George C. Kenney, USAF (Ret)

FIRST JAP KILL IN THE SOUTHWEST PACIFIC

There had been a lot of rivalry among the P-38 pilots as to who would get the first official victory over a Japanese airplane in combat. The P-38's had been patrolling over Lae for several days, calling the Japs on the fighter radio frequency and insulting them by saying: "We are the P-38's. We are taking over the patrol of the Lae airdrome from you and if any of you bowlegged so-and-so's don't like it and have guts enough to argue about it, come on up and we'll accommodate

General Douglas MacArthur, Supreme Commander of Forces in the Southwest Pacific, is pictured here with Lt. Gen. George C. Kenney, his air deputy and commander of the 5th Air Force, as the two conferred in Australia on January 9, 1943.

you." This is a polite version of what they said.

Until this particular date, the P-38's hadn't been able to get a rise out of the Nips, so they were carrying a couple of 500-pound bombs under each wing to dig a few holes in the runway with before they left.

One Jap pilot evidently got sufficiently insulted and taxied out to take off. One of the P-38 pilots, a big, good-natured New Orleans Cajun named Ferrault, dived down to take him. At about 2,000 feet he realized that he was carrying a couple of bombs, so he hurriedly released them and pulled up out of the blast effect to be ready to tip over again and shoot down the Jap as soon as his wheels left the runway. At the top of his climbing turn he looked down and saw the two bombs hit the water at the end of the runway, which ran all the way to the beach, and splash the water up just in time to catch the Jap plane as it was pulling off the end of the runway and spill the Jap into the water for a total loss.

When the kids returned, I asked Ferrault if he had nerve enough to claim "the first Nip brought down in air combat in this theater by a P-38." He grinned and asked if I was going to give him an Air Medal. I had promised one to anyone who got an official victory. I said, "Hell, no. I want you to shoot them down, not splash water on them." I then asked the rest of the kids if they thought Ferrault was really entitled to anything more than credit for about three hours' combat time. They were fairly sure I was kidding so they all agreed with me. Ferrault was a bit uncertain himself when I left. Later on that evening I went over, got the gang together, and gave Ferrault his medal but told him that he'd better keep the whole thing quiet. That outfit kidded him for weeks.

THE UNPREDICTABLE PAPPY GUNN

On August 28, 1943, we ran a test on a B-25 equipped with a 75-mm. cannon, which Arnold had sent over to me to try out. I assigned it to Pappy Gunn, who fell in love with it at first sight. Pappy attached himself to 25 B-25's, escorted by nine P-38's, who were going on a barge hunt in the Cape Gloucester area. It turned into quite a party for all concerned.

Two Jap destroyers just off Cape Gloucester looked to Pappy as if they were placed there for his own special benefit. Picking out the largest of the two vessels, Pappy scored seven hits with his 75-mm. cannon, but much to his disgust the destroyer didn't even slow down. A 75-mm. gun, which, after all, fires a shell that is only about three inches in diameter, was not enough to worry a destroyer. The two B-25's flying on his wings then told Pappy please to step aside while someone did the job who knew how it should be done. A 1000-pounder skipped into the Jap warship and split her in two. Another 1000-pounder sank the other destroyer, and the B-25's continued along the New Britain coast looking for barges. They found and sank eight barges and two large motor launches, while the P-38's shot down eight out of 15 Jap fighters that tried to interfere.

Pappy flew along with the gang, sulking and all mad because they had shown up his pet gun installation. Returning over the Jap airdrome at

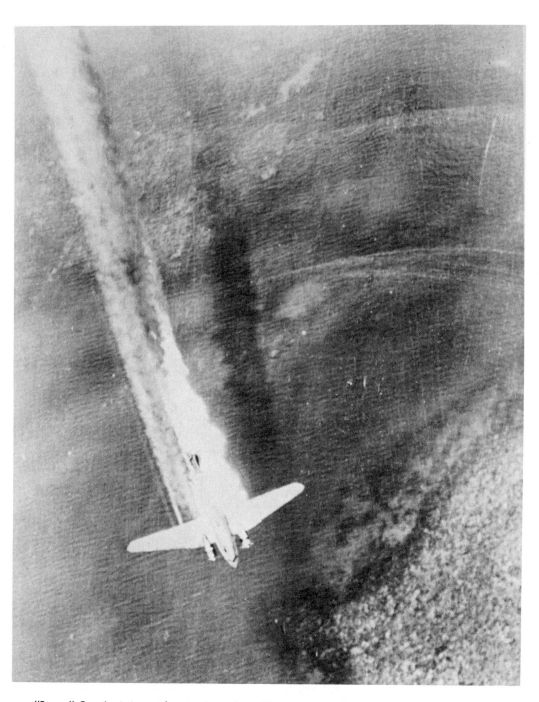

"Pappy" Gunn's victim on the airstrip at Cape Gloucester was identical to this twin-engine Japanese transport heading down into the sea near the Celebes islands. Like many Japanese aircraft, this troop carrier took only a few shots in the right place to turn it into a blazing tinderbox.

117

Cape Gloucester, Pappy looked ahead and saw his chance to redeem himself. Just landing was a Nip two-engined transport airplane. Pappy opened his throttle, pushed ahead of the formation, and fired his two remaining rounds of cannon ammunition at the Jap plane taxiing along the ground. One of the high-explosive shells hit the left engine and the other the pilot's cockpit. The transport literally disintegrated. Pappy reported with great glee when he landed back at Port Moresby, "General, no fooling, as I passed over that Nip plane there were pieces of Jap higher than I was."

Black Day for the Jap

Just before dawn on the morning of August 17, 1943, the big takeout of the Wewak airdromes began. Forty-one B-24's and 12 B-17's pasted the Japanese airfields at But, Borum, Dagua and Wewak with 200 tons of bombs. Two of our B-24's were reported missing and another B-24 landed on the south coast of New Guinea with four dead crew members. The antiaircraft gunfire over Wewak was reported extremely heavy and accurate. Two hours later 33 B-25's with 83 P-38's as cover made a simultaneous attack on Borum, Wewak, and Dagua. Sixteen B-25's, scheduled to hit But, had run into bad weather and did not make the rendezvous. Lt. Col. Don Hall, the same big-nosed little blond boy that first used my

parafrag bombs at Buna in September 1942, led the B-25 line abreast attack on Borum. Coming in over the tops of the palm trees, Don saw a sight to gladden the heart of a strafer. The Jap bombers, 60 of them, were lined up on either side of the runway with their engines turning over, flying crews on board, and groups of ground crewmen standing by each airplane. The Japs were actually starting to take off and the leading airplane was already halfway down the runway and ready to leave the ground. Off to one side 50 Jap fighters were warming up their engines ready to follow and cover their bombers. Hall signaled to open fire. His first burst blew up the Jap bomber just as it lifted into the air. It crashed immediately, blocking the runway for any further Nip take-offs. The B-25 formation swept over the field like a giant scythe. The double line of Jap bombers was on fire almost immediately from the rain of .50-caliber incendiaries pouring from over 200 machine guns, antiaircraft defenses were smothered, drums of gasoline by the side of the runway blazed up, and Jap flying crews and ground personnel melted away in the path of our gunfire, in the crackle of a thousand parafrag bombs, and the explosions of their own bomb-laden aircraft. We hit them just in time. Another five minutes and the whole Jap force would have been in the air on the way to take us out at Marilinan.

Wewak suffered the same fate. Thirty Jap fighters were warming up to

Japanese troops huddle in their dugout gun positions as a B-25 swoops in low to drop its "parafrags" on the defenses of enemy airfield at Boram.

take off when 12 B-25's caught them by surprise and duplicated the kill at Borum. Only three B-25's attacked Dagua but once again surprise paid dividends and 20 more Jap aircraft were burned and crossed off the enemy list, with at least an equal number damaged.

We found out afterward that the Japanese referred to the attack as "the Black Day of August 17" and that they had lost over 150 aircraft, with practically all the flight crews and around 300 more ground personnel killed. All our P-38's and strafers returned to their home airdromes.

YOU COULDN'T LOSE WITH KIDS LIKE THAT

Right in the middle of my troubles . . . (Gen.) "Squeeze" Wurtsmith came in with a new problem. He said,

"General, you'll have to help out a couple of my kids. I'm afraid if you don't they are in for some trouble."

It seems that about a week previously a couple of former pilots of the 49th Fighter Group reported in to him at Nadzab. I had sent them home for combat fatigue about three months before. One had a Nip to his credit and the other had two official victories. Both had well over 300 combat hours. Squeeze said he recognized them and when they asked if there were any P-38's for them to fly and could they start flying again right away, he said, "Sure," and told them to report to their old squadron. They went off as happy as a couple of larks. During the next two or three days each one of them added another Nip to his score up over Wewak. Then their story leaked out. When they had returned to the United States, they were sent to a rehabilitation or rest center somewhere in Florida. After a few weeks of doing nothing but rest, they got bored and finally decided that they "had just thought they were tired," so without saying a word to anyone they simply packed up and left. Two weeks later they had thumbed their way to Brisbane. Their names, of course, did not appear on the cargo or crew lists of any of the planes they hitchhiked their way on. Our pilots would cover up for each other in a case like this, any time any place, and you couldn't stop it, no matter how many orders you put out. As a matter of fact, I liked the spirit so much that I wouldn't try to stop it.

The only trouble was that, when it came to drawing pay, they had no orders — they were AWOL, deserters; in fact, they had broken enough rules to qualify for a nice court-martial.

I told Squeeze to tell them I'd take care of them and dropped a note to General Bevans, the Air Forces Personnel Officer in Washington, asking him to get out some orders to make their trip legal and reassign them to me.

The details of how they managed to go from Florida to New Guinea in wartime without getting caught would have made a good story. You couldn't lose when your youngsters had a spirit like that.

DEALER'S CHOICE: DOGS, WOMEN OR PIGS

Col. Jock Henebry was running my advanced combat training show at Nadzab, where the newly arrived replacement crews got a lot of gunnery and bombing training against the bypassed Jap holdings at Rabaul and around Wewak. Their operations also assisted the Australian ground forces, who were investing the Jap positions and mopping up isolated enemy garrisons all over New Britain and New Guinea. Jock had taken over the job on his return from leave in the United States in December 1944. . .

Australian patrols around Rabaul

had been having a lot of trouble with Jap police dogs, who had been trained to give the alarm and even attack and try to hold intruders at bay until the Nips could get to the scene and dispose of or capture them. The Aussies had definitely located the dog kennels and had asked Jock to bomb them. Jock, who had spent over 600 combat hours in the Southwest Pacific making low-level attacks on Jap airdromes, troops, and shipping . . . carried out the mission successfully but he hoped there would be no publicity. He didn't want anyone to know that he had been reduced to bombing dog kennels.

A few days before, while visiting one of our old strips in the interior up around Mount Hagen, Jock had been approached by a delegation of native warriors. The chief, who boasted that he had an army of 500 spearmen and bowmen, said he wanted some air support in his projected campaign against a neighboring tribe that a few months previously had made an unprovoked raid on his tribe and had gotten away with a lot of women and pigs. He said he was pro-American so the supposition was that the enemy tribe must be pro-Jap. As an ally he wanted cooperation and, as an added inducement, he was perfectly willing to split on a fifty-fifty basis with Jock all the women and pigs of the enemy tribe that he captured.

Jock exhibited some high-power diplomacy in wiggling out of the proposed assignment. The presentation of gifts of costume jewelry, gold-lipped shells, and tobacco, followed by a pig roast and native dance, put everyone in good humor and the chief decided to postpone his campaign indefinitely.

THE RACE OF THE ACES

Bong, Kearby, and Lynch were the big three in the Southwest Pacific as February, 1944, began. Maj. George Welch, with 16 to his credit, had gone home in November, 1943. Capt. Daniel Roberts, who had knocked down 15 Nips in 11 weeks, was killed over Finschhafen on November 9, 1943, and Maj. Edward Cragg, also credited with a score of 15, was shot down in flames over Gloucester on December 26 of that same year.

The nearest fighter pilots to the top three now were Maj. Gerald Johnson, Maj. Tommy McGuire, and Capt. James Watkins, all crack shots, who were getting Japs at the rate of two or three in a combat and were in a triple tie at 11.

In the late afternoon of February 27, we picked up and decoded a Jap radio message which gave the time of arrival at the Wewak airdrome of a Jap transport plane carrying some staff officers from Rabaul. By the time we got the information, it was almost too late for an interception, but we gave the information to Bong and Lynch, who hurriedly took off and flew wide open all the way, arriving over Wewak about two minutes before the Jap plane was scheduled to land. The inconsiderate Nip, however, was ahead of schedule, had already landed, and was taxiing down the runway. Lynch dived to the attack but found that in his hurry to get away his gunsights had not been installed. He called to Bong to take the Jap. Bong fired one burst, the plane was enveloped in flames for a second or two, and then it blew up. No one was seen to leave it, before or after the attack. The two kids then machine-gunned a party of at least a hundred Japs who had evidently come down to greet the visitors. Subsequent frantic radio messages passing between Wewak and Tokyo indicated that the victims were a major general, a brigadier, and a whole staff of high-ranking officers.

On their return, Bong and Lynch came over to my New Guinea advanced headquarters and told me the story. I wanted to let Dick Bong have credit for an airplane destroyed in combat, but of course if it was on the ground it couldn't count on the victory scoreboard. We counted only wing shots in the Southwest Pacific. I asked Dick if he was sure that the Jap transport was actually on the ground when he hit it. Couldn't it have been just an inch or so above the runway? Maybe the plane's wheels had touched and it had bounced back into the air temporarily? Everyone knew that some Japs were poor pilots. Lynch stood there grinning, and said that whatever Bong decided was OK

with him. Dick listened seriously, as if it were a problem in mathematics, and then looked up and said simply, earnestly, and without a trace of disappointment, "General, he was on the ground all right. He had even stopped rolling."

Everyone was now watching the scores of these two and Neel Kearby. A few days after Bong's return from his leave in the United States, Kearby had shot down two Jap fighters, bringing his score up to 22. Neel felt pretty good until he landed back at his home airdrome where he was greeted with the news that Bong had shot down a Jap fighter that morning over New Britain. The score was now tied, but it was at 22. A few days later each of the three leaders added another victory. With Neel and Dick each at 23 and Lynch with 19, Eddie Rickenbacker's old World War I record of 26 didn't look so far away now.

On March 4, Kearby decided to break the tie. With his group headquarters flight, of Maj. Sam Blair and Captains Dunham and Banks, Neel headed for the Wewak area and trouble. Just west of the village of Dagua, sighting a formation of 15 Jap aircraft, he signaled for the attack. A quick burst, and a Nip plane went spinning to earth in flames. One ahead. Now for a little velvet for that lead position. Neel turned back into the Jap formation and, with a beautiful long-range shot from a 60-degree angle from the rear, got his second victim with a single burst. As he pulled away, three Jap fighters closed in from above and behind. Dunham got one. Banks got another. The third Jap poured a burst into Neel's cockpit from close range. The P-47 with 23 Jap flags painted on its side plunged straight down. It never came out of the dive and no parachute opened — it kept going until it disappeared into the jungle bordering on the Jap airdrome at Dagua.

Somehow I felt a little glad that Neel never knew that Dick Bong had added two more to his score that morning shooting down a couple of Jap bombers during a fighter sweep over Tadji, New Guinea. Lynch in that same flight had bagged a bomber and a fighter, bringing his total up to 21.

On March 9, Bong and Lynch flew another mission over the Tadji area to see whether or not the Japs were filling up the holes in the airdrome, which we had bombed heavily a few days before. They couldn't find any airplanes to shoot at in the air or on the ground, so looking for some kind of target, they spied a Jap corvette escorting a couple of luggers just offshore, heading west toward Hollandia. Burst after burst of the .50-caliber guns of each plane poured into the Jap vessel, which responded with its own deck defense guns. Suddenly Bong saw Lynch pull around and head for shore. One of his engines was smoking. Then, just as he got to the shoreline, Dick saw in quick succession a propeller flying off, Tommy Lynch taking to his parachute, and at almost the same instant, the plane exploding. Bong flew around for several minutes to see if he could discover any indication that by some miracle Tommy had survived. There wasn't a chance, and Dick knew it. The chute had burned up with the explosion and probably Lynch was dead before his body hit the ground.

Dick flew back and reported. I was afraid that seeing Tommy go might affect his nerve, so I ordered him to Brisbane to ferry a new airplane back to his squadron and sent a message to the depot commander there that if the airplane was ready to fly before another couple of weeks I would demote him at least two grades.

It turned out that I needn't have worried about Bong's morale . . .

On April 3 he got in a fight over Hollandia while with his old 9th Squadron, escorting a big bombing raid on the Jap airdromes there. A Jap fighter got into an argument with Dick and lost. Number 25.

On April 12 we again raided Hollandia with 188 bombers and 67 fighters. Twenty Jap fighters intercepted. Our P-38's shot down eight of them and listed another as probable. Two of the Nip planes that were definitely destroyed in combat were added to the score of Capt. Richard I. Bong, making his score 27, one more than the record set by Eddie Rickenbacker in France in World War I. The one listed as probable was also one of Bong's victims. He told me that the Jap plane he had reported as a "probable" in the combat of April 12 near Hollandia had gone into the water in Tannemerah Bay about 20 miles west of Hollandia. The reason it had been called a probable was that no one except Bong had seen it go down and his camera gun was not installed that day. Under the rules, he could not get credit for it unless the victory was confirmed by an eyewitness, or the wreckage of the Jap plane was found where he claimed it had crashed. He showed me on the photograph of the area exactly where the plane went into the water and said that it was a single-seater fighter of the type we called an Oscar, that he had hit the left wing, the pilot, and the engine, but that the plane had not burned.

When we captured the Hollandia area a couple of weeks later, I got a diver to go down where Dick had said the airplane went in. The diver located it almost instantly and we pulled it up. It was an Oscar. The left wing had 11 bullet holes in it, the pilot had been hit in the head and neck, two cylinder engines were knocked out, and there was no sign of fire. I put out an order giving Bong official credit for the victory — his 28th.

The Jap just naturally made you mad. It was his arrogance, conceit, ego-tism, and aura of superiority; it was for Pearl Harbor that you disliked him; or for what he had done to tens of millions of peoples in Asia; or perhaps, for what he had done to one of your own buddies, as was the case with Dave "Tex" Hill — one of the five original Flying Tigers who stayed on in China when the AVG was converted to the 23rd Pursuit Group of the China Air Task Force, AAF.

Nothing had changed for Tex Hill and the other four Tigers, except the name of their outfit and a bunch of green, new pilots to fill up the ranks of the 23rd.

One such new pilot was Johnny Alison, a fine young type to whom the veteran Tex Hill had taken a shine. It was on the night of July 29, 1942, during a Japanese bomber raid on the 23rd's Hengyang Field, deep in China, that Johnny Alison and his P-40 was seen going down in flames. Needless to say, it made Tex Hill mad and here is that story.

Two Can Play

Maj. Gen. Claire Lee Chennault, USAF (Ret)

NIGHT BOMBERS appeared again on July 29, and this time "Tex" Hill, "Ajax" Baumler, and Johnny Alison were up in P-40's to meet them. By staying low they hoped to spot the bombers' blue-white exhausts as they approached the field. Ground radio gave them plots on the approaching Japs, and Alison picked them up as they crossed the Siang River and headed out to maneuver for a bomb run. Alison pulled up to point-blank range on the lead bomber when they turned into their run on the field. In following the bombers' turn, Alison came out slightly above them and was silhouetted in the bright moonlight. A rear gunner of one bomber opened up at almost point-blank range, spraying Alison's P-40 from prop to rudder. A tracer scorched Alison's arm, his prop was hit several times, a large hole was blown out of the crankcase, and the fuselage punctured a dozen times. With his plane a wreck, Alison never deviated from his objective. He poured a stream of fire into the lead bomber and saw it suddenly stream oil like a bleeding whale and pull up in a climbing turn. Alison moved over and gave the Jap wingman a burst that blew him up in a swath of orange flame. He damaged the third with a similar burst. By this time Alison's plane was about finished. Because we were so desperately short of spare parts, Johnny decided to ride it down for what salvage there might be rather than bail out while he had a chance. At 2,000 feet the oil in his shattered crankcase caught fire.

He was then too close to the field to make a landing, and the last anybody saw of Alison he was streaking across the field at 200 feet, heading for the river with his engine ablaze. Everybody assumed he could hardly survive the inevitable crash. Ajax Baumler finished off the third bomber and got the fourth north of Hengyang. When Tex Hill landed and learned that Alison was presumed to be dead he was furious. Tex's war was always a very personal war, and he took the loss of a buddy extremely hard. When the Chinese net reported plots from the north early the next day, Tex led ten P-40's into the air with a cold determination that boded ill for his opponents. Meanwhile Alison had nursed his flaming P-40 to a crash landing in the river east of Hengyang. Johnny survived with a badly cut head to get the Distinguished

Pals Johnny Alison (left) and David "Tex" Hill lean against the trailing edge of a P-40 wing. At center is Albert "Ajax" Baumler, with Mack Mitchel, right. Original AVG Flying Tigers, they stayed on when the unit was converted to the 23rd Pursuit Group, AAF.

Service Cross for his night's work. He had been taken to a Catholic missionary who sewed up his head and put him up for a rest. Johnny, very much alive, watched the next morning's flight from the mission compound as Tex flew out to avenge his "death."

The Japs sailed in with 35 Oscars in a widespread loose V formation. From the opposite direction came Tex with ten P-40's behind him. Tex singled out the Japanese formation leader and then ensued one of the strangest sights ever seen in air combat. Tex headed for the Jap leader in a head-on pass with both of them shooting and closing the range at better than 600 miles an hour. It was like a pair of old-fashioned Western gunmen shooting it out on the main street of some cow town. Watching from the ground, a collision seemed certain. Neither would give an inch.

At the last split second before a crash, the Jap pushed over into a steep dive. Tex barely brushed over his cockpit. The Jap trailed a thin plume of smoke. He must have been badly hit, for he circled over the field and then deliberately pushed over into a vertical dive, holding it until he crashed into a row of bamboo dummy P-40's parked on the field. It was the first kamikaze on record. After the fight Tex landed through the smoke of the still-smoldering Oscar. He ambled over to the wreck where the dismembered body of the Jap leader (a major complete with samurai sword) lay near his plane. With the pointed toe of his cowboy boot, Tex poked at the blackened and severed head and looked squarely into the sightless eyes.

"You tried to kill me, you little rat," Tex drawled coldly. "Two can play at that game."

By late 1943 the situation in Burma was serious. Japanese armies had overrun Southern Burma and pushed northward. Struggling down from Northern Burma, leading a force of Chinese-American infantry was Lt. Gen. "Vinegar Joe" Stilwell, but progress was slow, and the going tough. In Western Burma, British ground forces were desperately battling to hold off the Japanese, now threatening the American airfields in Assam and poising for an invasion of India. Slowly the enemy was advancing to victory on all fronts in Burma and something had to be done.

It was at this point that Air Force Gen. Hap Arnold came up with a daring plan to transport a division of British Gen. Orde Wingate's crack ground troops behind the Japanese in central Burma. There they would fan out, cut the north-south lines of Japanese supply and communication and weaken the enemy, thus preventing further advances.

The daring plan called for the use of the untried American CG-4A *gliders to land engineers with airborne road-grading equipment at night in a flat savannah in the central Burma jungle, quickly build airstrips into which troop carrier planes could fly 10,000 of Wingate's fierce Chindit raiders and resupply them by air under the very noses of the Japanese.*

To organize and conduct this unique military operation Hap Arnold called in two of his proven China combat veterans, Col. Phil Cochran and Col. Johnny Alison, and gave them one simple order: "To hell with the paper work, go out and fight."

The American Air Commando glider pilots arrived in Assam with their gliders in early 1944 and began training for the mission. Two level spots in central Burma were possible landing areas. The men called them "Picadilly" and "Broadway."

Hours before the air commandos took off, on March 5, 1944, a lone B-25 flew over "Picadilly." It reported back that the Japs had strewn large logs over the entire landing area. Quickly the plan was switched and all gliders would now pile into "Broadway."

Loaded to maximum weight with the heavy mechanized road-building equipment, and a group of short, strong, fierce Gurkha Indian troops, the towplanes and gliders left their base at Assam and headed into the night toward the towering mountains and insidious jungles of Burma. There they would write the dramatic chapter of how the Jap lines were cut and the enemy hold on Burma was finally broken.

The Password Was Mandalay

Lt. Col. James W. Bellah, USA (Inf)

THIS is how Phil Cochran and his gang flew the vanguard of General Wingate's forces over the mountains in bright moonlight and put it down deep in the heart of Jap-held Burma. This is how some men died, but hordes of men lived to strike a vital masterstroke to save China and to help Stilwell and Wingate conquer Northern Burma.

Seven months of backbreaking, mind-searing work ended abruptly that last morning. Only hours were left — slow hours until takeoff. Jerry Dunn kept talking about death and I kept shutting him up. He'd smile and say: "If you talk about it, it won't happen."

There were two open spaces on the map, open spaces ringed with jungle and mountain. Let's call them Broadway and Picadilly. Nobody had ever been on the ground at either place — but there were photographs. The troop-carrying gliders would start down into those places shortly. Broadway and Picadilly had to be taken and held at all costs because the gliders couldn't go back. The tow ships, stripped bare to haul the heavy loads, had barely gas enough after release to get themselves back through the hostile night miles.

You would hit the ground and go into action and behind you, in wave after wave, would come the American combat engineers and more British troops and bulldozers and graders and jeeps and mules to build an airport between dawn and dusk, so that the next night huge troop-carrying power planes could fly in and start landing the Army.

In the vast glider park there were voices from Brooklyn and Carolina, London and the North Country, Liverpool, Texas and Nepal. But suddenly nobody seemed to have any nationality. Phil Cochran must have felt that complete loss of all the nonessentials of life. He closed the briefing with "Tonight you're going to find out you've got a soul. Nothing you've ever done or nothing you are ever going to do counts now. Only the next few hours. Good luck."

Dunn and I lay down on the ground in the shade of a glider wing while I loaded his tommy-gun clips with tracers. We were the first wave. Dunn talked about his wife in London. Every once in a while as he talked the whole thing would surge up inside me like a dental appointment when I was a kid. If it ever breaks, it splatters like blood into the outer reaches of your soul — and you run screaming. You have to stop it and when you do, you feel good inside. Real good.

The time drew on. Dunn slapped me lightly on the shoulder. "See you," he said and walked back to his glider. Chaplain Marlin F. Kerstetter came by and we talked for a minute. It was Sunday night. "As soon as you take off," he said, "I'm going back to hold my service, but I'll be in the second wave."

All the rank — Slim, Stratemeyer, Galdwin, Old, Wingate, Cochran and Alison — were in a huddle. It was coming up on time. Our troops were lined up to go aboard. Doc Tulloch, co-piloting with John Alison, looked over his medical equipment and suddenly Cochran called a quick, emergency briefing.

"We've got late afternoon reconnaissance photos. It looks as if the Japs have obstructed Picadilly — as if they were wise — so we're all going to pile into Broadway. All right — get going! And just remember the dope on Broadway — forget all the rest!"

John Alison came over on the run — John was a fighter pilot but he had checked out on gliders a few days before just to make this flight, for he was Cochran's second-in-command with the job of making an airport in 12

Famed British General Orde Wingate (center) briefs Air Commando glider pilots just prior to take-off for the heart of the Burma jungles. Col. Phil Cochran, standing with arms folded, was leader of the operations.

hours out of a jungle clearing. He got in and Doc Tulloch crawled in beside him. Magoffin and I climbed in and the detachment from the regiment under Wilson filed in behind us.

Everyone of us was in full field kit and armed to the teeth with carbines, tommy guns, pistols, knives and grenades. Uminski, with admirable enthusiasm, had fitted a tommy-gun stock to an air-cooled .30-caliber machine gun for hip and shoulder firing. A pirate crew, Wingate's army and Cochran's air commandos — in mottled

camouflage suits, with broadbrimmed rakish, paint-dabbled jungle hats — most of them with a growth of rank beard, which seemed to be one of the few local conceits.

There was no excitement, no eager babbling to quiet screaming nerves, no bravado — for this was no quickly cooked-up raid. This was an army, filling the great gliders row on row behind us — a force in heavy strength with hundreds of miles of night flying ahead of us over trackless jungle and jagged mountains — night flying completely over a formidable Jap force to be let down far behind in its rear. It was history in the making.

The gliders were towed in pairs on long ropes. Seese was flying the left glider in our tow. He carried Brig. "Mad Mike" Calvert with most of one of the brigade staffs aboard. Ground crews rigged the ropes as our tow ship taxied out like a great waddling duck. We were being hooked in when the Doc touched me and pointed ahead. "First tow airborne!" — there it was, clear of the treetops in the late afternoon sun with its two lumbering gliders weaving behind it. The second tow was roaring down the strip raising an enormous dust cloud, struggling and howling for flying speed, bouncing slightly, straining, straining and then tearing free of the earth and its own cloud of yellow dust and coming into clear silhouette above the treetops.

Our glider jerked and shuddered as our tow ship took up the slack on the ropes. Then we began to move down the strip into the dust. On both sides of the field the long line of troops were still filing in endlessly to fill the other gliders behind us. Suddenly, as our tow ship came to full throttle, everything blotted out in the dust — everything but John Alison at the controls and the faces of the men in the glider — a little bit drawn at the mouth, a little bit tightened around the eyes. We were racing to takeoff, bouncing slightly, straining on the end of the long towrope, shouldering heavily for flying speed.

Ahead of us the great tow ship was up a few feet to the left and slightly ahead; Seese's glider was airborne. Then so were we, with Alison bearing down heavily on his right rudder, sweating over it and shouting directions to Doc Tulloch to trim ship. We came up over the trees fighting for altitude and presently we settled into the long, slow, grind of wide circling to get our height for the mountains ahead.

The soldier beside me handed over his maps, saying, "Will you circle Broadway with your pencil — we're the Picadilly party." Everyone unclipped his safety belt and eased his pack. The Doc and I went into a huddle over the map and got Broadway lined in for everybody. Then we settled down to the long flying hours ahead — long, cramped, smokeless hours with God-knew-what at the end of them.

All of that vast activity that had been around us for days was gone now, and we were alone, in the setting Assam sun. It flooded the glider and tinted the inside of its fabric with rose gold. It picked out the red in the stubby beards of our party and shone in highlights on rifle barrels and knife hilts. It was quite glorious for a few minutes as we climbed for the mountains, then it faded into the quick jungle purple below and all of our faces were gone in the shadows of the evening.

High over the mountains, C-47 towplanes and gliders head into the approaching night. The landing, 200 miles into Burma, was scheduled to take place under cover of darkness.

Ahead all we could see was the blue blob of exhaust from the tow ship's starboard motor — the ship itself was shrouded in haze. All we could feel was the breathing of tightly packed men on either side and the animal shudder of the glider as it swung into the prop wash and swung out again. All we could hear was the thundering noise of our thrust through the air — gliders are as noisy as power planes.

Doc Tulloch touched me, saying, "Four thousand feet." I looked at my watch. We had been off for some time, with still a very long time to go. The moon was high over the clouds now — a great three-quarter moon. Presently it broke through its own silver wash into magnificent light above us and the bearded faces came out of the shadows into pale life again.

"Seventy-one hundred feet," Doc grinned exultantly. "That clears the mountains!" Then in a moment we hit turbulence and began to kick around and bounce like mad. The towrope looped back toward us and eased over our port wing. We bumped up and swayed out to the right and the rope snaked off straight ahead again toward the flame of the tow ship's exhaust. We were alone as far as we could see, but we knew that the rest of the wave was behind our spearpoint — that the succeeding waves would take off on schedule as their time came up — that the show was on and that it would go through.

We were at 8,500 feet now and in a few moments we were across the Burma frontier, with the mountains behind us. There had been village lights dotting the way as we crossed Assam, but once in enemy-held Burma the ground was completely blacked out. The thought flashed through my mind that if the Japs had even one night fighter pilot half as good as "Cats Eyes" Cunningham, we could all be done-in like sitting ducks, for we were sneaking the invasion in without fighter cover and in unarmed ships — counting entirely on audacity and surprise.

The moon was bright and high over Burma, with its almost forgotten war, far away from the rest of the world and very unimportant to millions of people. If we died — would it be worth the sacrifice? Purely academic thinking — all thinking is, once you are committed to action. But suddenly from it the whole reason behind all of the war was as clear as a bell stroke.

For centuries my part of the world has dreamed and thought and worked and fought for government owned by the individual — and to some extent has attained that ideal — and therefore dead or alive the individual doesn't count except insofar as he attempts by all his acts to maintain that individual ownership! That's what John Alison and the Doc and Magoffin and all the thousands of men behind us were doing up here and out here tonight — maintaining individual ownership — and the thinking stopped as if a door had closed on it with a loud crash.

John turned his head and shouted "The Irrawaddy River!" We crossed it and passed within a few miles of a Jap airfield and for minutes afterward all of us who could, plastered our faces to the windows watching for tracers or pursuit aviation. But they let us through that bottleneck — they must have thought us a night bombing mission in force.

There was a bright fire presently far off to the right of us on high ground and somebody passed the word that we were ahead of schedule — God bless tail winds on nights like this!

"Target in 20 minutes." All of us in that glider came alive — broke from our tight-packed, cramp-locked huddles. Bolts snicked sharply as cartridges snapped into chambers. Hangers on pistols crashed back and slid home again. Men straightened and got their packs adjusted — heavy jungle packs that would carry us out the whole way on foot if need be. The word passed for safety belts and the catches clicked to.

Ahead, the tow ship banked lazily and suddenly John Alison and the Doc called out together, "Lights — they've got the smudges lit!" The first glider was already down then. Halfway around in the bank, Alison hit the cutoff at a thousand feet and we were gliding free, coming in sharply for a landing in complete darkness. Seese's glider was free beside us and slightly ahead. Here we go — packed to the guards — with no power but gravity to bring us in. Here we go

into a blind clearing at better than a hundred miles an hour, howling down the night wind, deep in the heart of enemy territory, with a whole Jap army between us and home.

Trees — and we're over them! The lights — and they've shot past under us! A long flat shadowland ahead and we flatten for it, level off, sink toward it, strike it and bounce. The skids tear into it and the dust blots us out, streaming behind us across the clearing like the tail of a meteor. Then suddenly we have swung slightly right and stopped and the doors fly open and the security party is off on the run, fanning out on a perimeter of 360 degrees — moving toward the jungle that is all around us and that may burst into shattering enemy fire at the next breath.

"Gliders!"

Another tow ship is over us with its gliders cut off. You can see them over the distant trees, losing altitude fast, diving toward us, helpless to turn back or to go on beyond their glide — howling down into the clearing with their heavy loads — one of them with death reaching for it. It banks slightly before it quite clears the trees and a split second later there is a splintering, crushing thunderclap echoing across the night silences and the glider is gone.

We start a party toward the edge of the jungle, running toward the sound of the crash, passing the word back for the doctor. Paddybirds chirp sleepily in their nests and the moon is still high and white above — but in there, somewhere deep in that tangled growth, there is nothing but silence. We cut in partway and call — but no answer comes back. We circle down a fishtail in the clearing and call again. No answer — and not a sound — but the roar of more motors overhead and the slicing sigh of two more gliders cut free — and again two more — until the air above seems full of them for a moment.

The word is passed that the bulldozers are not down yet — plowed ground and buffalo wallows and a log or two have taken wheels off some of the landed gliders — all hands are ordered to manhandle them and clear the landing space for the other gliders coming in. Everybody turns to on the disabled ships, tugging frantically to get them out of the way. But a big glider with one wheel off is a hard thing to move. "Turn her port wing to the north then, and keep her red wing-tip light on! Lay on the next one. Heave! Here comes another tow."

Fifty men strain at the wreck but she doesn't budge. Skids dig in. "Haul up on the wing — hold her shoulder high — around with her tail. Sweat, you bloaters — lay on!"

"Gliders!"

Two more are howling down over the trees, roaring toward the congestion. One of the two sees it in time, zooms over it with the last of its speed and plows in safety just beyond. But the other crashes head on and welds two gliders into a ball of scrap.

Screams tear the night and the wrecker crew claws into the wreckage with bare hands to get at the injured. A British surgeon is already inside doing something under a flashlight, something quite frightful after his morphine has stilled the screaming.

And there is a quiet North Country voice in there, "Don't move me — this is where I hit — and this is where I die."

You don't have heroes in armies any more. You just have men.

John Alison was changing the lights, re-rigging them with Magoffin to give the following gliders a better runway to come in on. Indefatigable John was tearing all over the lot on his short legs — no longer the fighter pilot or the glider pilot — but the airport manager sweating himself soggy.

Brigadier Calvert had his command post set up in the jungle edge and his security patrols out in all directions. Quiet Calvert — with his soft English voice masking the most civilized of killers. Stringy Shuttleworth had his polished monocle stuck firmly in his left eye — a well-bred jungle stalker.

The first short-range ground patrols were back now — no enemy. There had been one distant shot — but there was no enemy in force as yet. John Alison had the landing strips laid out again to avoid the wrecked gliders and the lights re-rigged for the second wave. In the pause between, Doc Tulloch set up his dressing station and it began to fill up. Men hobbled in singly and between two pals. Men were car-

135

ried in on stretchers. There was no sound from them. There seldom is after the first shocked screams. Across the field, the British surgeon fought all night to save two men — and lost with the dawn light — and that angered him for he had fought well.

The breather was over and again the roar of tow ships filled the night skies — and again the gliders swooped in two by two — one with a bulldozer aboard to miss the strip in the darkness and to dive headlong between two trees that barely cleared the fuselage, to take off both wings and howl onward into the clear with the murderous bulldozer torn loose inside to slam onward unhinging the nose, heaving pilot and copilot up into the air, ricocheting out under them and letting the two men drop back unhurt!*

There was now enough of a security party down to hold that clearing for 13 daylight hours — the 13 hours necessary for the combat engineers to make an airport for power ships, so Alison got on the radio and stopped the final waves of gliders.

With the first fish-belly light, the bulldozers began to growl and the engineers were at it, grading and filling, leveling off hummocks, cutting the rank buffalo grass, hauling disabled gliders under the trees.

A British captain hobbled in on a broken foot. He had found his way in from a deep jungle crash with his ser-

* EDITOR'S NOTE: 30 men were killed and 33 injured in landings that first night.

geant weaving along behind him — both of them dazed. Two more men were alive in that crash they said, so Doc Túlloch got the position from the captain and machete in hand and stretcher-bearers behind him he started across the clearing to cut his way in to find them.

Word came over from the other clearing station that there would be a burial of British and Americans shortly because the jackals were already howling — the first time I ever heard them howl in daylight. There was a burial in one grave regardless of rank or nation, with John Michael Matthew, the little Burmese chaplain from Rangoon diocese, reading the service and everyone fervently following with the Lord's Prayer. Suddenly there were motors high in the air but nobody looked up or moved to take cover until the rough wooden cross was planted and the last spadeful of earth was in. Then they scattered in all directions. But it was only our top cover, cruising far above, during the daylight hours, according to careful plan.

All through the forenoon the engineers toiled in the gathering heat. Doc Tulloch was back empty-handed. The captain with the broken foot had been too dazed to keep his directions straight. Doc got another set of directions from the injured sergeant and went in again. But again the directions were wrong and again Tulloch came out empty-handed and dead beat

"Broadway," Burma. Landing in the jungle at night held many hazards as shown here — gliders crashed into each other. Thirty men were killed, 33 injured in the landings the first night.

from cutting through jungle growth for upward of ten miles.

Brigadier Calvert roughed in the casualty list as it was known to us and as we could guess it further from known factors of missing gliders. Yet suddenly it seemed amazingly small for what it had purchased. In another six hours thousands of troops would pour in in power ships on this airport of ours — that some of the first-wave men had died to secure.

There was the hum of flight motors in the sky suddenly and over the tree-tops came the tiny planes of Major Rehori, jaunty, frail and insolent in their perfect formation. They had come across the vast enemy-held terrain at treetop level, with belly tanks to get them there — the *Helldivers* had come to take out the injured.

We got one of them to cruise the jungle and it located Doc's crash. He brought in the exact bearing. We shot the azimuth and cut into the rank growth of jungle and after an hour of it, we found the crash. Jerry Dunn was in there — to stay. So were the rest. He had been wrong — you mustn't talk about it — you mustn't think about it. When you have an appointment in Samarra, you will keep it, whether you talk or not.

The American engineers toiled on throughout the long, steaming afternoon, smoothing the strip for the power ships, lengthening it — making the airport. Their officer lay in there in that jungle crash with the rest of them — the third officer they had lost to date. "Every time we get a job in Burma we lose an officer." They stood around for a moment, helpless, bewildered, angry deep inside themselves; then young Brackett, the last lieutenant they had, said, "OK — two more hours of daylight. Get going!"

The sun was low, sinking to the treetops, and the shadows were pooling deep across the clearing — that clearing far in enemy territory — so far that when you looked at it on a map you still couldn't quite believe that you were there. But you were — and it was no longer enemy territory — it belonged to us! It was an airport, ringed now with enough men to hold it for the time that was left to wait — test-lighted now for the troop-carrying power ships as the sun went down — and the lights worked.

A wrecked glider was the control tower — John Alison was ready in it, with his control radio.

All that airstrip needed was a name. Then suddenly it didn't need a name. It had many names — names from Brooklyn and Carolina, London and the North Country, Liverpool, Texas and Nepal — names of the men who had paid off to make it. Men who were there with it deep in the Burma jungle — who would stay there with it forever, watching over it.

There was a motor roar far up in the evening sky — the first of the troopships. They came in and circled for Alison's landing beam and got it, roaring down and taxiing off the strip to disgorge the Army. They came in faster than they ever could at LaGuardia Field — one after another, circling, cutting in their landing lights, roaring down on the lighted strip. You could count for a while, then you lost count, and you asked someone and the figure was unbelievable. And it still is, if you look it up in the official records.

Here was General Wingate's army — and Phil Cochran and his gang flew it over the mountains in the bright moonlight and put it down deep in the heart of Jap-held Burma — and the password was Mandalay.

The Japanese seizure of the Burma Road in the spring of 1942 threatened to put China and the American air units there out of the war. Little did the enemy realize that subsequent events would prove otherwise. The AAF's India-China Wing of the global Air Transport Command immediately began to airlift supplies over the unchartered extension of the rugged Himalaya Mountains — an operation that became known as the "Hump." Flying through passes 14,000 feet high, flanked on both sides by towering peaks extending thousands of feet further up, the C-47, C-54, C-46 and C-87 transport pilots wrote an epic chapter in air war logistics. These heavily loaded unarmed cargo aircraft overflew the most rugged terrain in the world where forced landings were impossible and crews bailing out had only the barest chances of surviving. In these mountains, sudden and wild storms brought heavy overcasts with deluging rains, hail and snow. At times flyers met violent winds over 100 mph. Below was wild hostile country.

Here, by a noted war correspondent, and today a radio and TV commentator, is a vivid description of a C-47 flight over this treacherous aerial resupply line.

Over the Hump

Eric Sevareid

THAT DAY there was not a cloud in the skies over North Burma, and that was bad. The Japs liked to catch unarmed transport planes like ours, flying "over the hump" between China and India, and the radio operator had just reported that four Zeros were somewhere around.

Teetering on a wooden ration box, I thrust my head up into the glass bulge on the top of the C-47, peering into the dazzling blue for signs of the Zeros. I could see a long distance in three directions over the greenish, jungle-covered hills, but when I gazed eastward, toward the China we had left an hour before, the morning sun blinded me. If we could spot the Zeros first, we had a chance. The pilot, Lt. George Hannah of Louisville, could slip the camouflaged plane down low into the valleys and try to sneak away. But if they saw us first and came at us out of the sun — well, another plane number would probably be rubbed off the blackboard in the operations shack at the Assam base in India; and the boys who regularly fly the hump into China would say, in that misleadingly casual tone I have heard so many times, "Hannah got his today."

The crew chief took my place and I stood behind the pilots, watching the ridges lapping toward us. The co-pilot, who had not made this run often, was a little nervous and would quietly suggest to Hannah that maybe we wouldn't clear that next one, a quarter-mile away. Hannah would say nothing, but turn and wink at his colleague as we cleared the ridge with no more than 40 feet to spare. That was the idea; on a cloudless day it was no good flying high, because that's where the Zeros played about. Instead, you just coasted over the hills, below the horizon of the next range, risking a sudden downdraft which might smash you, but making it tough for the Zeros to pick you out in the bewildering patterns of green and brown.

There was another risk. Hannah pointed down to a cluster of long, low, wooden buildings, thatched with palm and banana leaves. We were flying directly over some Japanese army barracks, almost within pistol range. I cannot describe the sensation it gave me; I know the meaning now of the phrase, "between the devil and the deep blue sea." We stared at the brush below, waiting for the first machine-gun tracer bullets. Hidden machine guns on the North Burma hillsides have downed more than one of our transport planes.

But this time there was no shooting. We roared on and suddenly, dead ahead, we saw a narrow, white gash winding across the hills. This was the "Ledo Road" which American army engineers are driving through toward its ultimate connection with the old Burma Road. We were over it in a moment and knew then that we had the protection of our own antiaircraft guns hidden somewhere in that impenetrable bush below us. In a little while our three-hour run from China was ended and we stepped out into the muggy heat of Assam. I never felt more relieved in my life and even Hannah, I noticed, was mopping the sweat from his ruddy face. He had that day completed his 96th flight over the hump.

Hannah is just one of hundreds of American boys who have been "sweating it out" over that route for the last two years. They are carrying gas, bombs and ammunition for Major General Chennault's 14th Air Force, and jeeps, guns, medicine and a thousand other items to keep China's flickering resistance alive. They have helped to hold the great bastion of the Chinese earth where one day, Lieutenant General Stilwell believes, Japan's ultimate fate may be decided.

Strangely assorted cargoes have been carried back out of China: ingots of tin ore and wolfram for America's factories; American soldiers on stretchers, some silent with wounds, others twisting and turning, racked with malaria; Chinese soldiers sent to India for training with modern American weapons, under American officers. These Chinese troops will go back into China on foot, fighting their way. Some are already doing so, clearing the Japs away from the advancing Ledo Road.

Few Americans know the story of the great hump flight, because the War Department had to maintain silence until now. Today the story can be told, because our protection of the route is more complete.

We have a long list of unsung heroes in this war, and the Air Transport Command youngsters who have flown the hump day in and day out ought to be placed near the head of this list. Most of them haven't even been able to let their families know what they are doing. "Just flying a routine transport run" — it sounds at a distance like a cinch, but I have heard our fighter pilots and bomber crews out there talk about the hump flyers, and I know the deep respect in which they are held. I remember Lt. Tommy Harmon, who fights in a P-38, saying at mess: "I would rather fly a fighter against the Japs three times a day than fly a transport over the hump once."

The ATC operations room is like a combat headquarters. Every night, when I was there, they jotted down the casualties or near-casualties for the day. It takes a particular type of lad to fly this route. His navigation must be excellent, because for most of the three-hour run he must maintain radio silence, and it is very easy to get lost over that rugged terrain, especially if he must fly among the

Framed against the rugged peaks of the towering Himalayas, a camouflaged C-46 Commando transport flies the "Hump" from India to China.

towering ice-covered peaks which extend eastward from the principal range of the Himalayas.

He must know his plane thoroughly and how it will react in all kinds of weather. He may leave India deciding to fly low over the Burma hills and find that an unforeseeable monsoon storm forces him up to 18,000 feet, where his plane may ice over in a few moments. If he has passengers, the crew chief must revive those who pass out for want of oxygen.

Most of all, he must have steady nerves. The brash, highly strung boy who makes a good fighter pilot will not do. To be attacked when you have a gun in your hand is one thing — anybody feels confident. But to know that a Zero is after you and that you are utterly defenseless, and still to keep your eyes ahead and your mind working logically to figure out your escape — that it something quite different.

Planes crack up on the hump, and so do flyers. Expert medical officers, such as Col. Don Flickinger at the India base, examine the pilots at frequent intervals; at the first sign of fraying nerves they are sent out for a rest — to the luxuries of Calcutta, or the cool lakes and pines of Kashmir. Some, like Hannah, seem to go on forever without a break in their nervous systems, but they are not many.

Those who complain that we are "doing nothing for China" would be surprised at the amount of stuff we are delivering by air over the hump.

There are scores of flights into China every day in the year. The Burma Road, at its very peak, carried about 15,000 tons of supplies into China per month. My guess is that the ATC is already approaching that figure. Of course, that is pitifully little. One big cargo ship a month would equal it.

Sitting about the barrack rooms you hear constant talk of crew members who are "hiking out." Boys who have had to bail out of their plane somewhere on the hump are trying to find their way across the ridges and through the jungles to the India or China side. I have heard endless discussions among the flyers as to what they would do if their turn came, what equipment they would try to salvage, where they would head for. It is constantly on their minds. They study carefully their excellent large-scale maps, noting the little red circles which indicate positions held by the enemy.

The record of rescues is getting better, partly because more head-hunting natives are learning that rewards of salt and cloth await them if they find and return the boys unharmed. And we have more crews now which do nothing but nose their C-47's day after day through the innumerable valleys, looking for a fluttering bit of white cloth which may be the signal of a lost American flyer. More and more boys are turning up, brought by horse-cart into China (Chinese peasants are quick to hide them from the Japs) or led into India by Naga natives.

I know how efficient the rescue work can be, once the search plane spots you on the ground. Flying over the hump last August, the plane I was in developed engine trouble and the 20-odd of us aboard had to bail out into the jungle. It took us 27 days to get out.

There are many stories of far worse experiences. You cannot crash-land your plane on the hump because there isn't a level, cleared spot to be found, but two American boys once managed to land on the side of a snow-covered peak, and lived. Both suffered broken ankles. They huddled in the wrecked airplane, eating their scanty canned rations, wrapping themselves in their parachute silk for warmth. Several times searching planes flew near but all their signaling was in vain.

When their food was nearly gone, they bandaged one another's ankles and stumbled and slid down the mountain. Only one who has tried to walk on a broken bone can imagine what they went through. By a stroke of luck, wandering Chinese discovered them one day, lying by a stream, without strength to go on, and 19 days later they were safe in an Air Force hospital.

It would not be honest reporting to ascribe all the troubles and tragedies on the hump to the enemy and the elements. Among the transport planes used was a new model, hurried into service because of popular pressure in America for more aid to China.

Fundamentally, it is a superb airplane, but it was very new then and all the "bugs" in it were by no means ironed out. This model hauled many hundreds of tons of supplies into China, but a good many of the planes crashed and lives were lost. In time, these planes are expected to be as reliable as the steadfast C-47.

There were other troubles. The heat and humidity in Assam are enervating. The food was wretched and the quarters were worse. The boys at the Assam base had almost nothing to look forward to at the end of their dangerous day. For a time morale sagged badly among the ground crews, there was little discipline, and the efficiency of maintenance and traffic control went down.

Then Maj. Gen. Harold George, chief of the ATC, came out from Washington and things began to happen. This quiet, stocky man with the determined jaw issued orders and replaced officers. He put a newcomer, hard-boiled Col. Tom Hardin of Texas, in charge, and overnight there was discipline. He also devised new methods of faster communication with the China base, and introduced night flying across the hump.

My first attempt to fly into China had failed, but soon I got a chance to try it again — this time under the most favorable circumstances. General George allowed me to fly with him and several other high-ranking officers, in his four-engined C-87. Now, I thought, all would go smoothly. There

143

were those four engines, instead of only two, and there were two of the world's best transport pilots at the helm — the men who flew Willkie around the world, Lt. Col. Robert Kight and Maj. Alex Klotz.

But after a comfortable flight of two hours, the weather abruptly changed as we neared our objective in China. The ceiling at the China base closed down almost to zero. We flew in endless circles at 18,000 feet, hardly able to see our wing tips in the fog. We strapped on our oxygen masks and goggled at one another as the minutes passed. When we were an hour and a half overdue, I was uneasy and began to calculate how long it would take me to get into that chute. I think Lt. Col. Rex Smith, sitting opposite, was enjoying my discomfiture. He pulled up his mask and leaned to my ear.

"You don't dare jump again, Eric," he shouted. "Nobody in New York would believe it this time. Even if they did, your office would just think you had gotten into a rut and your reputation will be ruined! You better go down with the plane!"

He knew what I didn't: that we had enough gas to go back to India, if necessary. Klotz wanted to, but Kight had an idea he could bring us down. Then we learned there were 22 other planes "stacked up" in the fog around us, all trying to get down. I listened in the headphones and could hear the steady voice of an officer on the ground. He was "stepping down" the helpless planes. "All right," he would say, "number 756, you can come down to 10,000. Four eight two, you can go to 9,000." He never put two planes on the same altitude level, and he was bringing them in, one at a time.

Then we learned by listening that one transport above us had a defective radio — while the pilot could send, he could not receive. He asked for a flight to come up, so he could follow it down through the mist. It was dispatched. He never found it. Then he was saying, "Got 20 minutes gasoline left." Then, "Ten minutes left, I think." His voice sounded very cool. Finally he reported, "I sure hate to lose this ship, but we're going to bail out. See you on the ground." Then silence.

After more than two hours of circling and cautious lowering, we landed safely and I learned that the boys who had "hit the silk" were reported to have come down 20 miles away. Chinese soldiers brought them to the airfield on a truck the next day. For all of them, this had been their first jump. But this is what they did: as they crossed the field, they saw a transport plane which had no crew. They walked into operations, trailing their dirty chutes, and said, "How about letting us take that plane back to India? There's some guys coming in for a poker game tonight."

In the far northern approaches to Japan, in Alaska and strung out along the bleak, volcanic Aleutian Islands, the 11th Air Force fought a curious and miserable war. It was a war of intermittent clashes with the elusive enemy, and a never-ending, weary struggle against the elements.

There was fog, a white blinding impenetrable substance, that enveloped the landscape and blocked from view surrounding mountains for as long as three months at a time. Then there was wind which seemed to blow from all directions at once. A weather bulletin reading "110-mile-an-hour winds with strong gusts" was not unusual. Parked aircraft had to be anchored to the earth. When the cold, driving, heavy rains made shallow lakes out of airfields, the lower ball turrets of the B-17's would be under water. When frequent snows and sleets desolated the mainland and the island chain, the aircrews wouldn't even bother to get out of bed. At 85 degrees below zero it was cold indeed, and when the temperature got up to 35 below out on Umnak, ground crews would jokingly complain about the "heat wave." Then, too, there were the williwaws — strong winds that built up on one side of the island and pushed downward with all the strength of several typhoons on the other side. You just didn't fly in a williwaw and only a greenhorn would spit into one.

For the 11th it was "up where the soup begins" — the worst flying weather in the world. It was not at all unusual for the daily weather flight to radio back to base "weather completely unfit for flying."

And so the greatest enemy, by far, was not the Japanese. On the ground, it was loneliness and boredom. In the air, weather and the constant gnawing thought that the endless stretch of water, from the edge of the airfield to target and return, was cold. It would let you live less than one minute if you went down.

The "Forgotten" 11th Air Force — the title it claimed for itself — contained a fighter and a bomber command made up of units of B-17's, B-24's, B-25's, B-26's, P-38's and P-40's.

Operating under the most adverse conditions, the 11th had given strong air support to our May, 1943 amphibious recapture of Attu (the outermost Aleutian island which the Japs overran in June of 1942 when they attacked Dutch Harbor and were repulsed). In the short but bitter Battle of Attu, the 11th lost only two bombers, and four fighters but it hammered the Jap-held Kiska Island until the enemy was forced to voluntarily withdraw from this stronghold in 1943.

From then on, targets for the 11th were in the distant Kurile Islands — the northern approaches to the Japanese homeland. Paramushiru, often called the "Japanese Arctic Gibraltar," was tops on the list and here is the story of the first strikes against it.

Bombs for Paramushiru

Maj. Louis C. Blau and Maj. Frank T. Gash

WHAT impressed everybody most about Paramushiru was the size of the targets.

Month after month we had bombed a thin rim of pinpoint targets around the curve of Kiska Harbor, but the army staging area on Paramushiru and the naval base on Shimushu Island were duck soup. If your stick overshot a warehouse, it plunked right down in the middle of a barracks area. You could hardly miss hitting something.

When we first learned we were to take a crack at Paramushiru we were still so busy bombing Kiska that there was little time to make any special preparations. It was to be just another mission. The plan was to bomb Kiska on the way over, take on some more bombs at Attu, and after bombing Paramushiru, drop another load on Kiska on the way back. In that way we wouldn't waste any time or gasoline.

Our information about the island that was supposed to be a Japanese Gibraltar, guarding the northern approach to Tokyo, was meager. As a result, our first mission was for reconnaissance as much as anything else.

Still, there was an extra thrill in that takeoff from Attu on July 19, 1944. The distance on the course plotted for the trip and return was only about 1,700 miles, not far as missions in the Aleutian area go. Whatever qualms we had over the lack of emergency landing spots between Attu and Paramushiru were compensated for by the thought that we were carrying the offensive to the enemy. It was our first crack at the Jap in his native haunts.

Our Liberators, loaded with 500-pound bombs, were in command of Maj. Robert E. Speer. The weather on the way over was mostly hazy, although occasionally it cleared to CAVU (Ceiling And Visibility Unlimited). We kept to about 12,000 feet as we approached the Kamchatka Peninsula. The peninsula is mountainous, somewhat like the Aleutians, but quite wooded. We rubbed our eyes at seeing a tree, some of us for the first time in a year. After following the coastline for a while, we cut off for our run to the target.

This first visit apparently was a complete surprise for the Japs. There was not a plane in the sky; none were even seen until after our bombing runs had been completed. Apparently not even the antiaircraft was on the alert, because only four or five bursts were seen. Either they didn't have any

Straight ahead of this attacking B-25 lies the Japanese naval base of Kataoka, on Shimuhu, northernmost Kurile island. It is 11 p.m. as this lead plane dove to attack ships in the Paramushiru Strait. Note midnight sun reflected in camera lens just ahead of plane.

more antiaircraft set up or the crews were out for coffee.

As we approached, the clouds became broken and when we got over the target area visibility was good except for a low-lying haze which obscured the effect of the explosions. However, many excellent photographs were obtained and some smoke could be seen by the rear gunners.

One flight of three ships made a run at 18,000 feet attacking buildings in the vicinity of the airdrome near Kataoka. Another flight, through a misunderstanding of signals, dropped none of its bombs on the first run but had plenty of time to get away its entire load on a second run at about 17,000 feet, concentrating on shipping in the strait.

Many fishing and naval vessels and eight or nine large transports were observed in the strait. Several bombs were seen to drop close to these vessels, one of them scoring a near-miss on a transport.

It was all over in less time than it takes to describe it. As we headed back home, five single-engine pursuit planes climbed up to intercept and two of about 20 float planes observed on Lake Bettobu, east of the naval base on Shimushu, got off the water but their heart apparently wasn't in it. They gave up the chase within two or three minutes. The mission returned to Attu without a single bullet hole or so much as a scratch from antiaircraft fire.

Our reception on the next trip, three weeks later, was quite different, to put it mildly. We bombed Kiska on our way over to the jumping-off spot in the afternoon and everybody spent most of the night checking guns, motors, bomb racks and the thousand and one things that have to be looked after on any mission. We had a hunch the Japs might be waiting for us a second time.

With the aid of photographs obtained on the first mission we had a much better idea of our objectives when we took off through the early morning mist on August 11.

Weather was CAVU most of the way over to the Kamchatka coast. We flew from 10,000 to 12,000, climbing to 18,500 as we turned south.

When we reached the tip of Kamchatka we found that both Paramushiru and Shimushu were overcast with a top of about 2,000 to 2,500 feet so we circled down to make a dead-reckoning run. After checking all stations over the interphone and finding everybody ready to go, all three elements headed for the target. Then we got a break.

The run is less than ten minutes. As we approached, the overcast became broken and we could see that over the targets the sky was clear enough to make a bombsight run as originally planned.

Then the No. 2 supercharger of Lieutenant Lockwood's plane went haywire and the No. 4 engine cut off altogether. He managed to feather the prop but started to lag behind the other two ships of his flight. After coming all that distance, however, he didn't want to turn back without dropping his load, so he advised his flight leader he would keep course and make the best speed possible.

The second visit appeared to be as much of a surprise to the Japs as the first, perhaps because our approach was hidden by the overcast until we came within a short distance of the targets. They seemed to be on the alert this time, however, because planes were seen to take off the ground while we were still on our run and it wasn't long until the air was full of Zekes, Rufes, Haps and Oscars. During the running fight that continued for about 45 minutes, there were observed several other types of planes including one Watanabe Zero, a float reconnaissance plane and one plane with fixed landing gear, painted silver with a black stripe on either side of the fuselage.

In the waters of the strait we could see a large concentration of ships. It was a beautiful sight, the fluffy white overcast stretching away in all directions except for the big blue hole over the target and the rugged mountains on the southern part of Paramushiru sticking up through the clouds. But the scenic effect was only momentary. It was suddenly broken by the Jap planes swarming up through the overcast like bees out of a hive.

The runway extends north-south on a low plateau north of the army staging area. The Zekes were parked on a string of little T-shaped hard surface platforms beside it. As we came over they took off, apparently as each plane got ready and without any regard for formation. They taxied straight ahead across the runway, taking off from a large area to the east which extended almost to the waters of the bay. The whole field — runway, parking platforms and all — must have been as level as a billiard table because they seemed able to get off in any direction.

The antiaircraft crews were on the job this time, and puffs of smoke started blotching up the sky before we were actually over the targets. They were black, apparently from large-caliber guns, and pretty hot toward the last. Fortunately, the fire was accurate only for altitude and not for course. It appeared to be of the barrage type, aimed for a certain altitude over the target. As at Kiska, the most accurate fire seemed to come from ships in the harbor, rather than the shore batteries.

While the antiaircraft fire did not bother us a great deal, despite its intensity, the Jap planes did. There were about 40 in all, mostly Zekes, armed with two or three machine guns and some with cannon. Six Mavis four-engine flying boats were on the water in the harbor and about 25 or 30 other planes could be seen on Bettobu Lake east of the naval base, but none of these took off.

The attacks lacked coordination

and were not always pressed determinedly but they kept after us until we were well on our way home, a few of them for 40 or 45 minutes.

They attacked alone or in pairs and some, probably the green pilots, veered away before coming in range, even when they had numerical superiority. Their favorite angles seemed to be five and seven o'clock from which they could use the two vertical stabilizers as a shield to protect them from the top turret and tail gunners. However, several times attacks were made from the front at about 11 o'clock, perhaps for variety. Most attacks were made from our level although occasionally one dived and came up from below.

Two of the Japs were credited to Lieutenant Lockwood's plane. Two Zekes, coming up from below, attacked simultaneously, one at 11 o'clock and the other at five. Lt. Merle E. Arthur, navigator, gave the one coming in at 11 a burst at about 500 yards. The Zeke broke off and trailed smoke as it went into a dive and exploded after diving about 2,000 feet. Staff Sgt. Walter Succov, tail gunner, and Sgt. David L. Carter, belly gunner, got the other one from about 900 yards. The Zeke pulled up into a stall and fell off on the right wing with flames coming from the engine. It dropped into the ocean. A Hap followed this one down, circled the wreckage and climbed up to follow the plane again, but staying at a pretty safe distance.

11th Air Force B-24's make it back to their Aleutian Islands base from a raid on the Kuriles. Arctic storm is setting in. In minutes visibility will be zero.

Lieutenant Lockwood's plane, still plugging along on three engines, was damaged considerably in these and other attacks and began to lose altitude. The crew had a field day throwing things overboard to lighten the plane, and the ship was pretty well stripped in short order. It descended through the overcast and was flying at only about 200 feet when the crew got one of those thrills that brings your heart right up into your mouth. All three motors quit together due to a vapor lock. With exceptional presence of mind, Lieutenant Lockwood quickly threw on his booster pump and turbos and held his breath. Sergeant Carter in the belly turret was only 15 or 20 feet above the white caps when all three motors started again.

The Pacific Air War was tough. And in the early months of combat, the pilots of all services—Army Air Force, Navy, Marines—fought in remote areas of a vast Far East region under a "Europe First" priority for combat aircraft, support equipment, and manpower.

The Marine aviation status in the Pacific was bleak at best. The Marine Corps in its entirety possessed less than 250 aircraft. Although more than 1,000 had been committed by Congressional action, only a handful were spread across half a world of Pacific Ocean area.

When the Japanese struck Pearl Harbor like a bolt of lightning, it all but wiped out Marine Aviation Group 21 at Ewa Marine Air Station in Hawaii.

Far to the east of Hawaii, it was a similar story. What emerged from the fire, smoke, and ashes of December 7, 1941 became the trademark of Marine air combat.

Courage-Guts-Skill

Gene Gurney and Mark P. Friedlander, Jr.

At Wake Island—2,000 miles east of Hawaii—the flyers of Marine Fighter Squadron 211 were proudly inspecting the twelve shiny Grumman Wildcats, which had arrived just three days before, and checking over their crisp new operating manuals, when the Japanese bombers poured destruction over the coral-white island. By the end of that day only five of the Wildcats were left. The Marine pilots bravely fought against overwhelming odds in the five remaining fighters, stopping a score of enemy aircraft and sinking two Jap destroyers. As a flying unit, VMF 211 (the "V" stands for heavier-than-air, "MF" for Marine fighter) stayed airborne for two weeks after the first attack; and when the last Wildcat had been destroyed the pilots fought as foot soldiers until Wake Island fell to the Japanese invaders.

Unrelenting, the Japanese gobbled up the Pacific, and by May 1942 the victorious Jap forces were reaching out for Midway Island, the last stronghold west of Hawaii. Available reinforcements were moved into Midway in a determined effort to halt the Japanese onslaught. A squadron of AAF B-17 Flying Fortresses were flown in to help meet the brunt of the forthcoming assault. On 3 June 1942 a Japanese task force was sighted and in the early Pacific dawn, through the scattered cotton-puff clouds, the American airmen rose to meet the Jap Navy. Westward, behind the screen of the small task force, the big carriers were sending forth the bombers and fighters to devastate the island defenses. The Army Air Force, the Navy and the Marines, in a combined effort, hit the Japs with everything they had. In the ensuing Battle of Midway, the greatest encounter between air power and sea power, the young flyers stopped the Japanese and turned the tide of battle in the Pacific.

In the heat of the battle, one of the future Marine aces, Captain Marion Carl, while making a firing pass at a Japanese bomber, was jumped by three Zeros. Rolling over, Captain Carl dove toward the ocean to shake his pursuers. In his official report he stated that in the evasive dive he "firewalled" everything (his throttle to emergency war power, his propeller pitch control to full increase r.p.m. and his fuel mixture control to the full RICH position) for maximum speed and in so doing not only outdove the Zeros, but gained enough airspeed to zoom back up to make a pass on the three of them, shooting one down—the first of his 18½ kills.

Another future ace, Lieutenant Charles Kunz, who that same day shot down two Japanese bombers, returned in a very unhappy mood in regard to his aircraft. In a report to intelligence he made the following comparison between the combat capabilities of the Marine's Brewster Buffalo (F2A-3) and the Japanese Zero fighter: "The 00 fighter has been far underestimated [in previous intelligence reports]. As for the F2A-3, it should be in Miami as a trainer plane, rather than be used as a first-line fighter." But in spite of any misgivings, those were their only fighting machines and fight they did, running up an impressive tally against the Japanese. When the battle was over, the American flyers had struck a decisive blow across the knuckles of the greedy Japanese hand of aggression.

Eight months later, on the other side of the Pacific, as our forces moved into Guadalcanal, one of the most unusual adventures of the Marine's air war was unfolding. When the Navy had to withdraw its support from the landings on Guadalcanal, the Marines were up against overwhelming odds in the fight to hold their hard-won positions. At Henderson Field the order came down to put everything with wings into the air. Under this all-out effort, Major Jack Cram requested permission to take his Catalina PBY flying boat on a bombing mission. Permission was granted, and reveling in his one chance to get into the fighting end of the shooting war, he sought, found and twice torpedoed a Japanese transport vessel twelve miles out at sea. From overhead half a dozen Zeros flashed down after the lumbering, gangly Catalina flying boat. His torpedo attack successful, Major

Cram, hugging the deck, hightailed it back to Henderson with the six Zeros making repeated stern sweeps, spraying the PBY with machine gun bullets. His situation seemed hopeless, so five of the Zeros slipped off to find more exciting sport, while one remained to finish the job. Grimly Cram droned on, with the Zero close behind pouring round after round into the PBY. By-passing Henderson Field, Cram skimmed over the treetops toward a fighter squadron auxiliary base with the Zero, almost in formation, shooting at him from behind.

Still unable to shake the Jap, Major Cram entered the traffic pattern at the fighter base. As he had hoped, a fighter (flown by Lieutenant Roger Haberman) was just entering the initial in the fighter overhead landing pattern. Haberman, seeing the strange sight, stretched his turn to become number three ship in the traffic pattern—directly behind the Zero. The strange procession rolled out on a long final approach and Haberman, without even bothering to pull up his gear, fired one burst into the Jap plane. The Zero burst into flames and crashed. Haberman continued his approach, landing behind the much-relieved Major Cram and his bullet-ripped PBY. The obliging Lieutenant Roger Haberman—a future Marine ace—was part of the "City Slickers" division of Captain Joe J. Foss' famed Flying Circus flight of VMF 121s.

Arriving in Guadalcanal in September 1942, Captain Joe Foss made history with his Flying Circus as he led his flight to seventy-two air-to-air victories, twenty-six of which he won himself. He had organized the two divisions of his flight into the Farm Boys and the City Slickers. Working together they became a team much feared by the Japanese aviators, and six of the eight men became aces. Their tally was impressive:

Farm Boys

Capt. Joseph J. Foss of Sioux Falls, S. D.	26
Lt. Greg Nash of Montrose, Calif.	8
Lt. William Freeman of Bonham, Tex.	6
Lt. Boot Furlow of Ogen, Arkansas	3
	43

City Slickers

Lt. Oscar Bates of Essex Falls, N.J.	4
Lt. Roger Haberman of Ellsworth, Wis.	7
Lt. Frank Presley of Encinitas, Calif.	6
Lt. W. P. Marontate of Seattle, Wash.	13
	30

"It's like football," the Marine ace said of his well co-ordinated team. "The ball carrier will end up eight yards behind the scrimmage line instead of two or more ahead if his team fails to co-operate and ward off the opposition. Whether you are going to shoot down any planes or even stay alive is determined by the boys you fly with."

Many of the stories about Joe Foss show that the man possessed a rare combination of fast reflexes, aggressiveness and luck. On one occasion

Foss had dropped out of formation with one engine about to quit. Dropping down into a cloud deck above the mountains he intended to stay in the protective "soup" until Henderson Field was clear—at that time it was under bombardment. Looking up through the light hazy clouds above him he saw a Grumman screaming down with a Zero on his tail. At about the same time Foss' sick engine failed and he feathered it. The Grumman ducked into the cloud deck and the Zero swung over in front of Foss. Kicking his ship around he pasted the Zero and it fell from the sky. Joe continued, with one engine feathered, on back to Henderson.

The most unusual air adventure of the Flying Circus occurred in January 1943 when they held off an entire Japanese air armada without firing a shot. Over one hundred Jap Zeros and Bettys were reported headed for Henderson Field in one last all-out effort to destroy the American stronghold. Foss and his Flying Circus went up to meet them (it was felt at that time that the report of over a hundred approaching planes was greatly exaggerated). When the Japs began to arrive, it became obvious that the Japs really had sent the reported hundred planes, and Foss called for reinforcements. In the meantime he gave his own men a very strange order—considering his normal love of a dogfight. His order was to avoid combat and instead to continue a "thatching" pattern over the field. This gave the Japanese the impression of an American decoy, and they scanned the skies for what they feared to be great numbers waiting in the sun for them to strike the handful of P-38s. Puzzled, the Japs circled back and forth between Savo Island and Cape Esperance—between the American and Japanese territory. Occasionally three or four Zeros would make feints at the Flying Circus boys but they were ignored. Finally, unable to draw the Americans into a fight or to figure out what type of trap awaited them, they did the incredible. They turned tail and headed home, dropping their bombs harmlessly in the ocean. No bombs fell on Henderson Field that day, and Foss had accomplished one of the greatest aerial bluffs in history.

But not all battles had been easy and the boys were constantly in the air tangling with Japanese bombers, fighters, and once even a "Washing Machine Charlie" when they attempted a night interception of the Japanese nuisance raiders that were robbing the Marines of their sleep and keeping them holed up in malaria-ridden dugouts. That particular flight, Foss and Roger Haberman had a closer call from their trigger-happy ack-ack people than from the enemy.

On 26 January, the commander of Guadalcanal decided that Joe and his boys had done enough and so the Flying Circus was sent back to Auckland, New Zealand and on to the States for a welcomed rest.

The big push back across the Pacific was gathering momentum and on Guadalcanal men and equipment poured in as the war in that area intensified. When, on 7 April 1944, the American radar warning system reported 160 Japanese planes headed toward the island, the Marines and Army Air Force were able to send up over 60 fighters to meet the approaching air fleet. It was during this engagement that Lieutenant James E. Swett broke the six-kills-in-a-single-action record of the 5th AF's Colonel Neal Kerby. (Lieutenant Swett's record of seven kills in a single action was later tied by Captain William Shomo, also of the 5th AF, and near the end of the war was broken by top Navy ace Commander David McCampbell who shot down nine in a single action.)

Lieutenant Swett, called "Zeke" by his companions, had seen combat in air-ground support missions, but had never faced an enemy in the air. A little nervous, and very anxious for the opportunity, he took off with the other American flyers to meet the Japanese that April day. Leading a division he went in with the group as part of the first wave to intercept the Zeros and Aichi dive bombers as they came over the water to Guadalcanal. Peeling off at 15,000 Swett led his men into the attack. After the first pass and break-off Swett suddenly found himself behind six Aichi dive bombers with the rest of his men nowhere in sight. As he stated in his official mission report: "I got on the tail of the first one and gave it a squirt [burst of fire]. He jettisoned his bombs and burst into flame. . . . I skidded and mushed in behind No. 2 while my tracers laced him. He smoked and burned and went down. . . . I had trouble getting the third one boresighted. . . . As the Aichi (No. 3) nosed over in his bomb run, my first burst smoked him. When he pulled out, I was still on his tail. A few more bursts and he exploded. Just as I pulled away, one of our AA guns on Tulagi drew a bead [at his plane] and wrecked one of my port guns. They almost blew it out of my wing."

With his F4F wing crippled and a machine gun damaged, Swett turned for his base. On the way he spotted another flight of Aichis (nine of them) on their way home, flying low and fast in a follow-the-leader pattern. Swett poured the coal to his F4F and, diving on the planes, sent the rear one down in flames (No. 4); closing the gap he sent No. 5 and then No. 6 down in flames. With three of nine down, and six total, he was just getting warmed to his work. He caught up with the next one (No. 7) and shot it down in flames. With five to go, he closed the gap between the next dive bomber. By this time the Aichi's rear gunner was awake to what was happening and was waiting for the American. They both fired at the same time, Swett with the last of his ammunition. Swett was wounded, the Aichi gunner was killed outright, and the Aichi (maybe No. 8) was last seen by Swett smoking as it headed for home. With his plane smoking badly, he headed back to Tulagi, but his fuel gave out two miles from shore, and he had to ditch the smok-ing plane in the channel. He was the twelfth man of both sides down in the drink that afternoon, so when the channel rescue boat pulled near his small escape kit raft, it approached cautiously, one sailor shouting, "Are you an American?"

"You're goddamn right I am!" shouted Swett.

The Navy man nodded, "Pick him up, it's okay. He's one of them loud-mouthed Marines."

For his work that afternoon, the 22-year-old Swett was credited with seven enemy planes and one prob-able, took a swim in the channel, suf-fered a broken nose, and received a Congressional Medal of Honor.

As early as 1943, B-24 "Liberator" heavy bombers ranged out from bases at Darwin, Australia, to pound Jap targets in the Netherlands East Indies. On June 24, 1943, for example, the 380th Bomb Group hit Macassar in the Southern Celebes and about a month later six of the Liberators flew the longest mission of the war up to that time when they struck the Jap naval base at Soerabaja, Java — a 2,400-mile flight.

One of the richest Japanese holdings in all of Southeast Asia was the oil refineries at Balikpapan on the east coast of Borneo which the Japanese military appropriated in their drive south after Pearl Harbor. A modern war machine moves on oil and it was from Balikpapan that the Japanese were receiving 35 per cent of the oil they needed to continue the war. Here was a high priority target for the American Air Forces. In a prelude of things to come for Balikpapan, Liberators of the 380th Bomb Group destroyed 40,000 tons of shipping in the oil port harbor on August 14, 1943.

The first weighty attack on the refineries themselves came on September 30, 1944. More than 70 Liberators of the 5th and 13th Air Forces led by Col. Thomas C. Musgrave, Jr. (now Major General, USAF) waddled off the single airstrip on newly captured Noemfoor Island in the Netherlands East Indies, each Liberator loaded with 3,000 pounds of bombs (for a gross weight of 68,500 pounds). This was 20,500 pounds more per plane than maximum specifications allowed; nearly a ton more than the B-24's had ever carried before on their longest range Pacific missions — to Truk and Yap Islands. The mission would be a crew-exhausting 16-hour, 2,600-mile round trip which promised to bring out desperate Japanese fighter and antiaircraft opposition.

These were the cold statistics of a major combat mission plan.

Soon to be forgotten would be the immensity of the task; the thousands of man-hours spent round-the-clock preparing the plan, readying the planes, briefing the crews; the lonely minutes during which long, long thoughts were projected into written words to be mailed "just in case"; the pathos, the toil, the sweat, and the apprehension about life and death among those who would go and those who would stay. The history books would not record these things.

And then the takeoff on a mission that would truly live up to the oft-repeated axiom of flight: "hours and hours of boredom . . . punctuated by a few moments of sheer terror."

This was Balikpapan.

Balikpapan

Capt. Donald Hough and Capt. Elliott Arnold

ON A blistering hot day in September, 1944, a few officers were called together at the headquarters of the Far East Air Forces in the Southwest Pacific and were told to make plans for a bombing mission: the target was to be the Dutch oil refinery at Balikpapan on the east coast of Borneo.

The officers went to a map. They put their fingers on the island of Noemfoor, in the Netherlands East Indies, from which the B-24's would take off. They found Balikpapan. They measured it. It made a round trip of 2,500 miles.

Now the heavy bombers in the Southwest Pacific were not unused to flying big distances. Planes in groups of twos and threes had flown that far in the early days, and once some 13 B-24's made a round trip of about that same length.

But there was one vital factor in the distance involved in this new mission that none of the earlier strikes had encountered: there were to be no less than 72 airplanes involved, and for the bulk of the run they would have to fly in formation for protection in attacking the most heavily guarded target in the Southwest Pacific.

And airplanes flying in formation have to jockey endlessly to keep their positions — and in this slipping back and forth they burn up gasoline.

For size of attack and for the mission involved there was only one other place in the world they could look for comparison: at the bombing of Ploesti oil refinery in Rumania on August 1, 1943. That didn't help much. That added up to a little over 2,000 miles, and that was considered a milestone in B-24 bombing at the time.

Before the big raid on Balikpapan could be launched, a base for B-24's was needed "up the line." In this dramatic combat photo, U.S. paratroopers are shown in the process of capturing Kamiri airstrip on enemy-held Noemfoor Island, Dutch East Indies.

This mission, as it was outlined to the officers on that summer afternoon, would take the formation from Noemfoor — which was the closest we could get our Liberators to Balikpapan at that time — across the northeast tip of New Guinea, across the Ceram Sea, past the Soela Islands, across Molucca Sea, across the Celebes, and finally across the Makassar Strait to the target. The planes would be in the air for more than 16 hours.

Stretched across the face of Europe it would be the approximate equivalent of bombing Leningrad from London and return.

And the trip would have to be made without fighter protection, because no fighters could fly the distances from the bases we then had available. And from the moment the big four-engined bombers left their bases they would be in enemy-controlled territory every inch of the way. It was known there were many enemy bases en route, all of them operational, many of them with clusters of fighter planes. And it also was known that Balikpapan itself was defended by the newest and deadliest of the Japanese antiaircraft guns.

For a target they had a dilly. Balikpapan, with its two main plants and its paraffin works, was Japan's largest refinery in the Netherlands East Indies, with a capacity of four million barrels of crude oil. It was estimated that Balikpapan, discovered originally by American oil men and developed with their skill, was supplying Japan

with 35 per cent of her war fuel requirements.

The men got down to work.

The order specified that each plane was to carry 3,000 pounds of bombs and full ammunition for the gunners to protect themselves. Best striking time would be just after eight o'clock in the morning, when atmospheric conditions should be most helpful. That meant a night takeoff.

The 72 planes were to be flown by two groups of the 13th Air Force and one group of the 5th Air Force, and men from all three groups cooperated in laying down the plans.

In view of the distances to be flown in formation, the planners decided to forget most of the flight characteristics of a B-24 over long distances, and to pretend they were starting out with a brand-new airplane. The problems of loading each plane would be so utterly different from anything attempted before, that for all practical purposes the Liberator might well have been a new type aircraft.

The first thing the men did was to get out all the data on weights and balances and figure out just what the airplane would weigh when fully loaded and gassed for the trip. The figure added up to the total of almost 70,000 pounds. Now the B-24 was originally designed to carry a maximum gross of 48,000 pounds, and with the knowledge gained over the years, normal overloading was up to 60,000 pounds. And that was for "normal"

Thousands of hours were spent tuning up the big Liberators for the strike on Balikpapan. Crew here is gassing up and checking the motors of their ship.

missions — the 1500- and 1800-mile strikes.

They went over the ship inch by inch and threw out what they thought could be spared. Little things — bomb hoists, extra bomb shackles, radio frequency tuning meters, tool kits, personal equipment. They finally got down to rock bottom — 68,500 pounds. They were more than four tons over normal overloading and they could lighten the plane no more.

Somebody remembered the Truk and Yap missions of which the boys still spoke dreamily as long missions, long and heavily loaded missions. They looked up figures. Each plane would weigh over a ton more than any plane that had bombed Truk and Yap.

Gasoline was the next problem. The exact amount of fuel used in these missions is a secret, but it can be revealed that more than 700 gallons of gasoline above the normal load was needed for each plane. A gallon of gasoline weighs six pounds.

To get the most mileage from the gas it was necessary to put the center of gravity at a place where the ship would fly the easiest. The factory-determined center of gravity, with normal gasoline load, was useless under these new conditions with the additional weight distributions. To add to that problem was the fact that an instrument takeoff at night and instrument flying for the first few hours of the trip would be necessary.

Still working on the theory that as far as all previous specifications went they were going to handle what would be tantamount to a new airplane, the airmen next called in the civilian factory representatives from Consolidated, the builders of the B-24, and conferred with them. Every scrap of information from the factory now was carefully studied with the representatives on hand.

The center of gravity decided upon could not be constant, because, as the airplane burned up its gasoline, as the gunners fired their ammunition, the load would lighten and the weight would become redistributed. Especially as the gas tanks in the different parts of the ship emptied.

Individual airplanes were loaded as they would be for the mission and flown in test runs. It was found necessary after exhaustive experiments that a special series of directions be contrived, taking into consideration each hour of flight and the changing conditions attendant on each hour. Instead, for instance, of each man wearing from the start his parachute, his emergency ration belt, his medicine kit, flak suit, helmet — even his canteen — a special and definite place in the ship

was chosen to place these things. Even the men themselves were redistributed in the airplane, away from their normal stations.

Then the factory representatives were called upon again, together with the most experienced pilots in the theater, along with engineering personnel, to figure out the best power settings to get maximum mileage. Flying an airplane is not a mechanical job — some pilots get much more mileage out of their gasoline than others because of their more expert handling of the controls and for this mission no such latitude could be permitted because the gasoline leeway was too critical to permit it.

The speed of the airplane was set at 150 mph and the planners figured out a theoretical chart of power settings to get maximum range. Taken into consideration were the takeoff, conditions of climb, cruising, approach to target, breakaway, descent and cruise home, and for each hour of the trip a chart of changing settings was set up to allow for the changing weight of the plane as the heavy gasoline was consumed.

These weight-distribution and power-setting charts were printed for each pilot who was to take part in the mission.

Some odd things were discovered. For instance, flaps normally are used to slow up an airplane. With the load carried, however, it was found that for the first couple of hours of flight five degrees of flaps increased the airspeed three miles an hour. This fact was noted.

With a working plan to go by, the men outfitted six airplanes and loaded them as the new specifications called for. Six average crews were chosen — men who were not distinguished either for their excellence or their lack of skill. A flight plan was drawn up which would duplicate the projected Balikpapan mission in mileage and route — except that it was flown over territory that was either friendly or neutral. The planes were sent out, with a daylight takeoff, to test the theories.

The airmen who planned the show sweated out that mission. It would tell them whether they had been right or wrong, whether the show was feasible or not. The mission would have to be undertaken in any case, but this test flight would indicate whether there was going to be an inevitable bailout or a chance for home.

The planners were exhausted. They had received word of the Balikpapan mission-to-be just nine days before the day designated for the strike. During that time some of the planes were changing from one base to another — from one island to another — in the general strategic shifting of air bases in the Southwest Pacific. Only the flight echelon had moved to its new base, forward, and the water echelon was still behind. Not all the equipment had arrived. The men had to plan for and work on the Balikpapan show in the midst of this move, a move which always entails a great amount of confusion and difficulty.

The six planes returned to base. All of them had made the flight successfully. They had carried the extra heavy loads of gasoline. In the planning, each plane was allowed a surplus of 400 gallons. So close was the planning that the plane which returned furthest off schedule had burned just 75 gallons more than estimated. The closest of the six planes was just two gallons off estimate.

The airmen breathed easier. The mission, at least on logistics, was feasible.

Then the navigators sat down to plan the route. There were high mountains in New Guinea and they couldn't fly the planes straight across. They decided that the planes would take off individually, just after midnight, fly individually all night, and then rendezvous at daybreak at a selected assembly point. Formation flying at night was ruled out — it would tire the men too much and burn up too much gas.

Rendezvous was pinpointed over the middle of the Celebes. Daybreak was the hour. Celebes was entirely enemy-held and the rendezvous was within 40 miles of a Jap airdrome known to be operational.

The rendezvous was about 1,035 miles from the point of takeoff. It was about 220 miles from the target. The first 12 planes were given just 24 minutes to assemble at rendezvous and start out in formation to the target.

The sections that followed were given similarly rigid schedules. That meant that individual navigators had to navigate for almost 1,000 miles at night and reach a given point within 24 minutes of each other.

It was arranged that the leader of the first section, Col. Thomas C. Musgrave, Jr., would circle the assembly point, fire a red flare, flash an Aldis lamp, and that would be a signal for the others to gather for the remainder of the trip to the target. For formation over the target a javelin step-down was selected. This called for three-plane elements, each element slightly lower than the one in front of it.

The formation made for a beautiful bomb run, keeping the pattern tight and neat, but it was more dangerous than other kinds would have been as far as protection against enemy fighters was concerned. In that formation, planes cannot give each other maximum protection.

The weather officer, nicknamed "Thunderhead" in honor of the stuff he usually reported, was called in for a preview of the weather to be expected. He went into a huddle and emerged with the following prediction: a series of high towering cumulus — the dreaded cloud monuments that airmen fear and avoid. These would continue through the night. There would also be thunderstorms. However, over a ten-year range, the weather, it was estimated, would be better that time than at any other time in the year, and from the weather

angle also, the mission was feasible.

The men who would have to fly the mission were getting so they winced every time they heard the word "feasible." It sounded so awfully weak. . . .

Last-minute preparations were perfected. One of the groups was based elsewhere than on Noemfoor. The planes from that group were to collect on the Noemfoor strip with the others and all would take off from there. Each plane had to be airborne exactly 60 seconds after the one ahead of it. While planes were taking off, the ones which preceded them would be en route to rendezvous. Delays in takeoff would add up at the end of the night flight and if the schedule were not maintained, planes would have to circle pointlessly over rendezvous, burning precious gasoline. With 72 planes taking off from the same strip, if there were an average delay of only 30 seconds a plane, that would add up perhaps to a delay of more than half an hour over assembly point.

Crash trucks, derricks, bulldozers, all were brought down to the strip. So heavily were the planes overloaded it was feared that one or more might crack up on the night takeoff. Orders were issued that if a plane cracked up it was to be hauled off the strip immediately so as not to delay the others. Planes that got into trouble after takeoff had to keep in the air until the last plane got away before landing again. Ambulances were stationed near the field. Medics went to the line to wait for emergencies.

At two o'clock on the afternoon of September 29, the first briefing of all aerial engineers was undertaken. Then the pilots and copilots were called in. The reasons for every item of change in them were analyzed. This was not the usual "poop" which might be conveniently disregarded once the airplanes were aloft. A parachute *had* to be moved from here to there at exactly this time — this had to be shifted there and a man must move from this point to that point. This all had to be done, or a gallon of gasoline, ten gallons, maybe more, would be wasted. The tiniest deviation from the charts might mean the difference between a safe return and a bailout over enemy-held territory.

The engineers were given refresher courses in transferring fuel. The ordinary wing and wing-tip tanks were to be augmented by bomb-bay tanks holding several hundred gallons each and tests had disclosed that a few of the airplanes flew nose heavy, at a slight angle; it was thought there might be some difficulty in transferring gasoline with the planes pitched at that angle.

At seven-thirty that evening the main briefing took place. Everybody who was going on the mission was told officially for the first time what the target would be. There had been a lot of rumors but this was the first official announcement. The men opened their eyes slightly, sighed, some of them, and said nothing.

They were told exactly what light-ing facilities would be available for takeoff. In the event the Nips came over to strafe and bomb during take-off the enemy was to be ignored as far as possible and takeoff to proceed on schedule. Planes were to circle in a definite pattern before relanding if they developed mechanical trouble. If the mechanical trouble was so serious that the planes couldn't stay aloft until the last plane took off, the pilot was to run his faulty ship over the water, bail out with his crew and let the ship crash. Nothing, nothing at all, must interfere with the mission. There was only one strip for this particular show and top priority for all movement on it was for planes taking off.

The men were told that from the moment they were airborne they would be over enemy territory 100 per cent of the way. They were given dictionaries of native words in case of forced landings.

The first plane was ordered to take off at 0030 — just 30 minutes after midnight on the morning of September 30, 1944.

Meanwhile the strip itself had been readied for the show. Palm trees at the far end of the strip had been cut down, tops had been removed, so the weighted planes would have plenty of clearance. A field hospital was taken down and moved away from the end of the strip. Final instructions were given: 20 minutes before each individual time of takeoff the planes were to start engines, crew check for combat readiness, and then the pilots to taxi into position.

It was a beautiful night. There was a moon. The palm trees were silhouetted against the light sky. You could see clearly and plainly. The men liked the moon. They would have it only for a few hours but what there was of it was welcome. There was tension in the air. Rumors spread. From all over Noemfoor — or at least from the portion of it that we owned — men gathered. The linemen, looking over their airplanes, patting them, stroking them gently. Other flying men, ground personnel, men from other branches of the service — they were all looking at the long line of airplanes. Most of the airplanes were unpainted, shining silver in the moonlight. Some still had the old camouflage.

Then at the right moment the first airplane rolled up to the head of the strip and the motors roared until the island itself seemed to quiver and then the giant lumbering craft moved on down the strip and gathered speed and then was airborne and climbing slowly. The mission was started.

The first 24 airplanes were airborne in exactly 24 minutes. Despite the load there was no accident. The last plane of the 72 got off safely. There was a long-drawn sigh from the men on the ground. So far so good. Then, a little later, two airplanes returned with mechanical failures. The men climbed out of the planes almost in tears. Seventy airplanes were off on the show.

In the air it was a long night. Fre- quently the navigators figured when they had crossed their tiny points of land by the towering cumulus clouds which usually stack up over land. The navigators sweated. The men moved like clockwork inside the planes deftly moving things from place to place — often a matter only of inches — as the charts required.

Dawn broke over the Celebes. It was one of those incredibly beautiful mornings that occur only in the tropics, thousands of feet in the air. The morning was purple and red and the clouds tinted with pastels; then the sun rose above the clouds. The men blinked their eyes. With the first light they were crossing the Celebes, on schedule.

The first section of 12 planes was collected at rendezvous point within 13 minutes. The navigators had flown 900 miles in the dark and had reached their pinpoint within 13 minutes of each other. It was the kind of navigating that brought lumps to the throats of pilots and men scattered throughout the ships.

Then suddenly Musgrave, in the lead ship, found he had unexpected company. Two Jap twin-engined airplanes began to parallel the formation, just out of gun range. The men knew why they were there and why they made no attempt to attack the bombers. They were flying along, radioing course and speed and altitude for the Jap antiaircraft at Balikpapan. The Americans watched them bemused. There was nothing they could do.

A Jap airdrome, Mangar, was to be used as a checkpoint. It was an ironic thing to choose as a checkpoint but there was nothing else. The field was just 30 miles north of the target. Shortly after the turn on Mangar the lead plane was to be turned over to its bombardier to fly over the target for the bomb run. The other planes were to follow in formation. When the formation got to Mangar it ran into unexpected weather.

The clouds were closed in ten-tenths below them. That means total coverage. The clouds were packed together until they looked like the top of a soap bucket. You couldn't see anything through them. The planes flew the prescribed course to the target. So far the enemy had made no attempt to stop them. The element of surprise had been more successful than anyone had dared to hope.

But then, just before the formation got five miles from the target, when it was already settled into the long bomb run, into the climax of the mission, into the job for which the airplanes were made and the men trained, the Jap fighters came up in droves, like specks of hailstorm, and hit them.

It was an attack that dry military parlance calls "determined and sustained." The men call it "eager." The Nips were eager beyond anything that anyone had ever before experienced. They came to within 25 feet of the big bombers, blazing away with all their guns. They flew into and through the formation. They got above the bombers and went into almost vertical dive, every gun shooting as they came down. It all seemed as though they had been sent up with orders to stop the raid, to turn it away, at all costs. Balikpapan was vital to the Jap war and the Jap knew it.

The planes plodded on. The gunners were shooting away. A Jap plane here and there went down. Finally the planes came to the target area itself and to the bullets and cannon shells of the enemy airplanes now were added the shells from the anti-aircraft on the ground. The flak was thick and heavy and the Jap fighters ignored it and kept attacking through it. That in itself was unusual. It is more normal for fighters to break away when their flak takes over, but the Nips disregarded their own ground fire and pressed in.

Then came a heartbreak. When the bombers finally arrived over the target itself, it was almost completely covered with clouds.

Musgrave saw a small hole in the clouds and through it a portion of the target. The Nip was throwing up shells from his new 120-mm ack-ack guns and each time a shell exploded it crashed open with a terrific noise and if it came close enough the concussion rocked the ships back and forth. The air was filled with phosphorous bombs, incendiaries.

The easy thing to do was to drop

the bombs in the general target area. The hole had closed in but the men knew roughly where the target was and could have dropped their bombs, sure of hitting something, then got the hell away. That would have been the easy thing to do.

But the men had been briefed on pinpoint targets within the refinery, on the small vital nuclei which would put the whole thing out of business for a while. The mission had been planned too laboriously, the trip had been too long and too hard to sacrifice accuracy and deadliness at the last minute.

Musgrave ordered the bombardier to hold his bombs. He swung the formation in a great arc to the east. He would try to come in at a new angle. It didn't matter if the new attempt gave the Nip fighters a field day, if it gave the ack-ack just that much more time to try to shoot them down.

A few minutes later the formation approached from a new angle. The planes and flak had followed it all the way. Following Musgrave, the formation circled for 45 minutes until they could see exactly what they had been told to bomb, and then, and only then, did Musgrave give the word and the bombs were released.

Later reconnaissance pictures showed that the bombing had done just what it was supposed to do. In that mission — and in the three that were to follow in short order — almost half of the Balikpapan refinery was destroyed and the remainder was put out of action for more than six months.

Their bombs away, the planes turned and started for home. The Jap fighters were remorseless. They attacked for one solid hour without let-up. Now that the bomb run was over the bombers could devote themselves entirely to scrapping with the enemy fighters. The boys shot down seven of the Nip planes and counted nine probables. We lost two Liberators, and many others were damaged. Some were damaged so badly they had to make forced landings en route, but when the mission was ended only one crew and half of another crew were missing. The rest were rescued.

The furious Nips swarmed all around. The stories some of the men told when they returned have become sagas among our flying men in the Southwest Pacific. The planes had been over target, in all, for more than an hour. Time over target, normally, is counted in minutes . . .

Over the target a lead ship of the elements got it and nose-dived into Balikpapan town before anyone could bail out. First Lt. Oliver L. Adair, pilot of another ship, pulled into the lead to take the missing ship's position. At the same time Adair's ship was hit in an inboard engine and the wing and tail and fuselage were hit. Oil spurted over the red hot cylinders and started to burn. Flames were blazing in a 50-foot tail behind the airplane. Despite this, Adair shoved up

169

Aerial view of the major Japanese oil-producing and storage center at Balikpapan, Borneo. First bombs of the 13th Air Force strike are sending up clouds of smoke and dust.

the power on his three remaining engines and moved into the lead.

His right-waist gunner, Staff Sgt. Charles F. Held, had his gun shot out of his hands. The mount was destroyed and the ring site knocked off and the back end of the gun broken apart. He rigged up his parachute for a cushion. He held the loose gun against the chute pack and grabbed the hot barrel with his other hand and fired bursts at the attackers.

"I couldn't aim, but my tracers were coming close enough so the Nip knew the gun was still working."

He could only fire a few bursts at a time. The recoil would jolt him back against the other side of the plane and when he returned home finally his chest was black and blue, covered with bruises from the pounding and the hand that held the barrel of the gun was burned through the glove that he wore.

Everybody on that ship prayed. Once the boys heard the copilot, Second Lt. Raphael F. Baird, try to wisecrack in his throat mike to cheer up the men, and then give up the attempt, and instead, whisper, "Oh, my

God, let me get out of here, please God, let me get out of here . . ."

The top-turret man, Staff Sgt. Wilbur L. Bowen, said later, "Half the time I was praying hard enough to save half the people in the United States. And half the time I was cursing hard enough to put a good bishop in hell. When I saw three planes coming in at once with their wing edges sparkling I just prayed they wouldn't hit us. And then when one of my guns jammed I would pound on the magazine and cuss in the worst way I knew how."

On the way home they had to chop out the ball turret and the top turret to lighten weight. Working with axes and a machete they chopped the top turret into small pieces and threw it out. Then they worked for three hours on the ball turret. They got nearly everything out but some braces and armor which the ax wouldn't cut. One of the men pulled his automatic pistol and shot away the rivets that held the metal together.

The main gas tanks were full of small leaks. The men stopped them up with bits of candle, rags, a pencil, a broken screwdriver. There were holes in the hydraulic brake line they couldn't see.

The pilot figured he could make a normal landing. He ordered seven of the crew on the flight deck. The ship went in to land on Morotai. It settled for a perfect landing. The brakes held long enough to slow the ship down to 85 mph and then the left brake broke its line and the right brake locked and the ship jerked to one side toward a bank.

It plowed through palm trees. One stump flew into the bomb bay and hit Held in the leg. One of the props on the ship cut through a parked truck as the driver raced for cover. The nose wheel buckled and flew back into the bomb bay to hit Held in the other leg.

Twelve seconds after the ship had buried its nose in a sandbank every man was out of the ship. Held got out of the top escape hatch, hit the top of the ship, and did a complete flip-over into the dirt.

And from a latrine in the path of the bomber a first sergeant ran out — his trousers still below his knees . . .

On the ground at Noemfoor men were sweating out the mission. There were thousands of them packed among the palm trees. Pilots from a nearby night-fighter squadron were there. They said the bomber boys had sweated them out time and time again and now they were there to help sweat out the bomber boys.

And then the planes came in. The first five planes in their perfect formation. Riddled with holes. Parts of the tails and wings and turrets gone. But in perfect formation.

Capt. William J. Stuart, Jr., Operations Officer for one of the groups, burst into tears as he recognized his own ships. He stood there rigid, the tears pouring down his face.

"I'm not ashamed of it," he said.

"Goddammit, I'm not ashamed of it."

EDITOR'S NOTE: Three days later the B-24's returned to Balikpapan to face swarms of fighters and a hail of antiaircraft fire. The two raids had cost 37 Liberators.

On October 10, 1944, 106 Liberators from five Heavy Bomb Groups escorted by 36 P-38's and P-47's fitted with extra long-range fuel tanks struck the refineries for the third time. The Japanese put up 90 fighters in defense, lost 61 of them to the guns of the B-24's and P-38 fighter escorts. High-scoring ace Dick Bong got two. One P-38 and four B-24's were destroyed.

Again on October 14 and 18 the Liberators pounded Balikpapan, accompanied by P-38 and P-47 fighters.

The five attacks put the refinery out of commission for six months and when it did resume production, it was only at about half capacity. The plants had been critically damaged. In early 1945 another air campaign destroyed the oil center completely, eliminating for the Japanese their prize spoil of Asian conquest. It wasn't long before enemy gas tanks began to run dry.

By early 1943, American air units in China were reorganized into the 14th Air Force under Brig. Gen. Claire Chennault. It was a small air force by normal standards, having grown out of the American Volunteer Group and the China Air Task Force, and it would remain the smallest air unit facing the Japanese throughout the war. Cut off from the main lines of supply by the Japanese occupation and control of the Burma Road, Chennault's men depended on airlift over the Himalayas for everything from gas and bombs to medicine and spare parts.

Thus, literally a tiny island surrounded by a sea of Japanese air and land forces, ill-supplied and ill-equipped in men and aircraft, the 14th wrote a magnificent record. It was short of miraculous that the fighter and bomber pilots under Chennault not only survived the 5 to 1 odds against them but also carried the air war to the enemy with an array of guerrilla air tactics and techniques the enemy was not prepared to cope with. It was men like Chennault's fighter chief, Col. Bruce K. Holloway, who studied the enemy's strength and weaknesses, their combat habits and battle psychology, and fought them accordingly with methods that were not in the book.

The strategy of the 14th as well as the 10th Air Force in Burma-French Indochina and Malay, was basically a hit-and-run strategy keyed to surprise. Use of the feint was highly successful. Chennault would send one unit to the west to draw the Japanese air defense in that direction, then strike swiftly, suddenly, and at low level, on targets in the opposite direction. *Using a wide variation of this technique (sometimes the feint was the main blow) he kept the Japanese air defense guessing and, more often than not, they guessed wrong.*

The Japanese airman was perhaps the best disciplined in the world. He was bound to the rules. He knew nothing but to obey. He was courageous and followed instructions to the "T." And when you knocked out his plan, put him on his own, he was lost for he had no initiative, no resourcefulness of his own. He was not an individual. He fought by the book. This is why Chennault's guerrilla air warfare, built on the elements of surprise, of suddenness, of variables, and of innovation was successful in China.

Chennault's Guerrillas

A Picture Story

14th Air Force pilots listen intently to the old master, Claire Chennault (center), down on the line. Admiration and pride are inadequate words to describe how his men felt about him. And, the feeling was returned.

Explosion jolts this rail bridge over the Song Thuong River in French Indochina, while two more bombs are seen hurtling from the bays of the low-flying B-25. This was one of nine bridges. wiped out on March 5, 1945, in an effort to cut off and bottle up a Japanese supply and troop movement.

Depth charges, acquired from the Navy, are scattered in a pattern across a jungle thicket in Burma, known to be occupied by Japanese troops. Depth charges created horizontal blasts on striking the ground, shredding foliage and underbrush. This was one of the many weapon innovations of guerrilla air war.

Before the 10th Air Force was through, a lot of enemy trackage looked like this; a result of "spike bombing."

Spike bombing was an effective technique for track busting. Long pointed spikes, welded onto the front end of bombs, would keep the missiles from bouncing, dug them directly into the track bank. Delayed-action fuses would allow the low-flying mediums to escape before the blast.

B-25's of the 14th Air Force "Air Apache" Group caught this Japanese destroyer escort off the coast of Amoy China on April 6, 1945, on a wave-top prowling mission. Violent explosion rips midship as the B-25 pulls away from its skip-bombing run. Below, Japanese sailors frantically crawl over the side of the doomed vessel a few minutes later, as many already bob in the surrounding water.

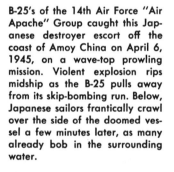

Col. Bruce K. Holloway, center, displays the Flying Tiger flag of the 23rd Fighter Group in China. At far right is Chennault. Holloway, Chennault's deputy and one of the key guerrilla air tacticians and China aces (14 victories) is now an Air Force lieutenant general. At left, Colonel Vincent and "Ajax" Baumler.

In a hit-and-run guerrilla air surprise attack, Chennault's fighters catch Japanese airplanes on the ground at Shinchiku Airdrome, Formosa, on Thanksgiving Day, 1943.

In October, 1944, the Japanese thought Chennault's 14th Air Force East China bases had been destroyed and they moved huge portions of their warships and shipping into Hong Kong harbor to escape Admiral Nimitz' Pacific Fleet. They were wrong. Operating out of secret bases, fighters and B-24 bombers swooped over the lush target. Smoke and fire pour from the Kowloon docks and rail yards. Center, Japanese fighter vainly rises to attack.

There were many curious and offbeat missions to be flown in the Pacific. The very nature of the area and its vastnesses required that they be carried out. One of the most unusual took place in the rugged, wild cannibal-infested mountainous areas of central New Guinea.

Too many planes and crews were mysteriously disappearing over this trackless area and we needed an emergency airstrip somewhere in the high interior for bomber and fighter crews to home into when that became necessary.

Borrowing a leaf from the Air Commando operation in Burma, glider pilots of the 433rd Troop Carrier Group at Nadzab, New Guinea, flew their motorless craft into a place on the map they named Hidden Valley, an unknown mile-high flat field nestled in the mountains. To get there, the CG-4A cargo gliders, attached by a 5/8" nylon rope behind C-47 towplanes, had to maneuver through narrow canyons crisscrossed by tricky air currents with only a few feet between wing tips and towering solid rock walls on both sides. Their heavy cargo included sacks of salt, hand tools such as shovels, picks, native interpreters from various tribes in the Markham Valley, armed native police guards, sacks of pretty seashells and shiny trinkets they hoped would be fair barter with the natives, most of whom had never before seen white people. This little-known 5th Air Force operation went off without mishap and Capt. Manford Susman, Air Force reporter who accompanied the expedition, tells how the cannibals were persuaded to help build the airstrip.

Into Hidden Valley

Capt. Manford Susman

I LOOKED back into the fuselage of the glider as we circled over the high country of New Guinea and tried to smile at my fellow passengers — four burly natives wearing the khaki uniforms of the Australian Native Administration. They couldn't see out but they knew what was going on and were just as nervous as the rest of us.

Below us, another glider — the first of four — was just banking in for its landing. I could see its shadow grow larger and larger against the tall, green Kunai grass. In a moment we'd have the answer to our $64 question — what was under that grass. In three seconds we'd know if it was smooth, landable meadow, or rocks. Or swamp. In two seconds. In one second — touchdown!

Looking down, I saw the nose of the CG-4A bite into the ground, slither along a few feet, and then stop. There was a pause while all of us in the air held our breath, and then the fuselage door opened and men scrambled out. They looked up at us, waved their arms reassuringly and fanned out into the grass to reconnoiter for the landings of the remaining three gliders.

Within a few minutes they had their walkie-talkie in operation and were sending us vital information: condition of terrain, wind direction, where to touch down. It seemed that the Kunai grass covered good hard ground and their only warning was to come in at higher landing speed than usual because of the 5,000-foot altitude of the valley floor.

We were over the first hurdle and life looked much brighter now that we knew we had a good place to land. The nervousness had come from the knowledge that, after a four-hour tow through mountain passes, our tugs didn't have enough fuel to return to base with us. There were no possible landing spots, except Hidden Valley now below us, within hundreds of miles, and between us and the only strip our tugs could land on was another, higher range of mountains — over which C-47's could not possibly tow gliders. In other words, we'd land safely in that patch of green, nestling between 13,000-foot peaks — or else we'd land unsafely. But land we had to.

Of course we had reconnoitered, photo-reconnoitered, and just plain buzzed the area for weeks trying to see, but we couldn't make sure. There were lots of questions, and one inescapable fact — as operations in the Philippines stepped up, more and more aircraft had to fly north over the New Guinea hump. It became imperative that we establish an emergency landing strip, an AACS station, and a weather detachment in the middle of the jungle. Too many pilots were taking off to fly that stretch of wilderness with no idea what weather conditions to expect, and with no communications after they got out of radio range of their takeoff point.

Engineering personnel flew over the area and put the finger on Hidden Valley for the very obvious reason that it was the only level ground within hundreds of miles. And then Chief Engineer GHQ SWPA was asked to construct an airfield there. After discussion with operations officers of Far East Air Forces, the chief engineer decided that gliders were the only answer.

So there we were, four glider loads of us, being cut loose one by one to descend into Hidden Valley, and now it was our glider's turn. I saw our pilot reach for the tow release handle over the windshield. He pulled and there was an impulsive, headstrong little movement from the glider and then we turned and started down.

We landed perfectly, as did all four gliders. In addition to the four glider pilots who had brought us in so beau-

178

tifully the party consisted of 20 natives and five whites.

On the way down we had noticed some natives crouching in the Kunai grass around the edge of the valley and we hoped they were friendly. No white person had been in the valley since 1938 and no natives had come out. Consequently, no one knew if the Japs had infiltrated into the area or if the natives were armed. One thing we did know for sure — we needed native labor to build the strip. Our interest in this fact was intensified when we realized that there was no way out of Hidden Valley for us until the strip was built. So it was with considerable apprehension that four of us, plus the native interpreter, headed toward the nearest group of villagers.

The interpreter said he wasn't sure he could speak the local dialect, and as we got close enough to make out what kind of people we had landed among he became even less sure. While we had expected to find a kind of hill native noted for his large size and comparatively advanced civilization, we found ourselves looking at wizened, pygmy-like people wearing no clothing at all except loin cloths. The interpreter swallowed hard and whispered, "These people are Kukukukas!" — naming the most fierce and treacherous cannibals in the interior of New Guinea.

It was a bad few minutes, but finally our interpreter managed to get across the idea that we came in peace. We later learned that the cannibals

were not particularly frightened of us because, seeing no bows and arrows in our hands, they assumed we were unarmed. When, the following day, we gathered the villagers together for an exhibition of firearms (to discourage any thought of ambush) their amazement knew no bounds. They were openmouthed at the disintegration of pumpkins and tin cans, but perforation of one of their battle shields by a .30-caliber slug caused a completely different reaction. They babbled and screamed at our interpreter who finally told us they wanted our help in their war with a neighboring village. In return they'd let us eat most of – or even all, if we insisted — of the enemy warriors. The poor interpreter spent another bad few hours trying to explain to them that to get the United Nations on their side they'd have to go through channels.

Mild as they were, our troubles with the cannibals were the worst we had. Although our gliders were crammed with items for trading — shells, trinkets, mirrors and salt — so barren were these people's lives that they wanted almost nothing. Still existing in the Stone Age, using no metals of any kind, they slept on the bare ground in pitiful huts, preparing food by simply throwing it into a fire. They couldn't even be forced into things, because they had no fear of death, visualizing heaven as a happy land so full of possums you could burn them like firewood. Their acquisitive instincts were completely undeveloped

Captain Susman (left) and glider pilot explain modern rifles to head-hunting pigmy warriors. They had never before seen firearms.

and none of our trinkets interested them at all. Salt was our best item of barter and by using it we finally got some of them to work. Salt became the medium of exchange. The natives were very clumsy with tools and constantly cut and bruised themselves. But three days of clearing, draining, leveling, filling — and cursing — had us a strip suitable for L-5's. The following day two L-5's landed, carrying gas for their return trip in the rear seat. We named the field Eunice Airstrip and the L-5's went to work ferrying out the glider pilots.

We'd run out of salt and needed various other supplies including meat.

In the beginning we'd tried to buy pigs from the natives, but met a peculiar resistance to the idea. It seemed that their pigs were their most prized possessions and they had no intention of parting with them. Our interpreter explained that we needed meat, and they seemed to understand. Muttering that they'd be right back, the party of natives disappeared toward their village. Our mouths were watering at the thought of some nice fresh pork — and then they returned. With them were several girl children from the village. "Meat," said the headman happily. "Meat for you to eat."

We radioed for more salt and some

kind of eatable meat. It arrived by parachute, as did many of our supplies thereafter, without the loss or damage of a single package.

More salt meant more workers and the strip progressed. Two weeks after our arrival, a C-45 landed bringing supplies and personnel. In the party was the chief engineer responsible for the construction, Brig. Gen. J. L. Sverdup, and the Air Surgeon of the AAF, Maj. Gen. David N. W. Grant, who wanted to observe the general health of the Kukukukas with reference to jungle diseases. With drainage and clearing of the strip completed by hand, we requested mechanical equipment to help us complete the job.

It arrived in two gliders carrying a bulldozer, a roadscraper, and operating personnel. Within a few hours the machines were at work. When the bulldozer's engine started the Kukukukas were astonished when it failed to take off and fly away. In another week — approximately three weeks after the initial touchdown — a C-47 landed with fuel for the scrapers, medical supplies and a few essential commodities like mail from home.

Today Eunice Airstrip is a going concern which has considerably reduced the hazard of flying the New Guinea Hump. There's a regular milk run plus quite a few casual landings, and the weather boys and the AACS station are installed for a long stay. As for the Kukukukas, they're at work on an official request for the United Nations to lend them soldiers to fight their neighbors in return for a number of potbellied little girls "suitable for eating."

The Douglas C-47 twin-engine transport, first flown as the civilian DC-3 in the early 1930's became the workhorse of the war. This grand old 140-mph transport chugged through the airways of every combat theater trucking anything in combat gear and supply that could be squeezed into its interior. It became affectionately known as the "Gooney Bird" around the globe, a reliable, sturdy, stable airplane that would fly anywhere, in any kind of weather. And if it wasn't the fastest mode of travel, at least it would get you there.

Although the Gooney Bird carried no armament, there were tales of strafing missions, with its crew shooting rifles out of its cargo-compartment windows and occasionally men told of bombing runs in the Gooney, a simple matter of kicking explosives and drums of ignitable fuel out of the rear cargo door and onto the heads of unsuspecting enemy troops. Indeed, the odds makers said it could do anything but dogfight with enemy fighters.

And then one day over the Burma "Hump" a pair of emboldened Jap Zero pilots swooped down on a lumbering overloaded Gooney Bird for an easy kill. One went spinning into oblivion, the other fled.

When the tale of what happened reached back to the base, even the most inveterate die-hards closed book on the Gooney Bird and slowly shook their heads. And here is the story.

A Gooney Gets a Zero

Lt. Col. Carroll V. Glines and Lt. Col. Wendell F. Moseley

THE CREW and their airplane had been overseas for about two years and had fought their own particular kind of war through North Africa hauling supplies to the front and taking wounded men back to the rear lines to the hospitals. That phase of the campaign ended, however, when they flew paratroopers to Avellino for a drop in the hills.

It was an urgent call for help from the China-Burma-India Theater of Operations that changed the routine life of one particular C-47. She was sent winging her way along with some other C-47's eastward from Africa to Burma to haul supplies over the "Hump."

Two weeks after the airplane arrived in Burma, hardly a sufficient amount of time to become familiar with flying conditions over the ragged mountains or the fighting tactics of their new enemy, Scrugham and Jost

The Douglas C-47 Skytrain transport, affectionately known as the "Gooney Bird." It was the workhorse of World War II.

suddenly found themselves in a tangle to the death with a pair of aggressive Zeros hellbent to add a fast transport to their tally.

"We were flying a routine cargo mission — no passengers — when two Zeros jumped us," Scrugham reported.

"I didn't take time to try to figure out what was happening. Instead, I swung the C-47 into a dive and hit the deck as the Japanese fighters peeled off after us for what they thought would be a sure kill.

"The first Zero made his pass at us but we were too close to the ground and he zoomed up without hitting us.

"The second Zero came right down on us. When he got within inches of our airplane I jammed the throttles forward another fraction of an inch and got just a little burst of speed.

"That character must have been trying to ram us because he never swerved. With the added speed I had given my airplane I caused him to miss hitting us dead center, but he didn't miss entirely and we felt the old C-47 shudder like she was going to shake herself to pieces for a minute.

"The Jap plane, after he hit us, kept right on going and we watched him explode as he hit the side of the mountain. But we still didn't know how much damage he had done to our plane. I moved the controls, first the elevators, and found that we had excellent control there. But when I kicked the rudders nothing happened. I knew right then that the Jap had knocked our rudder off. We looked at each other in the cockpit and talked about climbing as high as we could and bailing out, but I moved the controls some more and between the elevators and the ailerons we seemed to be able to control the old bird all right. So we decided to keep right on flying rather than have our airplane suffer the same fate as the Japanese Zero.

"Now that I think about it," Scrugham continued, "it never occurred to us to worry about that other Zero. We were so scared that his buddy had fixed us up so good that we completely forgot about him.

"All my life I guess I'll wonder whatever happened to him. Maybe he thought we had some new kind of secret weapon when he saw us knock down the other Zero, and he simply hightailed it for home to report it to his superiors. At any rate, he didn't bother us."

Whenever two brilliant tacticians of aerial warfare got their heads together it meant trouble for the Japanese in China. This happened in December of 1944.

Maj. Gen. Curtis E. LeMay, recently transferred to the China-Burma-India Theater, had taken over the newly established XX Bomber Command after a uniquely successful combat tour in B-17's over Europe. Here, in China, he headed a powerful force of America's newest and most potent air weapons, the long-range B-29 Superfortresses, which were arriving from the States in increasing numbers and settling down on mile-long airfields that were scratched out by hand from the rocky soil by hordes of loyal Chinese men and women. Here also, in the same theater, was the cagey veteran of China air combat, Maj. Gen. Claire L. Chennault, whose book of tactics had held the entire China-based Japanese Air Force at bay for four long years with a handful of aircraft and pilots.

The old tiger, with the cunning wisdom of years on the hunt, and the young tiger, with the power, drive and skill of youth, met at Chennault's headquarters in Kunming, China. The plan they concocted was to mark the beginning of the end of Japanese air power in China, as well as establish a strategic bombardment technique that would bring the whole Empire of Nippon to its knees within the coming year.

Hankow, China: The First Fire-Bomb Raid

Maj. Gen. Claire Lee Chennault, USAF (Ret)

... WE FINALLY lowered the boom on the great Japanese base at Hankow, key to the entire Japanese position in the interior of China. For six months I had been pleading with Stilwell and Arnold for a coordinated B-29-14th Air Force mission to destroy this spawning ground for Japanese military power. Not until Stilwell was ousted from his command in China and Al Wedemeyer succeeded him could I even get a hearing for my detailed plans of the mission. Wedemeyer heard my story, gave me his full support, and almost immediately secured Joint Chiefs of Staff authority to use 100 B-29's against a China target of my selection. This was a graphic demonstration of what it meant to work with a superior's support instead of facing indifference or active opposition.

Appreciating my six-month effort to flatten Hankow, Wedemeyer gave me full responsibility for planning the mission. Curtis LeMay, who had come from the bomber war over Europe to succeed K. B. Wolfe in command of the Asia-based B-29's, came to my headquarters in Kunming to thrash out the details. Despite his ghastly ex-periences leading unescorted B-17 raids over Germany, LeMay still saw little need for fighter escort of his bombers. We also argued over the bombs and tactics to be used. I wanted the B-29's to carry a full load of incendiaries to burn out Hankow as the Japanese had burned out Chungking five years earlier. I also wanted the B-29's to bomb from below 20,000 feet to insure accuracy and upset the enemy defense that would be set for them at higher altitudes. LeMay wanted to go in at high altitude and carry conventional high-explosive bombs. We finally compromised on four out of each five B-29's dropping an incendiary bomb load from above 20,000 feet. Each fifth plane would drop demolition bombs. The plan was to have the B-29's lead off with their fire bombs against the big warehouse district that stretched back from the docks and waterfront and contained all the enemy's surplus stores in central China. Everything the 14th Air Force could get into the air was to follow an hour later in a mopping-up operation aimed at wiping out the Japanese air power around Hankow. Our photo cover showed an average of 200 fighters and

Tons of bombs sprinkle earthward from 20th Bomber Command Superfortresses in the big daylight attack over Rangoon, Burma. Airmen said it was a "near-perfect mission."

50 bombers on Hankow's four major fields. Hankow was ideally located so that every unit of the 14th except the 69th Wing, then engaged on the Salween, could reach it. It was the first and last time during the China war that the 14th was able to concentrate virtually all its strength on a single target.

A force of 77 B-29's opened the attack on Hankow shortly before noon of December 18. They attacked in seven waves ten minutes apart. By the time the first 35 Superfortresses had unloaded their incendiaries, Hankow was swathed in a blanket of black smoke that completely obscured the city. Visibility was so bad by the time the final B-29 attacks were made that few bombs of the last four waves even hit inside the sprawling bulk of the three Wuhan cities. Japanese fighters appeared an hour after the Superfortresses had finished. Liberators bombed the main airfields outside the city from high altitude while B-25's went down low through the smoke to strew frag bombs over the satellite fields and pump cannon shells into hangars, gas storage tanks, and barracks. Smoke was so bad that the B-25's were flying on instruments until they broke into the clear only 200 feet above the river. Mustangs and Thunderbolts fought a pitched battle with Oscars and Tojos over the billowing smoke clouds. Flights of Chinese-American Wing P-40's patrolled over Japanese staging fields within a 100-mile radius of Hankow holocaust. Bag for the day was 64 Japanese planes without American loss. We put a total of 200 14th Air Force planes over Hankow and vicinity that fiery afternoon, the largest force we were ever able to muster on a single coordinated mission.

The raids of December 18 destroyed Hankow as a major base for the Japanese army and air force in central China. Fires burned for three days, gutting the docks, warehouse areas, and large sections of the foreign quarters. For a month afterward I kept the major strength of the 14th over Hankow, using fighters from three

wings and all our B-24's and B-25's. Fighters kept after enemy air power while the bombers pinpointed some arsenals and warehouses scattered outside the main burned areas and across the river in Wuchang. On the final Liberator mission against Hankow January 30, 1945, not a single enemy fighter rose to intercept. Our photo cover for that month showed an average of five fighters and no bombers on the Hankow fields. The backbone of enemy air power in the vital Yangtze Valley was broken and the bulk of the supplies on which the Japanese armies in central China planned to live and fight through the spring and summer of 1945 were destroyed. Starvation crept down through East China from the blackened ruins of the Hankow warehouses like a slow paralysis, marking the beginning of the end for the Japanese armies in the corridor.

The December 18 attack of the Superforts was the first mass fire-bomb raid they attempted. LeMay was thoroughly impressed by the results of this weapon against an Asiatic city. When he moved on to command the entire B-29 attack on Japan from the Marianas, LeMay switched from high-altitude daylight attacks with high explosives to the devastating mass fire-bomb night raids that burned the guts out of Japan and brought the Japanese to their knees even before the atomic bombs were dropped.

Out of every war there emerge a few legendary characters whose real lives read like a myth. In the Pacific air war one such was Lt. Col. Paul I. "Pappy" Gunn, a man remembered by airmen throughout the theater as the grand-master storyteller of all time.

The ratios of fact to fancy in Pappy's spellbinding recounts of his personal exploits were never known, but one thing was sure, his stories had some basis in fact.

Before the war the lean, gaunt, swaggering Pappy Gunn was an airman of fortune in the Orient, and at the time of Pearl Harbor, operated a small airline in the Philippines where he lived with his wife and children. He knew the Orient, and especially the Philippines like the back of his hand.

When the Japanese overran the Philippines, Pappy made his wife swear to God he was dead. Then he left home and volunteered his services to the Air Force to help air-evacuate personnel and planes to Australia. It was during his absence that the Japs captured his family, interrogated them about Pappy's whereabouts, and threw them into the miserable Santo Tomas prison camp. When he learned of this it made Pappy mad and gave him reason to hate the Jap like he had never hated anyone before. And when the Japs posted notice through the Islands, putting a price on his head, dead or alive, Pappy declared personal war on the Empire.

It was in Australia that the paths of Gen. George Kenney and Pappy Gunn crossed and soon there developed a close relationship, for Pappy was a crack pilot and a mechanical genius. He became the General's trouble-shooter, the great practical experimenter and prover of Kenney's unorthodox tactical air schemes. Among the innovations Pappy worked on were modifying the B-25 to carry 12 forward-firing .50-caliber machine guns and adapting it to a 75-mm nose cannon. There were also other wartime air weapon modifications that his ingenuity fostered.

Pappy bubbled with ideas on how to beat the Jap. He knew no fear. He had two great passions: to kill Japs and return to the Philippines. Kenney's problem was to keep him on the ground, for Pappy would join any outbound combat formation regardless of unit.

At times throughout the war he mysteriously disappeared for days. Then the stories would go around that Pappy had gone back to the Philippines, slipping into some clandestine airfield there on a highly secret intelligence mission or to settle a personal grudge. Like most adventurers of fortune, Pappy led a charmed, bizarre life that will never be completely known.

The world heard about General MacArthur's dramatic return to the Philippines to fulfill a pledge he gave at the time of his forced exit in

early 1942. But there was another hero's return, unnoticed and undra-
matic. It also took place on the beaches of Leyte. It was that of Paul I.
"Pappy" Gunn, and it was not exactly like Pappy wanted it to be.

Back to the Philippines

Gen. George C. Kenney, USAF (Ret)

BY THE MIDDLE of September 1944 the decision had been made to return to the Philippines on October 20. The landing was to be on the island of Leyte, in the vicinity of the port of Tacloban, in Leyte Gulf, on the east coast. In the meantime we started working on the oil refineries and storage tanks at Balikpapan on the island of Borneo, from which the Japs got most of their aviation gasoline. We knew they had more than 3,000 airplanes in the Philippines and we wanted to stop their fuel supply and keep as many of them on the ground as possible when we went ashore.

As soon as Pappy heard the news, his fertile brain began producing. His first scheme was to let him take one of the B-25's that we had remodeled to carry 12 forward-firing .50-caliber machine guns, fly it to Manila, and shoot up the 300 Jap planes that our intelligence crowd said were parked wing tip to wing tip on both sides of Taft Boulevard. This street, which ran along Manila Bay, was straight for about two miles and the Japs were using it for a landing field and for

storage of airplanes. An attack would certainly pay off, but the trouble was, we didn't have any airplane with range enough to make the round trip, even from our most forward airdrome at Biak, in Dutch New Guinea. This didn't bother Pappy, however. His plan was to arrive over Manila just at daybreak and, using incendiary ammunition and bombs, burn up every airplane on Taft Boulevard. He admitted that he couldn't make it all the way home, but had the place marked on the map for me where he would run out of fuel, ditch the B-25 and be picked up by one of our rescue amphibians, or maybe I could arrange with the Navy to have a submarine make a rendezvous with him. The spot he pointed out to me was more than 500 miles short of home. I vetoed the idea.

A couple of days later Pappy was back in my headquarters again.

"General," he said, "you can't turn me down this time. I've got it all figured out. I'll fly the B-25 alone. That will save some weight. The top gun turret won't be necessary, so I'll take that out and save another couple of thousand pounds. Then, the incendiaries from the machine guns will do the job, so I won't need to carry another ton of bombs. With all that weight saved I'll rig up a couple of 300-gallon gas tanks and hang them one on each wing and it figures I can make the round trip. How about it, General?"

Pappy almost wept when I turned this scheme down, too. I explained to him that I couldn't afford to take even one of our B-25's out of action for two or three weeks while he made all the changes in it for his bright idea. In the meantime, Admiral Halsey's carriers were scheduled to make a couple of raids on the Jap airdromes around Manila. Furthermore, Pappy's figures on the projected range of his remodeled B-25 didn't allow for any margin of safety. If he ran into head winds either coming or going he would wind up landing in the Pacific Ocean. Then we would lose the airplane, and if the water was too rough for one of our flying boats to land we would lose him, too. Pappy left completely dejected but was back the next day.

This time he had decided to become a ground soldier. The idea was that I would make a deal with the Navy to put him on a submarine which would set him ashore in a rubber boat some night on the east coast of Leyte about 20 miles south of Tacloban. I was also to get a letter from General MacArthur instructing him to organize an army of Filipinos to attack the Japs from the rear as we made our landing on the shore of Leyte Gulf. With his knowledge of the country and the people, and armed with General MacArthur's letter as credentials, to Pappy there was no doubt as to the virtue of his scheme or the prospect of a brilliant and successful operation.

For the next half hour I tried to explain to Pappy that we had more than half a million troops out there who might resent his winning the war single-handed. Furthermore, it was rather doubtful whether the Navy could recall a submarine at this late date just to carry him to Leyte and, even if they did, he wouldn't have time to recruit and train his private army before October 20, when we were due to land there. He started to talk about the guerrillas who were all ready to go into action if he could just get there to lead them, but I solved the problem by giving him another job.

"Pappy," I said, "I want you to recruit from the maintenance outfit back in Australia a special picked gang of about 50 men who can do anything. They must be able to shoot, dig slit trenches, build a shack to live in, lay steel mat for a runway, rebuild wrecked airplanes, overhaul engines, live off the country, and fight with fists, knives, or rocks. When we go ashore we are going to be working on a shoestring and we are going to need some smart tough guys like you to keep going. I'm going to move that

Lt. Col. Paul I. "Pappy" Gunn, one of those colorful, legendary characters who walk through the pages of every war. He became General Kenney's troubleshooter and helped immeasurably in training guerrillas.

outfit out of Australia soon anyhow, but in the meantime go on down there and train 50 real shock troops for me. I'll want them up here by October 13 to load on a boat, so get going."

Pappy grinned happily and took off. On the afternoon of the 12th, two C-47 transports landed at Hollandia near my headquarters. Pappy had sent a message that he was coming in with his gang, so I went down to the field to look them over. He had done the job. They looked tough enough to take care of themselves anywhere. Each one was armed with a pistol and a trench knife and carried a good-sized bag slung over his shoulder. I

asked Pappy what was in the bags. "Tools and spare ammunition," replied Pappy. "General," he went on, "these boys are what you asked for. They can do anything you want done, and if any Japs start interfering with them, they can handle that job, too. What do you want me to do with them?"

I attached Pappy and his gang to the air task force commanded by Col. "Dave" Hutchison, which would go ashore to organize the airdrome as soon as the place was captured. That night they loaded for the Philippines.

On October 20, four American divisions stormed ashore near Tacloban and at Dulag a town about 20 miles

191

to the south. Both places had an airdrome that the Japs had been using but they were badly pitted from the bombing by Halsey's carrier boys and both were too small for the number of airplanes I intended to put on them.

By the next day Gen. Verne Mudge's 1st Cavalry Division had captured the Tacloban strip and the bulldozers and graders went to work filling up the bomb craters and getting the ground leveled off. The place was nothing but a sand spit a little more than a mile long and about 300 yards wide. We would have to cover it with steel mat, and before that was laid we needed some coral or rock ballast on top of the existing soil to keep the steel mat from buckling under the impact of airplanes landing on it.

Pappy told us of a coral deposit about two miles away and we started hauling it to the strip the next day when the trucks got unloaded. In the meantime his "spearhead" outfit had already patched up some wrecked Jap sheds on the edge of the field for use as repair shops later on and were constructing a control tower out of palm-tree logs to handle the traffic as soon as we were ready to fly in our airplanes. In anticipation of Jap bombing, they took care to dig plenty of slit trenches near where they were working. A couple of days later I admired this latter job tremendously when the Japs pulled a bombing raid while I was inspecting the construction work at the field.

Pappy was an invaluable man to have on this job. As soon as the steel mat was ashore and enough of the surface was ready he showed up with about 200 Filipinos and members of some Chinese Youth Society and put them to work carrying the heavy sheets of steel mat over where our men could fasten them in place. Each day he recruited more local labor until finally we had more than 1,500 Filipinos on the job. Pappy was all over the place, keeping things moving and working himself harder than anyone else.

The Japs didn't ignore us by any means. For the first five days they bombed us four or five times during daylight and generally twice at night. We had managed to set up a radar which gave us about 15 minutes' warning but to Pappy that didn't mean stopping work. Everyone stayed on the job until the Jap airplanes appeared and then dove for the nearest slit trench. As soon as the bombs hit, Pappy would jump up and yell "Come on, let's get back to work and get this field fixed up so our planes can come up here and chase those bowlegged so-and-so's away." The quotation is not exactly what Pappy actually said, but it expresses what he meant.

We had about 500 feet of steel mat in place when I got a hurry-up call from Colonel Hutchison. Twenty-four landing craft had beached on the edge of the strip and unloaded supplies, guns, ammunition, and troops right on the airdrome, stopping all work. Another 28 ships were reported coming in during the night to do the same thing. I went out to the strip to look over the situation. The place was a mess, all cluttered up with troops, trucks, crates, and boxes piled six to ten feet high. The only item I could not find was more steel mat which we needed to complete surfacing the airdrome.

I got hold of one of the army brigadier generals who was looking after the unloading of supplies and told him to hurry up and clear the airdrome. We would help with all the military and civilian man power we had, but beginning the next morning Colonel Hutchison would take his bulldozers and push back into the water anything still left on the place which interfered with getting an airdrome built. In the meantime, we were setting up machine guns on the beach with Pappy Gunn in charge, with orders to stop any more landing craft from coming ashore. Pappy had volunteered for the job, giving as his reason that being an old Navy man he was the best one qualified to meet such a situation.

To make sure that my action was legalized and that no more stuff would be moved in on the Tacloban strip, I saw General MacArthur and told him what I had done. He immediately passed the word to both the Army and Navy commanders that he wanted the place used as an airdrome, not as an unloading point. Actually all these supplies belonged at a point on the beach about five miles south of the airdrome but the ship captains wanted to unload anywhere they could and get away from the beach before some Jap aviator bombed them while they were sitting ducks and unable to dodge. I couldn't blame them for feeling that way, but we needed an airdrome, and we needed it quickly.

We mobilized every soldier and Filipino we could get our hands on and started clearing the strip. By morning we were beginning once again to make an airdrome and two more barge loads of steel mat had arrived to start the final surfacing.

General MacArthur's orders had stopped any more unloading of supplies except for these two barges so that Pappy's machine guns were not needed to preserve the peace. He acted as though he was disappointed at losing this opportunity to use them, but actually he and the rest of us were so anxious to get the airdrome in operation that he forgot all about the incident and went back to work harder than ever.

A few days later Admiral Halsey commanding the 3rd Fleet supporting the Leyte landing lost the aircraft carrier *Princeton*. He radioed us that he was sending about 30 of the carrier's aircraft to Tacloban, as he had no room for them with his fleet. It would be just after dark when they came in to land and we had only about 1,500 feet of the airdrome completed and no landing lights. We notified him of the situation but it was too late. The planes were on their way. The next thing we knew they were radioing for landing instructions. By this time it was dark with low clouds, a thousand feet of ceiling, and drizzling rain.

Pappy came up with the bright idea of tying flashlights to a couple of sticks with which to signal the planes to a landing. He said that as he was a graduate of the Pensacola Naval Training Station and had a lot of carrier training, he could bring them in. We told him to go ahead. Pappy's improvised system worked and all of Halsey's planes got down safely.

The Navy planes came in in flights of six. Three of the flights had already landed, when the fourth flight began to circle the airdrome with their landing gears down and their running lights on. I was standing there with Colonel Hutchison watching Pappy with his improvised signaling equipment and admiring the job he was doing. As the first plane landed we suddenly realized that there were still six planes up there in the circle. A Jap light bomber had tagged on to the end of the formation in the dark and had let down his landing gear and turned on his lights like the rest. Just then, instead of landing, the Jap who was the next plane in position to turn in for his final approach headed out over the water, slapped his bombs into a big landing craft loaded with drums of gasoline, and got away. Pappy's landing job for the rest of the aircraft was made much easier. We

didn't need any landing lights for the next half hour.

We got our airplanes on the Tacloban strip on October 27. Thirty-four P-38 fighters from my crack 49th Group flew in and our troubles were over. The Japs made an occasional raid after that, but their unopposed field days were over. We also flew in plenty of mechanics and supply men, and Pappy's men became guards around the airdrome. We had already picked up a couple of Japs just outside the airdrome who were wearing Filipino clothes, and with all the local labor working there, we didn't dare to take chances on sabotage. The boys took the guard duty in their stride like everything else. Pappy had done a real job for us when he selected and trained that outfit.

As soon as we got the Tacloban strip in shape for operations Pappy began to get impatient to get into the war again. He started by trying to argue Colonel Hutchison into letting him have a B-25 bomber to pull a solo raid on Manila. From talking with the Filipinos around Tacloban he was sure he knew where the headquarters of the Japanese commander, General Yamashita, was and one bomb might eliminate him and wind up the war. Not having any luck with Hutchison, he appealed to me. I reminded Pappy that General MacArthur had declared Manila an open city so that we couldn't drop bombs there anyhow. Furthermore, killing a top commander wouldn't be enough even to slow down the war, let alone end it. We had shot down the number-one Jap Admiral Yamamoto back in 1943, but it didn't stop the Jap navy from operating. Besides, the mission Pappy wanted to try was a suicide job anyhow and with his knowledge of the Philippine Islands and the people, he was worth more to me alive than any Jap general dead. The thing that finally quieted him down, however, was when I asked him what would happen to his family at Santo Tomas if he were shot down and his body identified, or if he were captured and tortured into talking. This really began to worry him. He became so afraid that the Japs would find out that he was alive and with us at Tacloban, and would either kill his family or move them out of the Philippines, that from then on he avoided all the press correspondents as if they had the plague.

Colonel Hutchison played it safe and to make sure that Pappy stayed out of trouble, he issued a direct order to him not to fly without his permission and passed the word to everyone else on the field to watch Pappy to see that he didn't steal an airplane. "Hutch" told me that he was sure if he ever allowed Pappy to go out with a bombing formation, the next thing he'd hear would be that Pappy had become "lost" from the mission he was supposed to be on and had ended by dropping his load on the Japanese army headquarters in Manila.

On the afternoon of October 30 I was out on the airdrome with Colonel Woods, our boss engineer, with a map of the area spread out on the top of my jeep explaining where I wanted an extension of airplane parking space constructed when I happened to look up. About 500 yards away, just lifting over the palm trees at the south end of the strip, were four Jap planes abreast with the lights beginning to twinkle from the machine guns mounted in the wings. They had come in low and the radar had not picked them up, so we had no warning of the attack. Woods and I dropped flat on the ground behind the jeep as the Japs swept along the runway strafing and dropping bombs. The jeep didn't get touched but a truck ten feet away had its tires punctured, the gas tanks set on fire, and the driver wounded. Two men were killed in an antiaircraft machine-gun pit about 50 feet to one side of us. Two airplanes were set on fire and destroyed and two other men working on the strip were killed and ten more wounded.

One of the wounded was Lt. Col. Paul I. "Pappy" Gunn. He and Colonel Hutchison had also dived under a jeep but it didn't give much protection. A piece of phosphorus from one of the Japs' incendiary bombs struck Pappy and imbedded itself in the upper part of his left arm. We rushed him over to the field hospital, but before the surgeon could dig the fragment out of his arm the damage had been done. The phosphorus had burned deep into the flesh, severing nerves, muscles, and arteries in the process. That night even Pappy could not stand the pain and had to be given sedatives. The next morning we had him flown to Brisbane, Australia, where our best hospital, the 42nd General, was located, to see what they could do for him.

Pappy was out of the war. I hated to lose him, but the kids missed him, too. Pappy's stories would be told and retold for years, but they wouldn't be told as the old master could tell them.

EDITOR's NOTE: After the war Pappy returned to his Philippine stamping grounds and the airline business. He was killed when his war-surplus C-45 crashed in the jungle of Luzon during a violent thunderstorm. With him at the time, and also killed, was the son of Gen. Carlos P. Romulo, distinguished Philippine statesman and one-time President.

"Killing is impersonal as hell in an airplane," said a famous Marine ace in the South Pacific. It was good that this was so, for the American fighter pilots were largely just a bunch of kids not long out of high school, merely doing a job. They were not killers as the newspaper headlines sought to establish. And so long as air combat remained impersonal these kids could not be beat.

Take Dick Bong, top American ace of the war.

Dick, a farm boy from Minnesota and fresh out of cadet training, was full of zip and vinegar. He came to General Kenney's attention in 1941 when wide-eyed citizens reported a P-38 fighter loop the looping around the center span of the Golden Gate Bridge in San Francisco and "dragging" Market Street below the office building levels — all of which created panic on the streets below. Then an irate housewife in suburban Oakland called the General to report a P-38 had buzzed her house and knocked the washing off her backyard clothesline. Kenney, commander at Hamilton at the time, ordered the offender to his office for disciplinary action.

In walked a pink-cheeked, towheaded kid named Dick Bong, and as penance Kenney ordered him to report to the housewife in Oakland for one week's domestic duty.

Later, when Kenney was ordered to the South Pacific to take over command there in mid-1942, he was promised 50 P-38 fighters and was told to handpick the pilots from anywhere in the Air Force. First on his list was the "stunt-flying bad boy" Lt. Richard I. Bong, for in this young man Kenney sensed the qualities that made a fighter pilot.

Bong reported to Kenney's 5th Air Force and in December 1942 got his first Jap. In two years of combat duty, from southern New Guinea to the Philippines, broken only by a rest leave in the U.S., Dick Bong shot down 40 Jap aircraft to become America's all-time ace.

196

For Dick, aerial combat was a game like football. He was out to win. In the early days of his tour he was a jovial, jolly, whiz kid who never passed up a good poker game or a chance to raise hell with the boys. But combat changes a lad quickly, and those close to Dick observed this change as the rugged, exhausting missions piled up and his victories grew. He became less talkative and would silently watch the boys play poker, speaking briefly if spoken to or replying with just a shrug of his shoulders.

General Kenney saw a change in Dick Bong, too. Although the kid still had what it took to be king of the South Pacific skies, and despite his plea to ᴗe allowed to stay on until he got 50 Japs, Kenney made up his mind. Dick Bong would go home.

And then one day on the edge of an airstrip on Mindoro Island, there occurred an incident that proved to General Kenney the rightness of his decision, and to Dick Bong that it was time to quit. Here is the story.

I Take Bong Out of Combat

Gen. George C. Kenney, USAF (Ret)

I SENT for Dick, to tell him he was definitely and finally out of the combat and going home. His official score was now 40 enemy aircraft destroyed in the air. Everyone knew that he had knocked down at least that many more which he had reported destroyed but for which there were no witnesses. They had nearly all been shot down over the ocean so we could not even find the wreckage to serve as evidence. If Bong said he had shot down a Jap, we believed him, but the rules called for a confirming witness or definite evidence before official credit for the victory could be given. He was eight ahead of Maj. Tommy McGuire, my number-two ace who was tied with

the top score of the leading American fighter pilot in the European theater. It was improbable that anyone would equal Bong's score before the war ended in Europe or in the Pacific. Forty was a score that would be tops for any American aviator for all time. It was doubtful whether any future war would last long enough for anyone to get as many as 40 official victories again.

Since arriving in the Southwest Pacific Theater, Dick had flown 146 combat missions and had nearly 400 hours of combat time. In some theaters, pilots were allowed to go home for keeps after 25 combat missions.

Dick wanted to make it an even 50

197

and I sympathized with him. I didn't think there was a Jap in the whole Empire who could get Bong's airplane in his gunsights, but ever since Neel Kearby and Tommy Lynch had been lost, General Arnold kept sending me radio messages and letters asking me to take Dick out of combat before it was too late. General MacArthur had mentioned several times that he would hate to see Major Bong listed among those shot down. He knew Bong, had followed his string of victories, and liked the kid. The whole 49th Fighter Group, and in fact the whole 5th Air Force, wanted me to send him home. I, too, was beginning to worry about sending that pitcher to the well too often. After all, he had repaid Uncle Sam many times for what it had cost to make a fighter pilot out of him. Why not send him home and let him marry the girl and be a live hero? There was no use letting him plead with me about staying in combat. It was too easy for me to give in, so as soon as he showed up I put the cards on the table.

He was going home. There would be no more combat and that was that, so I didn't want any more arguments. Forty was a nice even number and he was to quit talking about 50 or any other number. I wanted him to go home while he was still in one piece, marry Marjorie, and start thinking about raising a lot of towheaded Swedes like himself.

Dick listened without saying a word until I had finished. You could see

that a lot of things were going on in that head of his. A country boy who liked his family. Of course he wanted some more of Mom's cooking, he wanted to hunt and fish with his dad, he liked to chat with his friends in Poplar (Wisconsin). He was crazy about a girl named Marjorie and wanted to marry her as soon as the war was over. At the same time he hated to quit chasing Jap airplanes as long as the war was on, but if I wanted him to go home it was all right. He knew that I liked him and was trying to take care of him. He would do what I asked.

"O.K., General, I'll quit arguing and go home whenever you say," he said. "But I'd like to make one more trip to Mindoro and check over a couple of guys in the 7th Squadron of that 49th Group that need a little more gunnery instructions."

I knew that what he really wanted to go over there for was to say good-by to the old gang. That was natural. Of course he should.

"As a matter of fact, I think it is a good idea," I replied. "I am going over there on an inspection trip myself tomorrow and I'll need some fighter escort on the way, as we will pass over a couple of hundred miles of Jap-held territory. I'd rather have you than a squadron of any other fighter pilots, so borrow a P-38 from someplace and come along. I'll let you know when I'm ready. In the meantime better get your stuff together and packed for that trip home."

Two top fighter pilots of the Pacific in early 1944 were Maj. Richard I. ("Bing") Bong (above), and Maj. Thomas J. Lynch (below). Close friends, they often went out on combat sweeps together in their P-38's. On March 9, 1944, Bong (with 23 victories) and Lynch (with 21) took off on a mission to Tadji. Offshore was a Japanese corvette and they raked it with their .50-caliber guns. Lynch was hit by shellfire and headed for shore. Just as he bailed out his P-38 exploded, killing him instantly. Bong started for home to report the tragedy.

With Bong out of combat, McGuire expected that his opportunity had come, but there just weren't any more Nips to be found south of Luzon. The incessant airdrome attacks had just about depopulated every Jap field south of Manila. With our new airdrome under construction in Mindoro, however, the gang was looking forward to hitting the Nips around Manila and Clark Field.

On the afternoon of December 22 we opened that campaign with more than 200 bombers, strafers, and fighters destroying nearly 125 Jap planes on the ground and shooting down eight out of the nine airborne fighters that tried to interfere. We had no losses. Our attacks the next day cost the enemy another 33 in combat and 58 more on the ground. We lost a P-38.

On Christmas Day our attack was intercepted by 70 Nip fighters. It cost them 39. We lost five P-38's but recovered three of the pilots. Tommy McGuire, leading his squadron which had just moved to Mindoro, shot down three of them to bring his score to 35. For the first time the "eight behind" jinx was out of the way.

The next day we raided Clark Field again. Only 20 Jap fighters contested this time. Our escorting fighters shot down 13 of them. Three of the victims fell to Tommy McGuire, back in there still leading his squadron. That ran his total up to 38, now only two behind Bong's record of 40.

The next morning I sent for Mc-Guire. I told him I was taking him off flying, as he looked tired to me. Tommy protested, "General, I never felt better in my life. I've gained five pounds in the last month. Besides, I'm only two behind, and ——"

"That's just it," I said. "You are tired and you won't be rested enough to fly again until I hear that Bong has arrived back in the United States and has been greeted as the top-scoring ace of the war. As soon as I get that news, you can go back to work. If I let you go out today, you are liable to knock off another three Nips and spoil Dick's whole party. What do you want him to do, land at San Francisco and have everyone say, 'Hello, Number Two, how's the war going?'"

Tommy laughed but he didn't want to spoil anything for Dick, so it was O.K. He'd relax, take it easy, get a lot of sleep for a few days, and then — he hoped the Japs wouldn't run out on us for a while yet. By the way, when was Bong going home?

"I'm taking him over to Mindoro on an inspection trip tomorrow or the next day," I replied, "and I'll see that he is loaded on an airplane bound for the United States as soon as we get back. I'm going to make a courier out of him, with top priority, so my estimate is that you should be sufficiently recovered in about a week to go back into combat. Now that that is settled, how about having lunch with me?"

Since I had acquired the former chef of the St. Francis Hotel in San Francisco as my cook, everyone liked to be invited to my mess. Tommy said he sure hoped my estimate as to the duration of his "illness" was correct, and he couldn't think of anything he'd rather do in the meantime than eat a meal with me.

A couple of days later, shortly after daybreak, with Bong in a borrowed P-38 acting as my escort, I took off to inspect the new airdromes around San Jose, Mindoro.

All the way from Tacloban airfield in Leyte to Mindoro Dick's P-38 criss-crossed back and forth above my B-17. Those keen blue eyes of his would have spotted any enemy airplane miles away and my own machine gunners would have been merely spectators at the combat. However, the trip was without incident, as I had expected, or I wouldn't have taken a chance on his getting into another fight. We landed at the San Jose field shortly after noon and taxied into the parking area.

As I shut off the engines, the siren sounded, and over the radio I heard the warning "Red alert." We hadn't time to get our radar warning net in place so this meant that in ten minutes at the most Jap airplanes would be over the area.

Col. "Jerry" Johnson, in command of the 49th Fighter Group, led the alert squadron into the air to make the interception. It took place almost directly over the field at around 15,000 feet. Johnson, the crack shot, opened the attack. The leader of the Jap formation was set on fire by Johnson's first burst, and as he pulled over to take on another victim, the Jap leader pilot, unable to stand the flames, jumped overboard. The Nips didn't wear parachutes or at least never used them over our territory, as it was against their code to be taken prisoner, so the plunge meant certain death.

The Jap pilot hit flat on the steel plank surface of the airdrome about a hundred feet from where Dick and I were standing. It was not a pretty sight. I watched for Bong's reaction. I had predicted a long while ago that if he ever found out that he was not shooting clay pigeons, I would have to take him out of combat. This was a nice kid. He was no killer, and his pet peeve against the newspapermen was that they kept referring to him as the "pilot with the most kills." As he watched Johnson's victim plunge to his death, I believe it was the first time he realized that he, Dick Bong, had been responsible for many similar occurrences. He walked over to some bushes at the edge of the field and for the next five minutes was violently ill.

There wasn't anything I could do, so I stood there waiting and more than ever convinced that tonight was the time for Dick to start home. He came over to me. The lad was quite evidently upset. He was no longer the happy-go-lucky, snub-nosed, tow-headed country boy. He had definitely aged in the last few minutes. This was a rough, dirty game that he had been playing, and I instinctively sensed that

201

he didn't want any more of it.

"General," he asked, "when are you going back to Tacloban?"

"About seven o'clock tonight," I replied. "We will land about nine thirty."

"Well, sir," he went on, "the group here could probably use my P-38, and as you are making a night flight back, you won't need any fighter escort so if you don't mind I'll go back with you."

"Certainly, Dick," I said. "Be here at seven thirty and in the meantime I'll radio back to see that you have a seat on that transport plane leaving for the United States at midnight. Also I'll have a letter to General Arnold ready for you, to deliver to him in Washington. That will make you a courier and give you top priority all the way back. In the letter I am going to ask him to let you go home to get married and have a honeymoon. After that I'm asking him to send you to the Materiel Division in Dayton, Ohio, to learn something about jet engines and jet airplanes and then transfer you to the Lockheed plant in Burbank, California, where they are producing the new P-80 jet fighter. You were talking the other day how you would like to play with a jet, so this will give you a chance to do it. How about it? Does this sound all right or is there something else you would rather do?"

A couple of big tears welled out in spite of his trying to hold them back. He brushed them off hastily and rubbed his eyes as though some dust had gotten into them.

"Oh, General, that's fine. I want to keep on flying. I just don't — sure I'd like to try flying a jet. I'll bet they are pretty hot. I —"

I put my arm over his shoulder and said, "Aw, shut up. I'll see you at seven thirty and don't be late."

He left for the 49th Fighter Group Headquarters while I got a letter ready for him to take to Washington.

After finishing my inspection and conferring with General Whitehead in regard to the part the 5th Air Force was to play in the coming operations in Luzon, I went down to the strip to take off. Bong was waiting there for me. The trip back was uneventful. Dick didn't act as though he wanted to talk, so after a few remarks to try to make him feel at ease I said I guessed I'd take a nap and promptly dozed off until we landed on the strip at Tacloban.

Just before midnight that night, December 29, 1944, armed with my letter to Gen. Hap Arnold and six bottles of Coca-Cola that I managed to scare up at the last minute, Maj. Richard Ira Bong boarded the Air Transport Command flight back home. I said, "So long, Dick, I hope to see you again before too long. Say hello to your mom and dad for me."

I never saw him again.

EDITOR'S NOTE: Dick Bong arrived in the U.S. on January 6, 1945. He received a hero's welcome from coast to coast as America's ace of aces.

Upon hearing of Dick's safe return, General Kenney sent for Tommy McGuire, Bong's closest competitor (with 38 Japs) and told him he could go back to combat. The next day McGuire led a couple of green replacement pilots on a fighter sweep over Jap airdromes on Cebu and Negros islands. Breaking a cardinal rule of combat, McGuire swung into combat at low altitude without dropping his auxiliary 160-gallon gas tanks. He spun in and disappeared in a tremendous explosion of fire.

Meanwhile, Dick Bong had been assigned to the Lockheed plant in California to test the new P-80 jet fighter.

On August 7, 1945, the day after the A-bomb had been dropped on Hiroshima, General Kenney was at Kadena airstrip, preparing to take off for Manila, absorbed in the events surrounding the forthcoming surrender of Japan. He was handed a radiogram. Maj. Richard Ira Bong was dead. His P-80 jet fighter had flamed out on takeoff. It was a day of sorrow for the whole 5th Air Force.

The Japanese put up a desperate battle in the air over Leyte. Offshore the carriers of two fleets, the 7th of Vice Admiral Thomas C. Kinkaid and the 3rd of Admiral "Bull" Halsey, protected the U.S. 6th Army that was meeting heavy opposition from 20,000 enemy troops, and drove back a powerful Jap carrier attack force in the Battle of Leyte Gulf.

By the end of 1944, 5th Air Force fighters had shot down 314 enemy aircraft, losing only 16.

In quick succession Mindoro Island and Luzon were invaded by MacArthur's ground forces. Air attacks, including those made by Third Fleet carrier aircraft, on Luzon from Leyte and Mindoro airstrips had put some 1,500 Japanese planes out of action. When our forces stormed ashore at Lingayen Gulf, little air opposition was met. Thus the main effort of 5th Air Force flyers on Luzon was given to support of our ground forces. Low-level strafing and dive-bombing of enemy troops strongly entrenched in mountains and hill country was no easy job.

Lt. Russell D. Giesy, P-47 pilot with 5th Air Force's V Fighter Command, was on such a strike against Jap ground forces in the rugged Balete Pass area of northern Luzon, when his engine quit.

A Stroll on Luzon

Lt. Russell D. Giesy

I TRIED to stretch my glide toward our lines but I was losing altitude so fast I decided to bail out. A brisk wind began carrying me toward the Japs, despite my pulls on the risers to change direction. As I neared the ground I heard snipers' bullets whizzing past me, but I hit treetops without stopping any bullets.

The chute hung momentarily, then let me drop about 20 feet to the ground. I was dazed for a moment, then got up and started running. Within a few seconds I came to my senses, however, and took out a miniature compass an intelligence clerk had given me a few days before. After checking this and figuring I was east of Highway 5, the main road, I walked across a ravine and up the other side to a wooded ridge. I decided to keep on the ridge, rather than risk being spotted directly on the road.

About this time things started happening. I ran across some enemy foxholes and, as I started down the side of the ridge, I spotted a lone Jap standing nearby. I heard Jap voices behind me. As I started back around the ridge, an artillery barrage cut loose showering shrapnel all over the place. After several moments of indecision, I ran down an incline and smack into a Jap camp which, fortunately, proved to be deserted for the time being. I saw a pistol and belt lying on one equipment pile, and since I had no pistol with me, I was tempted to stop for it, but decided to keep running.

I crawled up the next ridge and found two unmanned Jap machine-gun positions directly in front of me, one about 50 feet away and the other some 100 yards farther along. By now, I was so exhausted I rolled about 20 feet into the brush to wait and rest.

Soon two Japs came running up the same trail I had used and stopped within a few feet of my hiding place. One of them went over to the nearest machine gun, but the other stood near me for an hour and a half. I spent the entire time praying. Finally, he moved a little farther away and I decided to take a chance on clearing out. As I got up I saw the other Jap leave the machine gun and head in my direction. Turning quickly and hoping he would think I was his companion, I started walking down the trail.

The ruse worked and he came walking along behind me. Although he was armed with a rifle, I decided to slow down to allow him to catch up with me. I led him to the edge of a cliff, and when he was almost by my side, I wheeled and slugged him in the face with all my strength. He tumbled, screaming, down the cliff.

I turned and ran along the eastern side of the ridge. In my hurry I stumbled into a trench, and looked up to see a very surprised Jap officer two feet away on my right. He wore heavy horn-rimmed glasses and was holding a pair of binoculars. He reached for his pistol, and I struck him as hard a backhand blow as I could manage in my off-balance position. I felt his glasses crunch and he fell over backwards. I dove over the top of the trench and rolled down a steep incline.

At the bottom of the hill I found a

creek with about two feet of water. Several times I tried to crawl up the bank to gain the main road, which I could see at times, but I was too exhausted to make the grade. At last I came to a point where the creek bank leveled off and I climbed out to the road.

I had been walking in the center of the highway for some time when I came to a sharp bend. As I rounded the curve, one coldly spoken word broke the stillness of the dark, which had come about an hour before. That word — "Halt!" — made me the happiest I have ever been. I had reached an infantry outpost.

I asked the men why they hadn't shot me when I came stumbling down the road in the dark, and they said they knew I had bailed out and were hoping and praying that I would make it back alive.

The boys found a jeep and rushed me back to the regimental first-aid station where I was "wined and dined" and patched up. All in all, I couldn't have received more kind and gentle attention if I had been a newborn babe.

Beginning with the American invasion of the Philippines, the Japanese air forces dipped deep into their medieval past for a tactic that reaped a heavy toll of our invasion fleet. It was the kamikaze *or suicide attack. The word kamikaze meant "divine wind," which according to their traditions had swept down upon a Korean fleet centuries before and turned defeat into victory for the Japanese.*

The kamikaze was an instrument of desperation — inhuman, cold-blooded, final — and it indicated to American commanders that the Japanese would make an all-out stand in the Philippines.

They had sent their greatest military commander to take charge there, the man they called the "Tiger of Malaya," or known to Americans as the "Butcher of Bataan" — General Yamashita. And when Yamashita initiated the kamikaze air attacks, it was a sure thing the Japs had their backs to the wall.

The kamikaze pilot did not merely crash his aircraft into an enemy target. He deliberately flew to his death in a special explosive-laden aircraft — and in this sense he was a human guided missile. It is difficult for the Western mind to understand why the rank and file of Japanese pilots enthusiastically volunteered for the Kamikaze Squadrons, but neither can the Western mind visualize death as nothing more than a rose petal falling to the ground. Nor can it find comfort in a logic that would allow the family back home to rise in social prestige because of a suicidal death in battle of one of their kin.

205

Between October 25, 1944 — the first successful kamikaze attack by enemy pilots in the Philippines — and January 25, 1945, 424 planes, mostly Zeros, had sortied from Philippine bases for their suicidal plunges into ships of the American fleet supporting the invasion forces. At least 50 American vessels of all types were damaged by them, including six aircraft carriers, two of which were sunk. One of the Japanese air units, the 201st Air Group, stationed at Mabalacat Airdrome in the Philippines, had thrown hundreds of its pilots against the U.S. fleet since the original Leyte landings of October 20.

Now, with MacArthur's forces pouring ashore at Lingayen Gulf in Luzon, with overwhelming American Air Forces dominating the air, and with the Philippines all but lost, the 201st had five planes left for one last kamikaze mission. Here, by the commander of that unit, is the story of this last mission, and a look into the kamikaze mind.

Philippine Exodus:
The Kamikazes of Mabalacat

Capt. Rikihei Inoguchi, Commdr. Tadashi Nakajima and Roger Pineau

I WAS often asked by visitors to the base if it was not difficult to order the sortie of special attack pilots. Such a question was as hard to answer as the subject was hard to explain. There were many ramifications. The order to sortie, for kamikazes, was tantamount to saying, "Go out and die in battle!" If the order had been contrary to the will of the pilots, it would have been cruel beyond description, and I could no more have given it than I could have expected the men to carry it out.

In the course of the kamikaze effort there were dozens, scores — indeed hundreds — of special attack sorties launched upon my order. Neither my conscience nor the souls of those pilots could rest easy if their deed had been the product merely of command decisions. In these crucial moments of the Empire, however, dire circumstances called for extreme measures, and the young pilots rose to the situation. My ordering the sorties was but a function within the system, and my presence in the system was almost as defiant of rationality as the system itself.

In view of the special circumstances now that the 201st Air Group was practically disbanding, however, instead of simply designating the day's flyers, this one time I decided to call for volunteers.

I ordered all of the pilots to assemble in front of the shelter. When they had gathered I addressed the group, reviewing our situation and explaining how the splendid work of the maintenance men had provided an additional five planes.

"These are not in first-class condition," I pointed out. "In fact, two of them cannot carry a 250-kilogram bomb, so they have each been loaded with two 30-kilogram bombs. When these planes have been dispatched, our air battle will have ended and the rest of us will join in the fight as land troops. In making plans for this last special attack I want to know your wishes."

With this I paused to give them a chance for reflection. When it was clear that they had understood my message, I continued, "Anyone who wishes to volunteer for today's sortie will raise his hand."

The words were scarcely uttered before every man had raised his arm high in the air and shouted, "Here!" as they edged forward with great eagerness. I was startled, almost overwhelmed, by this demonstration. My heart beat faster and my chest swelled with pride at the dedicated spirit of these young men. I breathed deeply and tensed my facial muscles into a scowl to keep from betraying the emotion that flooded over me.

"Since you all want so much to go, we will follow the usual procedure of selection. You are dismissed."

As I turned to enter the shelter, several of the pilots reached out to grab at my arms and sleeves saying, "Send me! Please send me! Send me!"

I wheeled about and shouted, "Everyone wants to go. Don't be so selfish!"

That silenced them, and I entered the shelter to confer with the air group commander about the composition of the final list.

We were in complete agreement as to who should lead this unit. Lieutenant Nakano had recently been hospitalized with tuberculosis in Manila. Upon his release he had said to me, "I am now recovered, but there is no telling when I may have a relapse. If this recovery were complete I could wait my turn for duty at the regular time. But if the illness returns there would be no chance for me to serve. Therefore, please send me on a mission at the earliest opportunity."

Remembering his plea, I had kept him in mind for some short-range mission that would not tax his strength. This flight would not be long, and this was the last chance. Considering all factors, Nakano was the ideal man for leading the mission

The four other pilots were selected purely on a basis of ability. They were Warrant Officers Goto and Taniuchi for the first unit, and Lieutenant (jg) Nakao and Warrant Officer Chihara for the second.

Enemy air raids continued all this while, so that we hardly dared risk

Final moment in the life of a kamikaze pilot as he aims his Zero into the deck of the USS *Missouri*. Evidence toward end of war revealed that many kamikaze "volunteers" were wired to the rudder pedals and had their cockpit hatches locked from the outside, preventing escape at the last minute.

showing our heads. Enemy ships were swarming at Lingayen Gulf, and a landing there was imminent.

In preparation for a 1645 takeoff, the five planes, hidden at various points around the Mabalacat airfield, had their camouflage removed and engines warmed up. Now the training which had been practiced so enthusiastically proved valuable. The pilots moved swiftly. As the first plane started to roll, the others followed in close order.

The field was pockmarked with bomb holes, but following my hand signals, the planes were skillfully taxied to their starting places without mishap. As I waved my right hand in the signal for taking off, Lieutenant Nakano raised himself in the cockpit and shouted, "Commander Nakajima! Commander Nakajima!"

Fearing that something had gone wrong, I ran to the side of his plane to learn what troubled him. His face was wreathed in smiles as he called, "Thank you, Commander. Thank you very much!"

The simplicity of the words, the spirit of supreme dedication, robbed me of speech. I wished that I could find words appropriate to the exaltation of the moment, but no words would come. So, realizing that enemy raiders might appear at any moment and there was not an instant to lose, I wordlessly gave the signal for taking off.

Nakano's plane started forward with a roar. As the second plane passed in front of me the engine was revved down momentarily as the pilot screamed, "Commander, Commander!" I flagged him on with a vigorous wave of my arm, but through the din came back his shrieked farewell: "Thank you for choosing me!" I pretended not to hear these messages, but they tore at my heart. The scene repeated itself as each smiling pilot passed my position and I waved on the next: No. 3 . . . No. 4 . . . No. 5 — each did the same as he flew off to his destiny, leaving me behind in a cloud of earthly dust.

Assembling in formation, the five circled the field and then flew to the north with the evening sun of the Philippines glistening brightly on their wings. They must have felt the fervent blessings of their earthbound comrades who stood and watched as they disappeared into the afternoon sky. . . .

EDITOR'S NOTE: In this attack at Lingayen Gulf a minesweeper was sunk; two battleships, three cruisers, three destroyers, a minesweeper and a transport ship were damaged by kamikaze suicide attacks. No one will ever know which ones were the victims of Nakano and his four flyers.

While the Navy was tight-lipped about its kamikaze losses, this form of attack by Japanese air forces intensified. At Okinawa it reached its height and in the 81 days of the Okinawan campaign, Japanese suicide planes sank 35 ships and damaged around 299, killing more than 11,000 Americans and wounding three times that many. Attacks were not only aimed at the invasion fleet but also at airdromes, ground personnel, supply areas and key military land installations. While the Zero fighter was the primary kamikaze instrument and the most frequently used, many kinds of aircraft were employed by the Japs in this desperation tactic: obsolete and factory new models; piloted or flying (Baka) bombs — small winged aircraft with a ton of high explosives in the nose and without landing gear, released from a mother plane at some distance from the target and guided by the pilot straight into the target.

At war's end, on Kyushu Island alone, the Japanese had 790 special kamikaze planes and 850 regular planes adapted for kamikaze attacks waiting and ready to be used against American forces in the event an invasion of the homeland took place. Such an invasion, which was nullified by the A-bomb, would indeed have been a costly operation.

The "Baka" bomb — manned flying explosive carrying a ton of TNT in its nose. Japanese started using them in April of 1945 in attacks on American ships at Okinawa.

*". . . in ten minutes a man could walk to the end of his world
and find only sea and sand and coral . . ."*

Line Plunge Through Center

Maj. James F. Sunderman

THE Gilberts and the Marshalls, the Carolines and the Marianas — these island groupings marked the route of the great Central Pacific offensive which drove westward across thousands of endless miles of water toward the Philippines and Japan from Hawaii and the Fiji Islands. Across this broad expanse swept the Central Pacific forces under Admiral Nimitz, slugging right and left toward the four home islands of the Emperor.

For the crews of the seven bomber and three fighter squadrons of the 7th Air Force and the pilots of the swift Navy carrier task forces, the route was more familiarly known by the target names which read like the pages of a Martian dictionary: Tarawa, Makin, Apamama, Mille, Jaluit, Maloelap, Nauru, Betio; Wotje, Roi, Kwajalein, Eniwetok, Namur, Majuno, Rongelap, Likep; Truk, Ponape, Woleai, Yap, Kusaie, Hall, Oroluk, Puluvat, Mokil, Pengelap, Palaus, Pulawa, Ulithi, Nomonuito; Wake, Marcus, Tinian, Saipan, Guam; Okinawa and Iwo Jima.

Thousands of islands dotted the Central Pacific and the Japs had occupied all that were considered worth while. To dig them out of strongly fortified positions on each would have taken a decade or more and this was the hope of the Jap — to outlast us both in time and resources. Each bit of coral they had taken, and the jungle on it, was to be defended to the last man.

The 7th Air Force had been created out of the Hawaiian Air Force of Pearl Harbor days. For almost two years it sat idly in Hawaii, fighting what it called the "Pineapple War," while combat events passed it by. But all this ended with a vengeance on November 14, 1943.

On the dawn of that day, operation "Galvanic," the first of four code-named offensives began and the bitterly fought air drive through the Central Pacific got under way. For the next 17 months it was to be "one damned island after another" for the 7th.

This was to be the career of the 7th — strike out ahead, move forward on the ground. In the air — a navigator's nightmare — scores of long grueling missions to coral pinpoints in a world where unbroken horizons touched down to meet measureless miles of water; and survival, if you went down, could be an enemy far worse than the Jap. It would be combat from four miles up to treetop level; and you could watch the wounded on board die hard before you could get the plane back to base. And the weather — it would be calm and cloudless, or wild and weird, for here was the cradle of massive storm areas that crawled menacingly across the ocean surface and pushed billowy white thunderheads too high for overflight. And, when one of these sprawled across your flight path there was no alternative but to throttle back, and head into the black turbulance where violent winds, pelting rains and hail loosened the very rivets of the aircraft and tossed it like a feather in the March winds.

On the ground it would be 3,000

7th Air Force base on Kwajalein Island in the Marshalls. Here, truly, a man could walk to the end of his world in ten minutes and find only sea, sand and coral.

miles of stifling heat and C-rations, mosquitoes, flies and fevers, drenching tropical rains and few letters from home. This is the way it had to be for the 7th Air Force.

The overall strategy called for throwing the Jap off his guard. Only key bases were to be captured in the hundreds he occupied. The others would simply be neutralized by heavy, continuing air bombardment and then bypassed and left to wither and die.

"Galvanic" targets lay in the Gilberts. The B-24 Liberators and B-25 Mitchells of the 7th rose from their bases at Funafuti, Canton, and Baker in the Ellice Islands to hit Jap installations and airfields in preparation for the Marine landings on Tarawa and Makin. The pattern of the Central Pacific air war had its beginning here. The 7th was to provide bombing support for one invasion, and at the same time soften up targets far out ahead for future invasions. Simultaneously it had to protect the rear and flank of our westward advancing forces from the enemy on bypassed islands left in the backwash. The job was cut out. It was big, and it would be bitter, but once the offensive got under way, it rolled with tremendous speed.

"Galvanic" was followed by "Flintlock" in the Marshalls and historic names like Kwajalein, Mille, Eniwetok and Maloelap were among the targets pounded day and night by the long-range B-24's and the medium B-25's.

Next came "Catchpole" and it aimed at hammering Jap airfields and installations in the Carolines, the nestling bristling strongholds of Truk — "Gibraltar of the Pacific," Ponape, and Yap, along with Wake and Marcus, far to the north and northwest.

Fourth step on the Central Pacific road to Tokyo was "Operation Forager" designed to drive the Japs from the key islands in the Marianas group. Here was the real estate that lay within the B-29 Superfortress air-strike distance from the Japanese homeland. The primary objective was capture of Saipan, Tinian and Guam in the Marianas for B-29 air-base sites.

From "Galvanic" through "Forager," the 7th Air Force and the powerful, swift Navy carrier task forces ranged the wide Pacific, spearheading a bold amphibious island-hopping campaign straight toward the Orient.

In the Philippines this offensive met with the 5th and 13th Air Forces' drive up from the Southwest Pacific and the compass courses were set north to Japan. Formosa, Okinawa, Iwo Jima, Ie Shima, next came under air attack. These were the final stepping stones.

The Central Pacific forces' line plunge through center had left behind thousands of Japs on island garrisons hopelessly abandoned, waiting and starving, with no hope of supply or reinforcement.

It had opened a wedge in Japan's secondary Pacific defense line. The vitals of the Empire were now exposed to the long-range B-29's based in the Marianas.

"When we lost Saipan," said Admiral Nagano, "we realized 'Hell is on us, this is terrible.'"

True to Nagano's prediction, the closing chapter of the war would be written by air power from bases in the Marianas, and hell could hardly have the fury that was to be unleashed from B-29's out of Saipan, Tinian and Guam.

Truk Island, Japanese "Gibraltar" of the Central Pacific, was pounded constantly throughout the war — even after it was bypassed in the drive west. Here a B-24 flies through a flak-streaked sky over Truk.

Maloelap was a hornet's nest. This Japanese stronghold, just one of the many coral atolls in the Marshalls, was a name on the 7th Air Force's target board in a drive through the Central Pacific. Each time the Liberators and Mitchells headed there scores of Japanese fighters would rise to attack them. By the time Maloelap was completely neutralized on January 26, 1944, 89 Jap fighters had been shot down by gunners of the Liberators and Mitchells, 80 probable and 94 damaged. Scores more had been destroyed on the ground.

But the bristling little island exacted its price: seven B-25's and 11 B-24's lost; 48 Mitchells and 60 Liberators damaged. The combat drama in the skies above Maloelap was little different than that which took place above dozens of other atolls stretching across the Central Pacific. It was a rugged man's air war and the stories of the brave young men fighting it would fill a dozen books. One in particular had an impact throughout the Air Force all over the world.

Prayer, Guts, and Yankee Resourcefulness

Clive Howard and Joe Whitley

SOME of the battered Liberators and their crews were saved by amazing mixtures of prayer and guts and Yankee resourcefulness. The *Texas Belle* was one of them.

The target had been Maloelap. For an hour and a half after unloading its bombs, the *Belle* had fought a running battle with 30 Zekes.

Lt. Charles F. Pratte, the *Belle's* pilot, coaxed and prayed the shot-up airplane 400 miles back to the Gilberts. His only hope was a landing on one of the Tarawa airstrips. The *Belle's* hydraulic system was shot out; therefore, no brakes.

Construction on the strip Pratte picked had gone just far enough to accommodate fighter aircraft, and a sizable crowd was collected to witness the first landing by a Navy fighter. At this point, the *Texas Belle* came along and stole the show.

With no brakes, and with a field too short even for a healthy bomber, Pratte faced the almost certain prospect of piling up the Liberator on a coral heap at the end of the runway.

Tiny Maloelap Island in the Marshalls, with its cross airfields, was a major Japanese airdrome.

Dramatic photo of the *Texas Belle* as it nears end of its landing roll on runway after parachutes had performed the braking effect.

Or, avoiding that, he could boil down the short strip and into the sea.

To make matters just a little worse, one engine quit as Pratte came down for the landing. He managed to pull up and circle again. Then he got an idea. As it turned out, it proved to be one of the most original ideas of the whole war.

Going into the down leg, Pratte called out a series of orders over the intercom. They sounded like crazy orders; but orders, crazy or not, are orders. So the two waist gunners did as they were told. They rigged parachutes to their gun mounts and arranged the packs so that — if everything worked out as the pilot thought it might — the chutes would pop open in the slipstream. The tail gunner, also following instructions, rigged a chute to his gun mount.

As the wheels of the *Texas Belle* touched the runway at a speed well over 100 miles an hour, Pratte called out one more order. The gunners yanked at their rip cords and three parachutes simultaneously blossomed open like a series of sea anchors. The *Belle* was eased to a stop four or five yards from the edge of the ocean.

The stunt drew a special commendation from General Arnold, who, in a letter to General Hale, described the parachute landing as, "unique, so far as I know, in operational history." More important, it became an almost standard method for landing brakeless bombers, first, in the Pacific and, later, all over the world.

Nine months after the Central Pacific offensive began, it had rolled across the Gilberts, the Marshalls, the Carolines and was hammering at the Marianas. Here the Japs determined to make a do-or-die stand and it was here that one of the most spectacular air battles in all of history, certainly the high point in naval air combat, took place.

The powerful U.S. Navy Task Force 58, commanded by the veteran Vice Admiral Marc A. Mitscher, approached west of the southern Marianas in early June 1944. This massive array of American air power consisted of seven heavy carriers (Hornet, Yorktown, Bunker Hill, Wasp, Enterprise, Lexington, and Essex), eight light carriers (Bataan, Belleau Wood, Monterey, Cabot, San Jacinto, Princeton, Cowpens, and Langley), seven battleships, eight heavy cruisers, 13 light cruisers, and 67 destroyers. Mitscher's air units comprised 450 fighters, 250 bombers, 200 torpedo planes and 80 scout observation planes. It was the greatest air-sea armada ever assembled and to the Japanese a phoenix which had arisen out of the ashes of Pearl Harbor.

On the 11th of June, it launched a fighter sweep over the Marianas which destroyed one third of the defending Japanese aircraft. On June 14 amphibious assault forces swept ashore on Saipan.

It was a desperate moment for the Japanese and they began to pour air reinforcements into their Marianas bases. Chief among these was a powerful 73-ship surface fleet, including nine aircraft carriers (Taiho, Shokaku, Suikaku, Junyo, Hiyo, Ryuho, Chiyoda, Chitose, and the Zuiho), and the 74,000-ton battleships Yamato and Musashi. The task force was commanded by Vice Admiral Jisaburo Ozawa.

Ozawa had a total of 450 planes: 225 Zero fighters, 129 Judy and Val dive bombers, 87 Jill attack bombers, and 9 Judy reconnaissance planes. His fleet was 50 planes stronger than the Nagano force which had attacked Pearl Harbor on December 7, 1941.

On the 19th of June as Admiral Ozawa came within range of Task Force 58, he launched his planes in an attempt to destroy the American force. In the ensuing day-long air attack from both Ozawa's fleet and Admiral Kakuda's land-based units, U.S. Navy carrier pilots and gunners on the ships destroyed 402 Japanese aircraft, in what has become known as the Marianas "Turkey Shoot" or, officially, the "Battle of the Philippine Sea." At the end of the day Admiral Ozawa had 46 aircraft left, 26 Zeros, six Jill torpedo bombers, two Val dive bombers, and 12 miscellaneous types. Over 400 had been destroyed!

At the bottom of the sea lay the carriers Taiho, Shokaku, and Hiyo, along with two loaded fuel tankers, victims of air and submarine attack. Heavily damaged were the carriers Suikaku, Junyo, Ryuho and Chiyoda, and the cruiser Haruna.

The greatest carrier air strength the Japanese had ever mustered had been thoroughly beaten and the Marianas were ours for the taking.

Tales of personal heroics during the "Turkey Shoot" have emerged by the scores. Here written from official documents by three well-known naval reserve writers is a glimpse into that epic event.

The Marianas "Turkey Shoot"

Capt. Walter Karig, Lt. Comdr. Russell L. Harris, USNR, and Lt. Comdr. Frank A. Manson, USN

FIRST blood was drawn before sunrise on June 19 when fighter pilots from the *Monterey* (Capt. Stuart H. Ingersoll) intercepted two Japanese "Judy" (dive bombers) and shot one down. The skirmish was significant only to the extent that it alerted all the American forces present to the imminence of climax.

Sunrise came to Guam at 0542 — not quite a quarter before 6:00 A.M. — on June 19, 1944. Only about a third of the sky was cloud-masked: "ceiling and visibility unlimited."

Carrier planes flying CAP (Combat Air Patrol) over Guam reported tremendous activity on the island's airstrips, and suggested the advisability of deterrents being applied. The Japanese were hauling gassed-up, armed planes out of the tree-covered revetments and pushing them off into the air with all the determination of bees swarming.

Reinforcements were rushed to the Combat Air Patrol, and, between 8:00 and 9:30 A.M., shot down 35 of the enemy without greatly interrupting the Japanese' dogged labors to get every plane into the air at no matter what cost.

At 9:50 enemy aircraft were detected around the full circle of the radar screen, with a large group orbiting about 130 miles to the westward of Mitscher's flagship at 24,000 feet. The Admiral himself bellowed the call to battle over the TBS, the old circus war cry "Hey, Rube!" the signal to the fighters over Guam to rally around for a more important fight.

Aboard every carrier the squawk-box gabbled its "Pilots — man-your-planes" and from the American ships rose their own swarms, stingers poised. Bombers and torpedo planes, however, flew east. Their job was to make the airstrips on Guam worthless to the

This happy group of carrier pilots tangled with 21 Japanese planes, shot down 17 with no U.S. losses. Morale in naval air units aboard carriers was high.

shuttling Japanese, while the fighters headed for the enemy concentrations.

Comdr. Ernest M. Snowden, who commanded the planes on the *Lexington,* gives a vivid picture of what the approaching Japs looked like.

"We could see vapor trails of planes coming in with tiny black specks at the head. It was just like the skywriting we all used to see before the war. The sky was a white overcast and for some reason the planes were making vapor trails at much lower altitude than usual. That made it easier for our boys to find the incoming Japs. The air was so clear you could see planes tangling in the sky. Then a flamer would go down. We would hope it was a Jap and from the radio

chatter we could hear from the pilots, it seemed that the Japs were getting the worst end of it.

"One of our newest members of the fighter squadron, Ensign Bradford Hagie, shot down three Japs while ferrying from one carrier to another. Hagie had joined up with us as a replacement. On the day before he had motor trouble and couldn't land aboard *Lexington* because we were launching planes. A carrier cannot land and launch planes at the same time. Hagie put down on another carrier about 3,000 yards away. He slept on her the night of the 18th. Next morning he took off about 9:30 to fly back to his carrier. While he was in the air, he heard the report about the Japs coming in and decided to go for a little hunt. He shot down three, which isn't bad for a 3,000-yard ferry flight."

There were 70 enemy planes in the group taken under attack. They were met 60 miles from the guardian battleships, and by the time the distance had been cut by ten miles, half the attacking force was under water. It was three of the survivors that Hagie eliminated.

Another pilot who gloomily found his airplane apparently out of the fight was Lt. Alexander Vraciu, who had gained considerable combat experience flying wing for Butch O'Hare. His engine refused to make adequate speed, and the fighter control ordered him and five similarly indisposed aircraft to drop out and keep clear of trouble. But trouble headed for Vraciu and his five "orphan" brothers — a formation of Japanese planes, which, the cripples were told, were coming in fast in their direction.

Vraciu, his windscreen smeared with oil, shot off at a tangent from the monotonous circle he had been flying, followed by the five other fighters. One of the sextet could not keep up, falling behind and below.

In his mind Vraciu was going over every little detail of his lessons in how to win an air battle. Butch O'Hare had told him never to shoot at a Jap until he was close enough to do some good. Always go after the bombers first. Always aim at the spot where the wing joins the fuselage because that is where he burns most easily. Ignore enemy fire — they probably couldn't hit you anyway. Mix it up as long as you have the advantage, but the moment you lose the advantage, break away. Never dive on an enemy plane until you have looked over your shoulder. Good, practical teaching this — if one had a good, practicable airplane.

"Tallyho, three enemy planes," radioed Vraciu to base. "Keep looking," came the reply, "those aren't the dangerous ones."

Vraciu took another look, including down, and there they were, 2,000 feet below and on the port side. He grabbed his radio: "Tallyho — at least 30 rats (Jap fighters)."

He dove in for the kill, and then saw the enemy formation was composed of bombers. That meant fighters in the vicinity, and, remembering O'Hare's Rule No. 6, he craned his neck for a look over his shoulder and saw seven planes speeding toward him! Before he could gulp back the lump in his throat he recognized them as Hellcats. Now they were 12 against the 30 and five seconds later, Vraciu's exultant voice crackled through the radio phones "Scratch one Judy." He banked and came back at the other bombers all guns blazing. Two more tumbled wing over wing into the ocean.

"After we had been on them a few minutes they began to separate like a bunch of disorderly cattle," Vraciu related. "Every time one of the Japs would try to lead a string of others

The wartime-developed F6F Hellcat fighter began appearing in 1944 in the Pacific skies and became an ace-maker for our carrier pilots.

Many of the Japanese planes destroyed in the "Turkey Shoot" were Nakajima Jills, three-seater navy torpedo bombers which first came into combat around 1944 at Bougainville.

222

out of formation the Hellcat pilots turned into 'cowboys' and herded them back into the group. If they had been able to separate we wouldn't have been able to shoot down as many as we did."

Another pass and two more "meatballs" were dunked. A third run, and Vraciu's bullets tore into the Judy's bomb. The Japanese plane blew up in the air, sending Vraciu's whirling like a feather, but still his voice came clear: "Splash number six. There's one more ahead. He's diving on a BB. I don't think he will make it."

"He" didn't. The battleship's AA took care of that one.

Eight minutes later, with only 360 rounds of ammunition expended but most of his gasoline gone, Lieutenant Vraciu climbed out of his cockpit the Navy's ace, the six bombers bringing up his score to 19 planes shot out of the air and 21 destroyed on ground.

By late spring of 1945, Allied air power had rolled up to the gates of Japan. American Air Forces, on recently captured bases, ringed the four home islands of the Empire in a sweeping arc from the Aleutians in the far north down through the Western Pacific and up into China.

It had been over 3,500 miles (as the Air Force flies) and had taken 3½ years from the lower Solomon Islands, New Guinea, the mid-Pacific and Burma. Along those miles and throughout those years the Japanese were blasted, ripped out, torn up and driven back by air attack with almost monotonous regularity — base by base, ship by ship, plane by plane, troop by troop — everywhere they had planted their aggressive foot. The retreat had become unswerving, until now they stood with their backs to the wall, surrounded and hopelessly facing a final, inevitable, fatal air assault on their homeland.

Of all the tactics employed against the Japanese on the Road Back, attack-bombing at low level was the most effective. In every major landing operation, from Lae to Luzon (except Leyte) and from Makin to Okinawa, the carrier and land-based fighter bombers, the mediums and even on occasion the heavies, sweeping in a treetop or mast-high attack, caught the enemy air and sea forces by surprise, isolated the battlefronts, swept the beaches clean for invasion, and threw deadly firepower ahead of advancing land armies. It cleaned the ocean lanes of supply ships — the lifeline of the Empire.

It was mainly the job of the medium bombers, the men of the A-20's and B-25's. Day after day for them it was attack, attack, attack and curiously enough, per 1,000 hours of combat flying, this dangerous tactic brought lower casualties than other combat air techniques.

The concept of attack-bombing was a highly infectious thing among the bomber crews and the units to which they belonged. It instilled a spirit of offensive in American flyers that the Japanese had not counted on, and could not quite understand. Even few Americans, except those involved in it, knew what it really was, or what it meant.

The Spirit of Attack

From "Air Force" Magazine

To APPRECIATE the effects of this technique on the psychology of battle, one should see an attack outfit back at the base after a good bombing show. There is nothing quite like it; even the fighter crowd can't approach these men in mental attitude. Back at base they are as cocky and arrogant as they are precise and disciplined on the bombing run. Month after month, they do their jobs at wave-top or tree-top level, break in fast for surprise, turn on the full blast of their forward-firing 50's, watch the bullets splatter the defenses, feel the bombs leave the bomb bay and the plane rise sharply, bank and roar from the target and gain altitude, then watch the smoke and flames and debris they have left below. Regardless of how many fast, fleeting moments of action are experienced, the reaction is always the same.

No form of flying provides the exhilaration of low flying. The universal liking among pilots of buzzing the field tells part of the story. Add to that buzzing experience the power of eight forward-firing machine guns and four 500-pound bombs, the co-ordinated effort that goes with low-level formation flying and synchronized attack and a target staring you full in the face. The spirit of the offensive is built into the fuselage. Self-confidence becomes contagious, runs from pilot to crew to ground men. A bomb run becomes a personal fight, as near as an airman can come to hand-to-hand combat. There is no cloud bank between you and the enemy; you are right on his neck, close enough to thumb your nose in his face; most important, you can see the results of your efforts. It's a tough flying assignment, requiring maximum skill and precision work. It takes cocky flying, which sometimes breeds carelessness, but the careless die early and the cockiness matures into healthy self-confidence.

To avoid being caught by their own exploding bombs, low-level attack pilots dropped parachute bombs. The chutes slowed them down, allowing aircraft to escape. Here, on Boeroe Island, thousands of enemy planes were destroyed on the ground, as this Sally bomber will be in a few seconds.

Although low-level attack brought fewer casualties per 1,000 hours of combat flying than other tactics, it held out dangerous hazards nevertheless. Here an American A-20 on a treetop bomb sweep over Karas, Borneo, is caught by Japanese flak and begins its headlong plunge into the sea.

This historic photo shows the lead element of B-29's on the first raid over Tokyo since the Doolittle raid of 1942. Fujiyama, symbol of the Japanese Empire, towers far below.

PART III

THE HOMESTRETCH
AND VICTORY

"An air offensive against Japan itself would be decisive because all Japanese cities, centers of population, and agricultural areas, lie along the valleys of the streams, are congested, and easily located. In general, their structure is of paper and wood or other inflammable substances. They cannot depart from this character of construction because of earthquakes."

> — BRIG. GEN. WILLIAM MITCHELL
> U. S. Army Air Corps
> October 24, 1924

A buddy stands by to guard this crippled B-29 Superfortress from fighter attacks and escort it back to a safe landing at Iwo Jima.

Nagoya, Japan. Engine plant of the Mitsubishi aircraft plant burned to cinders by B-29 incendiary attack.

Introduction

THE HOMESTRETCH of the Pacific air war was primarily the long-range strategic air offensive against the Japanese homeland by the 20th Air Force combined with the tactical carrier strikes by the Navy's fast carrier task forces.

The air campaign against Japan itself began in June, 1944, under project "Matterhorn" — a plan to strike Japanese steel plants with B-29's from bases in China and India. It was "Matterhorn" that brought a new air force into the war, the 20th, composed principally of the four-engine, very long-range B-29 Superfortresses — untried and untested in combat — and long-range fighters.

The Superforts began arriving in India in April of 1944, flown by their crews from Kansas via the South Atlantic, North Africa and the Middle East; and 20th Bomber Command was established under Brig. Gen. Kenneth B. Wolfe, the first of a series of commanders including General LeMay. According to the plan, India-based B-29's would stage through newly constructed airfields in Chengtu, Western China, en route to Japan. After a shakedown mission to Bangkok, the Superforts mounted their first effort on Japan on June 15, 1944, hitting the Yawata steel mills. There were many problems and difficulties to be overcome with this new air weapon, and Matterhorn was not a great success. But it did teach valuable lessons on how to operate the big boys in combat, and most important, gave crews a chance to de-bug the complicated giant which had not been fully flight-tested when its combat appearance was demanded. The experiences in China came in handy when the final B-29 assault on Japan was begun from the Mariana Islands on the Pacific side of the Empire.

In the Marianas, crews began to fly in their Superforts in early October of 1944. First to land was "Jostlin' Josie, The Pacific Pioneer," flown by Brig. Gen. Haywood S. Hansell, Jr., Comander of the 21st Bomber Command. Four airfields there, two on Tinian, two on Guam, and one on Saipan, would eventually house the 20th Air Force, one wing per base, each wing having up to 180 aircraft and 12,000 men.

At first the giants flew training missions against Truk and other by-passed Jap strongholds in the Central Pacific. The kickoff to Japan proper took place on November 24, 1944, when 111 B-29's struck Tokyo. The initial months of the 3,000-mile round-trip, high-altitude, pinpoint bombing missions were not encouraging. Going into Japan at high altitudes the Superforts were meeting phenomenal, mysterious head winds (later found to be jetstreams) which increased their gas consumption and allowed less bomb load than desired. Many could not make it back to the Marianas, especially if damaged by flak or fighters, and they had to ditch at sea. Strong Japanese home fighter defenses would throw up 200 to 300 fighters against 75 to 100 ship formations. Losses were high in aircraft and crews, and achievements were low. Thus an intermediate base was needed between the Marianas and Japan. Iwo Jima was ideal. In February of 1945, Marines landed there and captured the island in a vicious campaign. From airstrips on Iwo, long-range fighters joined the B-29 formations over Japan and onto Iwo would land those Superforts en route home, if necessary.

In January, 1945, General LeMay was ordered to the Marianas from the 20th Bomber Command in India to replace General Hansell. LeMay's orders were to get better results. He tried a variety of tactics, largely against the aircraft industry but still the mission losses were unacceptable and the achievements were only one third of the maximum potential of the force in the Marianas. Out of 350 B-29's in the Marianas at that time, only 130 were getting to Japan. A radical change in operations was necessary.

Thus it was in March of 1945 that LeMay made an important decision — to send his mass formations over Japan at night in low-level incendiary attacks rather than high-altitude daytime strikes. It would mean less gas consumed, more bomb load per plane and negligible fighter opposition. At stake was the gamble of his men's lives and $200 million worth of airplanes on an unproven combat tactic.

On March 10, the first of such attacks took place when 324 B-29's (334 took off — 10 turned back) burned 15.8 square miles out of the heart of Tokyo, killing more than 80,000 people and destroying one fourth of all the buildings in that city. It was followed by four more in quick succession, two on Nagoya, and one each on Osaka and Kobe — wiping out a total of 32 square miles of urban area. Very minor losses in B-29's and crews were experienced. The LeMay plan was a fantastic success. The Superforts had finally found a way to destroy Japan.

This was not a campaign against the people. Circumstances forced such strategy since Japanese industry, partly destroyed in factories, was being relocated in thousands of homes and small buildings throughout the length and breadth of highly populated cities. And it was the destruction of the industrial potential of the enemy that had to be accomplished to bring the war to a close. The first four fire-bomb raids proved incendiary attacks could wipe out war production, as well as undermine the people's will to resist any longer.

And so began the great obliteration of Japan from the air.

Maj. Gen. Curtis E. LeMay, commander of the B-29 offensive against Japan. His decision to switch the tactics of his Superfort strikes from high-altitude pinpoint mission to low-level night fire bomb raids on Japan constitutes one of the great military decisions of all time.

Meanwhile, from February 16 through March, Admiral Marc Mitscher's Task Force 58, composed of 16 aircraft carriers, swept into Japanese waters to hit airfields on the Tokyo plains and on Okinawa, destroying 648 enemy aircraft and 30,000 tons of shipping. In conjunction, the B-29's diverted part of their operations to mining Japanese coastal waters, planting more than 1,000 tons of mines (12,000 mines) at the entrances of the Shimonoseki Straits, closing the Inland Sea of Japan to all large vessels, and in the Kure-Hiroshima harbor where the Jap fleet was hiding out.

All this air activity was aimed at sealing off Japanese forces in preparation for the landings on Okinawa, the final Allied stepping-stone to Japan.

The Okinawa campaign, March 18 to June 21, was the last and for the naval forces the most violent of all in World War II. It involved three separate carrier task forces (around 50 carriers) in addition to bombers and fighters of Gen. George Kenney's Far East Air Forces (the 5th, 7th, 13th), the 14th and the 20th Air Forces, and Marine Air Units.

The campaign was inaugurated by Task Force 58 carrier air strikes on

Kyushu and Okinawa, destroying 428 enemy aircraft. A few days later, on April 1, after heavy pounding from the air and the sea, Army and Marine troops landed on the western shores of Okinawa and captured the Yontan airfield in the first round of bitter land fighting that would last 81 days.

On April 6 the Japanese air force reacted violently to this invasion by launching against the Allied amphibious forces a series of 500 to 600 mass plane suicide attacks from bases in Japan. Between April 6 and May 21 the Japanese kamikaze forces made seven such mass attacks — the greatest air effort Japan put forth in the entire war. Fifteen carriers were struck by the human guided missiles, along with numerous surface ships, landing craft and warships. A total of 35 ships were sunk and 299 damaged by the kamikazes, giving the Navy the heaviest punishment in its entire history.

So strong was the Japanese air defense of Okinawa that from April 17 to May 11, 20th Air Force B-29's, at the request of the Navy, were diverted from their strategic bombing campaign to make 97 attacks on Kyushu and Shikoku airfields in what was to be a final step in the destruction of the Japanese air force. The diversion proved wise. By May 11, the 500-600-plane kamikaze forces had dwindled to flights of 50 or 60 planes and after that dribbled off even more.

For the entire three months of the Okinawa campaign, Navy carrier forces operated continuously within a 60-square-mile area northeast of Okinawa, launching their planes to support ground forces, intercepting enemy aircraft and hitting airfields on Japan proper. It was the most extensive carrier support of any amphibious campaign of the war. Carrier aircraft made over 40,000 combat sorties, destroyed 2,516 enemy aircraft, dropped 8,500 tons of bombs and 50,000 rockets on enemy positions. Marine Corps squadrons ashore destroyed 506 Japanese aircraft, expended 1,800 tons of bombs on enemy positions and 15,865 rockets. The carrier *Essex* logged 79 consecutive days of combat — a record in naval carrier operations.

Although direct air support to the Okinawa landings was given by the Navy, the principal task of the Army Air Forces in preparation for the invasion took place in areas far distant from the immediate operations. Elements of Far East Air Forces and the 14th Air Force attacked a variety of targets to prevent Japan's reinforcement of the Okinawa garrison. For example, in China the 14th Air Force struck at Japanese coastal shipping and in April, as enemy bombers were massing at Shanghai for attacks on our Okinawa invasion fleet, the 14th swept in to wipe them out. The Jap did not make a single attack from Shanghai against our Okinawa operation.

As the Okinawa show developed, loose ends were being tied up to the south and east. The 13th Air Force pounded the 7,000 Jap defenders around the Balikpapan oil center in

Borneo for 18 consecutive days. When Australian troops landed on the Borneo shores, not one was killed and only 20 were wounded. In China the campaign reached the final stage. For five weeks of concentrated effort, the 14th Air Force relentlessly hammered at Japanese forces, enabling Chinese ground troops to repulse a Jap land drive on the 14th's Chinkiang air base, supply center for the entire guerrilla airfield system in China. This virtually marked the end of the war there, for the Japanese began retreating from bases captured earlier, abandoning their last supply route to Malaya.

Step by step the circle constricted around Japan as all her outer defenses crumbled. By June 21 the coral of Okinawa was being blasted and shoveled, trucked and scraped into the world's largest air base. What the island meant as a base of operations was obvious, even to the enemy. It opened the front gate to the Japanese homeland and began the final blockade. From Okinawa air forces were able to roam the whole of the Nippon inner empire. This was mastery of the air, final and complete.

Air strength was being concentrated on "Okee" from all over the globe for the last push. The 5th Air Force

Tense moment aboard the carrier *Essex* as a kamikaze plane glances off the port side. During the Okinawa invasion, the *Essex* set an all-time record of 79 consecutive days of combat operations.

was completing its move from Luzon and Mindoro; the 13th was coming up from Leyte, Morotai, Borneo and Palawan; the 7th, an early arrival from the Marianas, was being reinforced by B-24 "Snoopers" from the 14th Air Force in China and A-26's from the 15th Air Force in Italy; B-29 service units from India and staff personnel from Great Britain were reforming the redeployed European championship 8th Air Force under command of Gen. J. H. "Jimmy" Doolittle, and the 8th was scheduled to receive the next 1,000 B-29's delivered from U.S. factories and training centers. Units of 9th Air Force were en route from France.

Indeed, Okinawa in the spring of 1945 was the Grand Central Station of air power. Everywhere on the island there was feverish anxiety to get operational. Groups took off on missions to Japan 24 hours after arrival, bags still unpacked. They had men, planes, bombs, mess kits, bedrolls, and slit trenches. Ships overcrowded the harbors; troop carrier aircraft shuttled in and out with cargo and personnel; the Air Transport Command terminal loaded and unloaded its C-54's. There just wasn't enough room on the island for everybody, yet somehow there was.

While all this was going on, the 20th Air Force B-29's from the Marianas continued their fire-bomb raids on Japanese cities incessantly. By June 7, productive capacity of the five major Japanese cities had been destroyed. The only large city left untouched throughout the war was Kyoto, historic center of Japanese culture and religion.

The 20th was now up to full strength — 1,000 Superfortresses and 83,000 men. Included was the 58th Wing, redeployed from China, and a special wing, the 315th, consisting of radar-equipped, stripped-down aircraft for special missions. With their electronic target-finding devices, the 315th completely destroyed the nine principal oil-refining and storage plants of Japan in 15 strikes, knocking out 6,055,000 barrels of storage tank capacity. One synthetic oil plant, at Ube, was not only demolished, but actually *sunk* because bombs broke dikes protecting the reclaimed land on which the plant had been built. Attacks were made at night in single-file formation, and all target areas were less than one-half square mile each.

Between July 10 and August 15, British Carrier Task Force 37 composed of four to five carriers, and U.S. Navy Carrier Task Force 38 (18 carriers), ranged unmolested off Japanese shores hitting airfields, war and merchant shipping, naval bases and military installations from the northern island of Hokkaido to Kyushu in the south. In this final carrier action of the war the Navy reported 1,223 aircraft destroyed (over 1,000 caught on the ground), 23 warships and 48 merchantmen sunk. Complementing the Navy sweeps, the 20th Air Force B-29 mining operations were accelerated sealing off Korea and North China shipping lanes by mining all principal Japanese harbors, an operation that accounted for close to one million tons of shipping. By the end of the war, Japan, at one time a great maritime nation with nearly six million tons of shipping (to which was added 3,520,568 tons during the war), had only 231 ships left (about 860,000 tons) and much of it in repair — so effective had been air attack (2,275,197 tons sunk), submarine operations (5,128,425 tons sunk), surface warships and mines.

By mid-July, B-29's were as thick as locusts over Japan, bombing day and night with virtually no aerial opposition. During the last month, only four U.S. planes were lost. When the largest cities had been destroyed, incendiary attacks were switched to secondary industrial centers. Formations of 50 to 100 Superforts would daily strike at separate targets. This hitting of many different places in all parts of Japan at once completely confused enemy fighter forces. They didn't have enough planes left to intercept more than one or two of the attacking formations, and were hoarding what aircraft they had left for use in kamikaze attacks against an expected U.S. surface invasion.

Toward the end of July opposition was so meager that General LeMay announced in advance what the target would be for the next day and warned the Japanese people to get out of town. On July 27, 60,000 pamphlets were dropped on 11 cities foretelling their impending doom. The next day, as promised, six of the 11 were hit.

Japanese officials admitted that the pamphlets alone caused conditions close to nationwide panic, scaring tens of thousands away from their jobs and into the hills.

In all, 58 cities had been burned out, a total of 178 square miles of urban area. Gone were 23 major factories of Japan's aircraft industry, six main army and navy arsenals, and numerous steel, petroleum and gas plants. In addition, 540 other important factories engaged in war production were obliterated as were thousands of small machine-tool shops, assembly plants and home industries. Materiel destruction in Japan staggered belief. In many cities wreckage existed as far as eye could see. It had taken the Superforts 37½ weeks to drop 157,000 tons of bombs. When August 1 rolled around they were prepared to let go an equal amount in the next three months.

Just as important as the elimination of factories and military centers, was the destruction of Japanese morale. The spiritual support for carrying on the war was gone. Faith in military and civilian leadership had disappeared. The two million homes burned down, the ten million people wandering aimlessly around the country without a roof over their heads or food to eat, the hundreds of thousands killed and injured in the firebomb raids made it clear to those who still lived that carrying on the war was futile. But there was no way for a mandate to be made known in the feudal society of Japan.

The Japanese Empire lay battered and bruised as the war entered the first week of August, 1945. Fighters from Iwo Jima, B-29's from the Marianas, aircraft of all types from Far East Air Forces on Okinawa and from carrier decks, ranged almost at will over the entire country, hard pressed at times to find targets. Even so, and ignoring advice of air leaders that Japan would soon surrender, preparations were being made in Washington and in the Far East for an amphibious invasion of the Japanese homeland, estimating a million American casualties in the operation.

Thus was the stage set when three Superforts from the 509th Composite Wing, based on Tinian Island, appeared over Hiroshima at approximately 8:15 A.M. on August 6. Three parachutes (carrying scientific instruments) blossomed out from one bomb bay, and a dark object hurtled down from another on its history-making 47-second descent. In a holocaust of atomic violence, more than 80,000 people were killed and the center of Hiroshima vanished from the face of the earth. Three days later, on August 9, the mushroom cloud arose again over Nagasaki. The next day, August 10, 1945, the Japanese government sued for peace.

The two atomic bombs had brought that decision to a head — a decision turning in the minds of millions of Japanese as far back as March 1945 and discussed by government officials for weeks prior.

On August 11, President Truman ordered Gen. Carl A. "Tooey" Spaatz, who had arrived earlier from Europe, to take over the United States Army Strategic Air Force (USASTAF — the combined 20th and 8th Air Forces), to cease all strategic air operations and recall all planes that might be in the air. This was done. By August 14, however, negotiations were still hanging fire and both General Kenney (Far East Air Forces) and General Spaatz were ordered to resume bombing.

And so it was that on August 14, 449 B-29's left the Marianas for a daylight strike, and that night 372 more from Guam took off, along with seven special mission Superforts from the 509th Composite Group and 186 fighter escorts.

It was this day that USASTAF sent 1,014 aircraft over Japan — thus fulfilling a pledge made by General "Hap" Arnold to the Japanese people earlier in the war that the United States would send 1,000 planes to bomb them.

There were no losses on this final gigantic mission, and before the last B-29 returned to its base, President Truman had announced the unconditional surrender of the Empire of Japan, and directed cessation of air strikes.

Between August 14 and "V-J" Day, B-29's and fighters from Iwo Jima sallied over Japan in great fleets in a "display of air power" — just in case. The planes carried ammunition, but no bombs.

When General MacArthur landed unarmed at Atsugi Airdrome in Tokyo on August 30, 98 B-29's staged an exhibition low-level flight — so fearsome a symbol had the B-29 become in the minds of the Japanese. And as the formal surrender ceremony took place aboard the battleship *Missouri* in Tokyo Bay on September 2, 1945, a massive formation of 462 B-29's circled in the sky above it — a significant and fitting perspective for the historic occasion.

Missions continued for General Spaatz's 20th Air Force and General Kenney's Far East Air Forces well into September. A constant stream of FEAF troop carrier aircraft landed occupation troops on Japanese soil. Except for a few more displays of air power over Japan, Korea and China, most B-29 flights were mercy missions, dropping supplies and medicine to POW camps throughout Japan, China, Philippines, Formosa and Korea. An estimated 4,470 tons were thus dispatched by parachute to 63,500 prisoners. Eight aircraft were lost with 77 casualties in this operation. One such mercy flight to a POW camp in North Korea ended in tragedy. The B-29 was shot down by a Soviet Russian fighter.

In sharp contrast, the giant Superfort which had rained from the heavens death and destruction on an empire, suddenly became an agent of humanitarianism, a servant of mercy, a symbol of hope and a return to peace.

It was at the Cairo Conference in November 1943 that the U.S. pledged to put the B-29 Superforts into action against the Japanese homeland and Manchuria from bases in China. This was "Matterhorn." And shortly thereafter one of the greatest industrial and training efforts ever concentrated on one weapon system was inaugurated in the U.S. for B-29 flight and ground crewmen.

By January of 1944, the first maintenance and repair men were shipped to India and in April the first Superfortress landed in India. It was followed shortly by the rest of the 58th Bomb Wing, the "Hellbirds," under command of the dynamic Brig. Gen. Kenneth B. Wolfe.

Meanwhile, in China, thousands of coolies were rushing the Chengtu airdrome into completion, breaking rock by hand, packing runways with man-drawn rollers, moving earth in small baskets. Superforts made scores of thousand-mile flights from India to China over the Himalayan Hump, bringing in their own gasoline, bombs and supplies.

On June 6, as Allied invasion forces poured ashore on the Normandy beaches in Europe, the shakedown Superfortress mission from bases in India hit Bangkok, Thailand and, although results were not good, the 58th was ready to strike Japan. Nine days later, on June 15, 1944 (the day we began the invasion of Saipan in the Mariana Islands to establish B-29 bases there), 15 Superforts took off for a night strike on the Yawata Steel Works on the Japanese homeland island of Kyushu. It was a long, suspense-filled pioneer mission, and as all such are, the unknowns ahead were greater than the knowns.

Among the 15 giant bombers was one named King Size *and in the bombardier's slot crouched a lieutenant whose salvo on Yawata were the first bombs to drop on the sacred soil of the Empire since the historic Doolittle raid in 1942. Here is the lieutenant's story as* King Size *climbed for altitude into the China skies and headed toward Japan.*

No Screen to Hide Us

Wilbur H. Morrison

RUGGED mountains surrounded the valley and we had to climb quickly to 10,000 feet to protect ourselves from the rocky linings of the clouds ahead. We flew along in daylight for three hours or so, watching the changeless scenery below us, worrying about the gasoline, and not thinking too much about the target itself. We had been told about the hundreds of guns and the idea of going over Yawata at 8,000 feet had sent shivers down our spines. However, with the exception of Loberg, we were all ignorant of combat conditions and for once ignorance was bliss. From time to time Albert recommended lower power settings and he and Loberg worked in complete harmony throughout the trip.

The sun set behind us and the deep-ening shadows obscured our view except for tiny blinking lights from the towns and villages below us. Riding on top of the clouds, with a universe of thousands of stars above us, we felt cozy and warm in our pressurized cabin. It was dark, except for the flashing lights of the automatic pilot and the fluorescent lights of the instrument panel.

At the coast, White picked up a checkpoint by radar which indicated we were on course so we set out across the Yellow Sea with renewed confidence. Now and then lights blinked on and off below us as some unsuspecting Jap ship passed beneath.

A darker mass appeared ahead in the enveloping blackness of night. A blur of solidity, with a few scattered lights, was visible as we drew closer.

"Dick!" I yelled.

"Go ahead."

"There's a large island just below us."

"That's Saishu. We're not far from Japan."

We made a turn to the left. I noticed a bright glow off to the right and called Loberg's attention to it.

"I wonder what that is," I said curiously.

The interphone clicked and Loberg's deep voice said, "It's the target. Those are searchlights."

I was fascinated, with a peculiar tense feeling forming in the pit of my stomach.

"Pilot to crew. We're coming up on the target. Put on your flak suits and helmets."

After turning on the I.P., the lights separated and formed distinctive thin beams of light, shooting higher and higher until their brilliance was lost in the atmosphere. Mingling with the searchlight beams were curving arcs of tracer bullets and wicked red flashes of heavy ack-ack firing at an invisible B-29.

The clouds had dwindled and there was no protecting screen to hide us, except for the cover of darkness that still surrounded us.

"Radar to bombardier, over."

"Guh . . ." My throat was stiff and tight, but at last the words came out. "Go ahead, Whizzer."

"We're coming up to land. The target should be just ahead."

I leaned over the bombsight and peered down. But the searchlights had been turned off and I could see only an indistinct blur below, with nothing to indicate where the target lay.

"It's too dark to see the target," I called. "You'd better count on a radar run unless I call you."

"I'll see what I can do. The return is not very good."

The darkness was rent wide open and batteries of searchlights combed the sky for us, wavering for a few seconds, and then swinging straight toward us with unerring accuracy. They enveloped us in blinding light. We felt naked and alone in an unfriendly world, but the intense light was no help in locating the target. On the contrary, the land below appeared covered with a milky-white film, interrupted here and there by flashes, which went off and on with precise regularity.

"Bombardier to radar."

"Yes."

"I still can't see the target. You'll have to make the run. I'm opening the bomb-bay doors and setting up the racks for release."

"Roger."

King Size lurched violently and then rolled to an even keel. I glanced nervously at Loberg, but the cause of it was soon evident. Red flashes appeared all around us and long strings of tracers arched up from the smaller-caliber guns on the ground. The searchlights never wavered but followed us with maddening intensity.

Wilbur Morrison, back row, far right, and the crew of the *King Size*. In late 1944, these men dropped the first bombs on Japan since the Doolittle raid. Their target was the Yawata steel works.

Giant mushrooming flares floated down on parachutes, lighting up the night in ghastly yellow.

"Left gunner to pilot."

"Go ahead, Scheinman."

"I just saw a night fighter fly over us."

"Keep a good lookout," Loberg cautioned. "The fighters can see us a lot better than we can see them. Make sure it's not a B-29."

The red flashes and the gray puffs of smoke were closer now and more intense. We were getting into the inner-defense zone and could expect to receive everything they had to throw up at us.

King Size rocked and rolled, and the bursts echoed against the sides of the fuselage. It seemed impossible we had not been hard hit, but we were not through it yet.

Making a quick decision, Loberg called White. "Will it be all right if I turn off a bit, and then go back on course?"

240

"Yes, sir," Whizzer said.

We turned first to the left, and then to the right, before turning back on the target heading.

Thicker and thicker grew the puffs of antiaircraft fire as we neared the bomb-release line. I glanced back at Loberg and it was then I became really scared. The white light accentuated the tight lines in his face, and his mouth was drawn rigid about his teeth. It wasn't a frightened look, but those lines expressed the emotion of a man cornered and fighting for his life.

The doors were open and the switches were on so I had nothing to do but sit and wait for bombs away, with my feet beating a rhythmic tattoo on the floorboards and my heart pounding like a trip-hammer.

"Bombs away!"

I quickly salvoed and pulled the door handle up as Loberg put *King Size*'s nose down and we dived away from the target. After what seemed like an eternity the refreshing blackness closed in on us again and we were safe.

We turned south, still inland, intending to pull out to sea as soon as we were clear of the target, but fate intervened in the form of more searchlights. A whole battery erupted into light below and those moving fingers were again probing for us. They swept the sky for a few seconds, then swung directly toward us, forming a cone with us at the peak. Loberg wheeled *King Size* violently, trying to shake

them, but it was no use. They clung obstinately. I felt the nose of the plane go down and I glanced at the airspeed indicator on my instrument panel. My heart seemed to jump into my throat. We were doing three hundred miles an hour, three ten, three twenty, and still we picked up speed until the indicator shuddered a bit as it touched three forty.

I glanced apprehensively at the ground and could plainly see houses and fields. "We're pretty low," I said to Loberg. "I can see the ground."

He pulled up sharply and the indicator fell off until it read 175. *King Size* groaned and creaked at this rough treatment, but we were out of the searchlights at last. Now we were too close to heavily defended Nagasaki for comfort, so we headed for the coast and flew out to sea for the return trip home.

There were only a few B-29's on the field as we circled and came in for our landing. After taxiing to the parking area, we climbed wearily from the plane to meet the grinning faces of our mechanics and Chinese guards.

At the interrogation we learned that we were the first plane of our group to hit the target, and second in the whole bomber command. Late arrivals over the target reported huge fires started by the pathfinders and we all agreed the mission was a success.

Despite the fact that we were dead tired, we were not inclined to go to bed. It was announced that an eyewitness account of the raid would be broadcast from the Chungking radio station, shortwaved to the United States by a correspondent who had flown on the raid.

The Chinese program ended and an American voice came through the loudspeaker. "The Empire of Japan is no longer isolated from the battlefields of the world," the voice said. "Tonight waves of B-29's attacked Yawata's large steel plant successfully despite heavy flak and night fighters. The strategic bombing of Japan has begun."

EDITOR'S NOTE: During the next five months, B-29's from Chinese and Indian bases struck at targets in Manchuria, Kyushu, Thailand, Burma, Korea, Formosa, Sumatra and on Singapore in a record 3,800-mile mission. Superfort reconnaissance sorties totaled more than the bombing sorties and provided a complete photographic report on all Japanese military and industrial installations from Kyushu and Manchuria to Singapore.

The China-based B-29 operations were uneconomical. It took 12 ferry trips over the Hump to enable each plane to fly one mission to Japan. But they accomplished one very important thing. The rush of war events required the B-29 to be sent into combat before it had been fully flight-tested. And it fell to the crews flying combat missions in China to debug the giant plane while they carried their war to the enemy. It was rough and costly in terms of men and aircraft lost, but the war dictated that it be done this way. The modifications found necessary in China were fully utilized when the giants began to fly out of the Marianas in formations of 600 to 800 aircraft.

In August of 1944, Maj. Gen. Curtis LeMay took over command of the B-29 20th Bomber Command in China and began smoothing out the rough edges of long-range, heavy-bomber operations. In January, 1945, when LeMay moved to Saipan to take command there of the 20th Air Force offensive from the Marianas, he applied many of the lessons learned in flying the Superforts out of China bases.

The B-29 strategic air offensive against Japan from bases in the Marianas was kicked off on November 24, 1944 when Brig. Gen. Emmett O'Donnell led 111 Superforts on a strike against industrial targets in Tokyo.

For several months following, Brig. Gen. Haywood Hansell, Jr., sent out his 21st Bomber Command Superforts on the 3,000-mile round-trip flight in daylight precision strikes. Losses to Jap fighters and flak over the homeland were not encouraging. Many of the big ships, damaged over Japan, could not make the long flight back to the Marianas and went down at sea. Despite air-sea rescue operations valuable crews were lost. An intermediate base was needed. From it fighters could rise up and join the B-29 formations en route to Japanese targets, and of equal importance, combat-crippled Superforts could make emergency landings there.

Midway between Japan and the Marianas, in the Bonin Island Chain lay an enemy-held rocky volcanic protrusion called Iwo Jima which the 7th Air Force B-24's had been pounding with regularity to keep Jap fighters from attacking the Japan-bound formations. It was ideal for the task required and on February 19, 1945 (after 20 days of consecutive air bombardment) U.S. Marines landed on Iwo to meet one of the bloodiest battles of the Pacific War. The predicted four-day campaign took four weeks. Unknown to us, the Japanese had run heavy reinforcements into Iwo shortly before our amphibious assault on the island.

The volcanic island was cut through with caves, crevices and passageways, strong natural fortifications from which the Marines literally had to dig and blast out the enemy.

Iwo gave us the base for P-51 escort of the B-29 missions, and soon the long-range Mustangs ran fighter sweeps over the homeland, directly joining the B-29 knockout blows against vital airfields and industry. As expected, the island provided a haven for B-29's which had gotten into trouble en route to or returning from missions over Japan. It also became a staging point from which the Superforts flew missions as far north as Korea, 2,000 miles from Saipan. By the end of the war 2,400 Superforts had made emergency landings on Iwo and more than 25,000 crewmen owed their lives to the island, exceeding by far the 4,900 lost in its capture.

Life on Iwo was no ball for the hard-working ground crews who kept the P-51's in the air and repaired the damaged B-29's. The dramatic Marine raising of the flag on Mount Suribachi did not mean the place was entirely secure, for the nature of the island, undercut with caves and hideaways, sheltered enemy soldiers for weeks and months afterward. And the ground crews, living in tents near the airfield, were never safe from groups of enemy soldiers who would come out after dark like rats, infiltrate the tent areas to forage or banzai charge the Americans in despera-

tion. One such incident occurred in the middle of a quiet night on March 26, 1945 when 400 Japs made a banzai attack on a fighter unit near the airstrip. S/Sgt. Harry Hamilton and nine other P-51 mechanics were asleep in their tent when it happened. . . .

Banzai!

From "Air Force" Magazine

A BLADE ripped the canvas and a grenade hissed in through the opening. It rolled across the tent and stopped under a packing case. Hamilton was blown out of bed and awakened on the dirt floor with his shoulder nicked. Bullets sprayed the tent at waist level. Rifle barrels poked through holes in the north and south ends of the tents and bullets peppered the double rows of cots.

"It was cockeyed. The whole affair," Hamilton said afterward.

The first thing he did, after finding himself on the floor, was to wrap a tourniquet about the leg of a badly wounded companion, a rather confused, automatic reaction which saved the man's life.

Cpl. Bernard J. Overesch, hearing the Jap at the south end of the tent, put a carbine to his shoulder and waited. A form then appeared and more bullets sprayed the tent. Overesch pulled the trigger and nothing happened. A shot from somewhere else felled the Jap, but not before one of the mechanics lay mortally

wounded and another seriously wounded.

Cpl. Hiram R. Savidge, aroused by the commotion, got up and modestly wrapped himself in a blanket. Later he found that a bullet had cut the blanket.

By that time the groans of one of the wounded mechanics was drawing fire.

"There wasn't time to be gentle," Sergeant Hamilton reported after it was all over. "I gagged him to keep quiet, then crawled to the south end of the tent."

Two Japs were standing just outside the door talking to a fatally wounded comrade. Hamilton drew a bead and pulled the trigger. This carbine also jammed. He grabbed another one. It jammed. That was too much. Hamilton began to swear.

Outside, the dying Jap stirred in protest: "Don't talk like that," he jeered. "It isn't nice."

The two other Japs were under cover then and Hamilton moved back to the center of the tent and cut a small slit near the ground. Through

Domelike Mt. Suribachi dominates the landscape around No. 1 airstrip on Iwo Jima. By spring of 1945, Iwo was a hornet's nest of American fighters. Protruding guns, upper left, are knocked-out Japanese antiaircraft.

this he could see a foxhole between his tent and the one adjacent. It was occupied by seven Japs.

On the other side three Japs were crawling closer to the tent. Hamilton fixed his sights on one of them. Suddenly a Jap officer dropped to his knees. In his upraised hand was a potato-masher grenade. Hamilton shifted sights to the officer and fired. The officer doubled up, still clutching the grenade. It exploded, and the other Japs laughed, as if it had been a boisterous joke.

Action then turned to a Jap who was reluctant to die. S/Sgt. Milwood Hlebof hit him first. The Jap gibbered. Cpl. Frank B. McCollum opened up with his carbine. He fired 15 shots and saw the Jap flinch with the impact of each one. When the clip was empty, the Jap still stared forward, babbling.

McCollum gave up on this particular Jap and Hamilton took over. "I fired two more shots into him and the guy still kept up his talking and hysterical laughter. I figured my carbine was shooting high so I aimed at the bridge of his nose. The bullet drilled him right between the eyes, and he folded up like a rag."

When dawn sunlight broke over the area, the battle was over and Hamilton suddenly remembered that the Jap officer he had shot had been wearing a saber.

"I ran out to get it," he told the correspondent. "But too late. Some souvenir hunter got there ahead of me."

245

Top Navy ace, Comdr. David McCampbell. Leader of Air Group "Fabled Fifteen," McCampbell downed 34 Japanese planes, destroyed 21 on the ground — the largest number of planes accounted for by an American pilot in one combat tour.

Second highest Navy ace of the war was Cecil Harris. In 81 days of combat, Harris downed 24 Japanese, getting four planes in one day on three separate occasions.

There is an old airman's saying: "Aviators don't last long after they get famous." In contradiction to this, top U.S. Navy aces in the Pacific seemed to live charmed lives. Flying from the carriers of the Navy's fast-moving task forces that roamed the Jap-held, island-dotted Central Pacific, Navy pilots shot down 2,400 enemy aircraft. They also destroyed over 6,000 on the ground in America's surge toward Japan and victory. The top four Navy aces were among 330 of their fellow flyers who earned that title in the Pacific. Uniquely, all four survived the war.

U.S. Navy Aces

A Picture Story

Lt. Eugene Valencia, third-ranking Navy ace, ended his combat with 23 Japanese planes to his credit.

Fourth-ranking Navy ace was Alexander Vraciu, with 19 enemy planes in the air, 21 on the ground.

It is a lonely and disturbing thing to make a decision that can change the lives of millions of people. Occasionally, throughout history, military commanders in the field have faced that heavy moment of responsibility wherein their actions may alter the course of war and reshape human affairs for generations to come.

One such moment took place in the quiet seclusion of a war room on Saipan, headquarters of the 21st Bomber Command in early 1945. The man was Maj. Gen. Curtis E. LeMay, commander of the B-29 strategic offensive against Japan. The decision dictated a switch in the B-29 combat tactics from high-level, precision bombing to mass formation, low-level fire-bomb raids on Japanese cities.

Involved was the commitment of his entire force, his highly trained crews, his costly strategic bombers, his own reputation and that of the Air Force, not to mention the gamble in laying on the line a predominant portion of his nation's military power at a critical time in the war.

Historians have ranked it as the most significant decision of World War II and one of the few top ones in all military history. It broke the back of the Japanese Empire, undermined the people's will to resist, and hastened the Pacific War to an end.

Here for the first time, is the full, detailed, incisive story leading to the historic decision and the events that followed.

The Giant Pays Its Way

Maj. Gene Gurney, USAF

THE ROAD to Tokyo continued to be a long one. Sixteen times General LeMay had sent his bombers to Japan. On all but one of the raids, photo reconnaissance planes returned with disappointing pictures. Not one important target had been destroyed by the 5,000 tons of bombs hurled from the planes of the 21st Bomber Command based in the Mariana Islands. Losses had been high. There had been little damage from flak, but fighter interception and the long overwater flights home had taken their toll. At the end of February, 29 of the command's Superforts had fallen to enemy fighters while flak had downed one; fighters and flak together took nine. Mechanical difficulties had caused the loss of 21 planes; 15 were lost due to unknown causes.

The men were becoming unnerved. "Ironpants" LeMay tried every tactical trick in the book while his crews cursed both him and their plane.

"Hell," he answered, "I'm not here to win friends. I'm here to win a war. And the only way to do that is for my men to drop the maximum weight of bombs on the target."

LeMay sent them up at night — at high noon — in formation — singly — a hundred at a time — two hundred at a time. Still reconnaissance planes brought back pictures showing targets untouched.

Then early in March, 1945, General LeMay decided on a bold change in tactics.

The B-29 had been considered the perfect tool for daylight precision bombing, and Japan the perfect target. However, there had always been strategists who favored the use of other tactics, and their number increased as the cost of daylight missions went up and it became apparent that pinpoint bombing with high explosives was not producing the results.

Because of their congestion and generally flammable construction, Japanese cities seemed a logical place for the use of incendiary bombs. And as early as March, 1943, tests got under way in the United States to develop a new and more effective fire bomb. At Dugway Proving Ground, Utah, a typical Japanese workers' village was built, complete down to the last detail, including books on shelves, furniture, fences and sheds. It was the work of a New York architect, Antonin Raymond, who had studied in Japan for 18 years.

The houses were accurate in every detail, including furnishings, such as grass and fiber mats which the Navy brought in from Hawaii. Five blocks, complete with streets, included 100

June, 1945. Death of a Superfort on the bomb run over Japan as it is caught by enemy fire and disintegrates.

residences and a few small industrial buildings.

A nearby Army post provided fire fighters with equipment believed identical to that available to the Japanese. In Japanese air-raid warden fashion, these men were stationed in the "village." As fast as the fire bombs were dropped, they went into action with their fire-fighting equipment.

In early 1944, a bomb was developed which the fire fighters could not cope with. Air Force experts knew they had the answer. It was a petroleum or jellied gasoline bomb (called *napalm*) perfected with the aid of the Standard Oil Company, duPont chemists and the National Research Defense Council. All that remained now was the problem of effective delivery.

The 314th Bombardment Wing had just arrived on Guam. It was commanded by Brig. Gen. Thomas S. Power (now Commander - in - Chief, SAC). Power had flown B-24's in Italy before becoming a highly successful troubleshooter in the B-29 training program of the 2nd Air Force. He took delivery of his wing's first 25 Superforts on February 23, 1945 and was immediately directed by General LeMay to participate in a maximum effort against Tokyo on the 25th — the objectives being to knock out the city's growing home industries.

Power's men had hardly unpacked; they had no training period to familiarize themselves with local flying conditions. Despite those handicaps General Power agreed to put up 22 of his first 25 Superforts to make an even formation and he led his unit on its first bombing mission, an event which was to help bring about radical changes in bombing tactics, and effectiveness of the B-29 air offensive against Japan.

The 22 shiny new bombers of the 314th Wing and 22 green crews took off from Guam and headed out over the ocean for the assembly point 300 miles south of Japan. The weather, passable at first, grew worse, forcing the formation down until they were flying on the deck. Rain was pouring faster than the windshield wipers could clear it away and as they neared the rendezvous point, planes were scattered in every direction. The weather had ruined the carefully worked out plan for bombing Tokyo.

Realizing that he had to get his crews out before there was a collision, Tom Power gave the order to climb and led the way up through the soup. At 15,000 feet he broke out between two cloud layers. Only one of his original wingmen had managed to follow him, but there were planes in from all other squadrons. They formed up and continued to climb. Finally the clouds thinned but by then they were flying in heavy snow. Power lined the formation up, and made the bomb run at 25,000 feet without ever breaking out of the weather.

All told, 172 Superforts made it to the target that day. Using radar they dropped their bombs, the first big-scale fire-bomb raid on Tokyo.

Japanese newspapers reported briefly that "130 B-29's appeared over the capital, inflicting only slight damages," including destruction of imperial property at Omiya Palace.

The next day Tokyo radio reported two B-29's over the city They were post strike reconnaissance planes. Against the snow covering the ground, the areas blackened by fire stood out clearly. Several small spots indicated adjacent blocks had been destroyed. One big black area covering a square mile dominated the photos; it had been totally burned out.

As General Power studied the reconnaissance pictures of his wing's first raid, he speculated on what would have happened if more planes had come in lower with a bigger bomb load. If a Superfort didn't have to climb to a high altitude, he reasoned, it could carry more bombs. With his operations officer, Col. Hewitt T. Wheless, he discussed the possibility of sending low-flying B-29's to Tokyo by routing them up the peninsula on the east side of Tokyo Bay on radar, then turning them toward Tokyo at a certain point. Each B-29 would have an assigned heading and speed and bombing time to insure the desired concentration of fires from the incendiaries.

"We wanted to get in below the level of the flak and above the range of the small cannon," said Colonel Wheless.

Word of the studies being made by the 314th reached General LeMay at

Flak over Tokyo was thick. This B-29 crewman inspects the riddled tail end of his Superfort after a mission to the Japanese capital.

21st Bomber Command Headquarters. Late one night — it was close to 2 A.M. — he walked over to the makeshift quarters which Power and Wheless shared. "Tom, what's all this talk about fire-bomb raids?" he asked.

Power explained the idea which he and Wheless had been working on. Wheless, who was asleep, was called out to join the discussion. General LeMay listened intently and asked them to work out an overall plan for a low-level raid. He gave them 24 hours to get it ready.

Power and Wheless went to work at once. By that afternoon they had outlined their idea for a low-level incendiary raid and turned it over to the boss. LeMay studied it, checked the reconnaissance photos of the February 25th raid, and looked once more at the weather charts. The success of precision bombing depended on visual conditions over the target. Almost all his missions had been forced to rely on radar because of bad weather at high altitudes over Japan, and weather during the spring months was going to get worse, not better. That meant more bombing by radar, and radar bombing was of necessity area bombing, not precision bombing. Against Japanese cities incendiaries would work better than high explosives in area-bombing missions. Coming in at a low level would greatly increase the effectiveness of his planes. It would save gas; it would be easier on the engines; and it would probably take the Japanese completely by surprise.

Perhaps, then, low-level incendiary attacks *were* the answer. Fire bombs could do the trick if they were spread thickly enough. But could the B-29's get in there at low level and get out again? He might, LeMay thought, be sending his men on a mission from which most wouldn't return. He alone could issue the orders. The responsibility for failure would be his and his alone.

Day and night LeMay worked on plans; he studied strike results, weather forecasts, intelligence reports — everything that might affect the success of a bombing mission. He was not an ostentatious worker. Sometimes he appeared merely to be sitting at his desk, staring off into space. A staff officer remarked: "The General does less work than any man in the Army. His desk is almost always clean. We can walk in on him at almost any time of day or night and find him writing letters to the wives and children of the men in his command who have been lost in action — or just sitting there, sucking at that oversize pipe of his."

"He doesn't appear to work much," said the captain who had been LeMay's aide for three years, "but he *thinks* more than any man I have ever known. In England he averaged no more than four hours' sleep a night for over a year. Here, on Guam, he will be on the job all day, see his planes off at dusk, stay up all night to get their reports, and at eight in the morning he is back at his desk, prompt, energetic, fresh. It would kill most men."

During the first days of March, General LeMay made the decision — probably the greatest one-man decision ever made in military history.

It came late in the afternoon. An all-day drizzle had turned the roads around the 21st Bomber Command Headquarters into a sticky red ooze. LeMay was alone in the War Room. Hours had ticked by as he sat there, huddled and heavy in a small chair, staring at the maps through those black, overhanging eyebrows. The plan, which was all but formed now, would mean death for the Tokyo industry and hundreds of thousands of Japanese.

Lt. Col. "Pinky" Smith walked into the War Room and stopped short, muttering an apology as he recognized who was there.

The briar pipe waved at him. "No, Pinky, don't go away. I want to talk to you. There is something I've been thinking about — a new way of hitting them up there in the Empire. And I want you to draw me a field order and a plan. Listen . . ."

Pinky listened intently to the quiet, slow words of his boss. What he heard dumbfounded him, made his flesh creep. Smith had been through this before. Once, back in India, he had heard men speak of LeMay as a "butcher" when they learned about one of his plans. Once they had thought of him as a "bomb-crazy madman." But both times LeMay's plans

had worked. They always seemed to work.

"He seems almost like a machine — or a god," said Smith. "Fire a thousand questions at him in an hour. If he'll answer, you can bet that 99 per cent of the answers will be right. He doesn't open his mouth often, but when he does you better listen well — and act. He means every single syllable." But this time the plan Pinky Smith heard was almost unbelievable in big bomber operations.

Finally LeMay stopped; his whole plan was laid out.

There was a moment's silence, then Smith said, "Later, General, when we get down to details, I will need some more information."

"Right. Call me when you need me. One more thing, Pinky, I don't want anyone — anyone at all, mind you, who is not absolutely vital — in on this. I want it kept as quiet as possible."

Smith relayed the General's words to key members of the staff. The comments flowed freely:

"We'll get the holy hell shot out of us. . . ."

"It's nothing but a suicide mission. . . ."

"If we tried this over Germany, we'd lose 80 per cent of our planes. . . ."

The new men — new to LeMay — said again: "He's crazy . . . It's impossible. . . ."

But day and night the men worked; intelligence, operations, ordnance, weather, target information, photo interpretation, maintenance and supply. Only a few down the line knew the plan. They were only told that certain information was wanted, and fast. It was their job to get it. A mission and men depended on its being right.

Quickly it took on shape and detail: wind velocities, bomb loads, gas loads, ammunition loads, man loads; airspeeds, magneto settings, oil pressures; star fixes, courses, Japanese landmarks, ocean landmarks, islands; radio frequencies, distress frequencies, code words, flash signals; number of planes, number of men, number of bombs, number of ambulances, number of doctors; initial points, aiming points, target areas, assembly points; start-engine time, taxi time, takeoff time, Japan time, Washington time, sunrise, sunset; enemy flak, enemy searchlights, enemy submarines, enemy interception, enemy espionage; enemy factories, enemy power plants, enemy canals, enemy docks . . . the Imperial Palace of the Emperor of Japan.

At last it was ready.

"Our bombers will attack in maximum strength and destroy the central industrial area of Tokyo on the night of March 9 . . ."

It was now the job of the wing commanders to go back to their units and brief the men who would fly to Tokyo.

Rosey O'Donnell returned to Saipan, Jim Davies to Tinian, and Tom Power to the 314th to give orders for — The LeMay Plan.

In unventilated war rooms throughout the command, 5,000 airmen crowded onto narrow wooden benches. They were sticky and sweating and uncomfortable, waiting.

In the War Room of the 500th Group on Saipan, for example, every crew bench was packed. Each crew spread over two of the hard, wooden benches, the men up front in the ship — pilots, navigator, bombardier, engineer — sitting on the front bench; left blister, right blister, central fire control, radio, radar and tail gunner sitting on the bench behind. Over each crew hung a sign with the airplane commander's name on it. Some of the names were now replacements for the dead and missing.

The walls of the high double Quonset hut were covered with maps, charts, and photographs of Japan, of the various targets, cities, and factories; of a few of the islands on the way up and back — and news maps of the Italian, French, German and Philippine theaters to enable the men to keep up with the war on other fronts.

At the far end of the Quonset was a big wooden stage from which the briefing officers spoke; back of it were more maps, more charts — and the cold, fatal blackboards covered with sheets of blank brown paper. Unknown to the crews, underneath those sheets of paper was the LeMay Plan — the "bad news for tonight."

The War Room was so tightly packed that those standing could barely reach into their pockets for a smoke.

Five hundred men — scarcely one of them 30 years old — dressed in khaki shorts and open shirts — waited in a kind of forced silence.

Something must be on, something big. There were guards at every entrance, and brown paper concealing the blackboards. The War Room was more crowded than it had ever been before.

"Looks like a big one tonight, Mac."

"Yeah, every guy and his brother is going out."

"Maybe we're going home. . . ."

"Can it! Here's the Old Man."

On stage, center, leaning on the lectern, sandy-haired, blue-eyed Group Commander Dougherty began to talk: "Gentlemen, for tonight we have a new plan. When you hear it, you won't like it. But after you think about it a while — it makes sense. It *should* work. The best brains and the best information have been put into it. And if it does work, tonight can do more than any one raid ever did to bring the end of the war closer.

"Here it is! Three hundred and thirty-nine aircraft from the 21st Bomber Command are scheduled to go to Japan tonight — the largest force of B-29's ever to take off from anywhere."

Every man in the room low-whistled, poked his neighbor and grinned.

"The 73rd Wing will furnish 162 aircraft; the 313th Wing 121, the 314th 56.

"Our bomb load will be all incendiaries. . . ."

The War Room vibrated with a symphonic chord made up of wolf whistles and owl hoots.

One after another the briefing officers spoke.

Group Commander: "Your target is Tokyo. . . ."

Intelligence: "Target information, size of force, tactics. . . ."

Weather: "Tonight there will be a front at last. Over the target there'll be 2/10th cloud cover. . . ."

Bombardier: "Your bomb load will be 12,000 pounds. . . ."

Navigator: "This will be a navigator's mission. . . ."

Engineer: "No auxiliary tanks will be carried tonight. . . ."

Radar Intelligence: "Your radar scope pictures will be set at. . . ."

Communications: "Distress frequencies and code words. . . ."

Thus the LeMay plan was explained to the men who would fly it.

Tonight they would go into Tokyo between 5,000 and 7,500 feet. Every other mission had been flown between 25,000 and 30,000. The altitude had been dropped five miles!

Tonight they would go into the heart of Japan singly. Every other mission had gone over the target in formation. It was formation, interlocking fire, that protected bombers from being slashed by enemy fighters.

Tonight they would go into Tokyo in darkness. For the last ten missions, even during the day, they had been unable to see the target.

Tonight they would fly to Japan,

254

and back — 3,000 miles and more — without any bomb-bay tanks of gasoline. On almost every mission to date planes had dropped into the swallowing Pacific because they ran out of gas on the way home. And all those planes had carried bomb-bay tanks.

Tonight they would carry nothing but fire. The bomb bay of every aircraft would be loaded with tons of fire bombs.

The men were dumbfounded . . . and frightened, at first.

LeMay, the famed high-altitude, formation-flying, precision-bombing strategist, had tossed aside every rule in his own book.

The men turned to each other: Will any of us ever get back? No gas in the bomb bays! Five thousand feet! Didn't they shoot the hell out of us at 25,000 feet?

The factual briefing was over. Group Commander Dougherty walked back to the lectern.

"Tonight there is *no other target* except Tokyo. Tokyo is our primary target, our target of opportunity, our target of last resort. Every single bomb *will be dropped inside Tokyo.*

"There will be no evasion tactics over the target. Enemy flak may be thick and heavy, but still there will be no evasion tactics because of the danger of collision. Tonight we shall have over 300 airplanes up there — so keep your eyes open.

"One more thing." The airmen held their breaths. *"No guns and no ammunition will be carried. Get that.*

No guns! No ammunition! First of all, if we carried guns, it is likely we'd fire on each other. Second, we will carry all our weight in bombs and gas. Third, intelligence reports indicate there will be no night fighters of any account. Therefore, *no* guns and *no* ammunition.

"Final poop sheets for pilots, final weather, and flimsies for radio operators may be picked up here at 5 P.M. That's all."

In tight, excited knots the airmen looked over the new incendiary bombs that they would carry for the first time tonight. Gradually a feeling of optimistic excitement swept over the crews. The first smash-in-the-eye details had flabbergasted them. Then reason and logic took over. Why would there be no guns, no ammunition? To reduce their weight and keep them from shooting each other. How could they get there and back without bomb-bay tanks? By saving weight and flying at low altitude. Why could they get in and out at such low altitude? Observations had shown an absence of barrage balloons, a scarcity of night fighters, a lack of automatic weapons for defense against a low-altitude night attack. And above all, there was the factor of surprise. Never had a B-29 attacked below 20,000 feet.

By and large the men felt that *maybe* the LeMay plan would work.

The crews filed away to their specialized briefings, splitting into trades: pilots, engineers, radio, radar, navigators, bombardiers, each to their spe-

255

cial rendezvous to learn the final information needed for their special jobs — information so technical that it was meaningless to another crew member.

Then came the final hours — the sweating hours, when the risk of the mission chilled the skin. Some men played ball; some slept; some went to the line and helped the ground crews ready the planes. Almost everyone wrote final letters — to his mother, to his wife. Some wrote a third. They had written this letter before, some many times, then tore it up when they returned. A little shamefaced and embarrassed they handed it to a friend. "Say, Mac, just in case. Mail it for me, will you? See you tomorrow, maybe. So long . . ."

The loudspeaker in the camp area crackled, announcing that combat crews could go to the mess halls. Perhaps the meal was a little better that afternoon. Takeoff time for the 73rd Wing was to be between 6:15 P.M. and 7:17 P.M.

The cooks, the clerks, the friends who would be left behind, looked at the combat crews as if they were seeing them for the last time and wanted to remember their faces. By this time everyone knew about Tokyo at 7,000 feet; about no guns or ammunition; about the job to burn out the heart of the capital city of Japan.

Chow over, the men picked up the flimsies from the war rooms. Still time left. Some men took showers, changed their clothing from the skin out. It was a habit with most crews to be especially clean when they went up to the Empire. Maybe clean clothes and clean skin would reduce chances of infection if they were wounded. Maybe it was simply that taking a shower and changing clothes used up time.

Then the trucks appeared, and the crews boarded them with their gear and bumped their way up to the flight line. Here they collected their flak suits, Mae Wests, parachutes, and checked over their thirty-odd pieces of personal equipment.

The light of day began to drain out of the sky into the ocean — the dull endless ocean that swallowed up everything; light from the sky, planes from the air, crews from your own squadron.

Time: 6:05. First planes take off at 6:15 P.M. Ten more minutes to go . . .

The tower operators, perched 100 feet and more above the field, chattered together. They were having a last-minute smoke — talking about something they saw in the month-old funny paper that morning. Below them, spread over the giant field, 162 B-29's were readying for takeoff. Out from the loud speakers in the glass-enclosed tower came the blaring chatter of pilots asking directions, calling back information. The tower operators paid no attention. The senior operator, Sergeant Spachtaholtz, looked at Sergeant Baden's watch.

O.K., let's go . . ."

Zero hour.

The first planes were ready, straining at the edge of the runway. Behind them, long lines of B-29's were formed, nose to tail, props whirling, navigation lights gleaming small and red and green and white. Giant fin after giant fin pierced the dusk as far as eye could see, dwarfing the men and jeeps that crowded the side of the runway.

Spachtaholtz, ex-steel-mill worker, stretched his small, thin body as he reached into the air to pull down his signal light. He touched the trigger — the lead B-29 saw a green light.

"Take off!"

Endlessly the B-29's flashed by, heading out to the ocean — and the Empire. Squadron after squadron crept out from the hardstands, joined the nose-to-tail procession down the runway. One port-side landing light hurled out a beam of yellow in front of each monster as it lumbered slowly, then faster and faster, down the 8,500-foot asphalt strip straining to lift 70 tons into the air.

Up in the tower the brass worried, watching the boys go out. But the traffic maze — 162 aircraft, $200 million worth of equipment — was handled quickly by the two quiet-voiced sergeants. They visually checked every ship for lights, bomb bays, engine fire; talked them into position, controlled their every movement; prevented disastrous traffic jams. Every

Business end of a B-29 as it approached outskirts of Tokyo. Bombardier is sitting up ahead of the pilots in the nose. On final run, bombardier took over, directed the course of the aircraft.

50 seconds another two planes took off from the parallel strips.

At 7:17 the 160th Superfort was on its way to Japan. Only two had failed to get off.

General "Rosey" O'Donnell was pleased.

Across the bay in Tinian, another 110 ships were airborne.

In Guam, the green 314th Wing had sent off 54.

The LeMay Fire Plan was headed for Japan. Shortly after midnight Tokyo would be blazing; shortly after midnight some of these planes might be shot down; shortly after midnight many of these men might be dead.

To the men left behind — the crew chiefs, tower operators, crash-truck men, ambulance drivers — it was a deserted feeling they had, drained of their purpose and importance now that their planes were gone.

Shortly an abort returned. Shamefaced, the crew piled out of the plane. Something had gone wrong. They couldn't make it. There was nothing to do now but go back to the tents and hit the sack.

Isley Field was empty.

In the Mission Control Room of each wing, scoreboards told the story in figures: the number of planes off, the aborts, the early returns. But no scoreboard tallied the scratched nerves, the numbed hearts, the bitten lips of the men who were on watch — the mission control officer, the air-sea rescue team, the teletype operators. On all the islands nervous radio operators were standing by to catch the first message. Telephone switchboards and teletypists were ready to flash to the wings the bad news of crashes and lost planes — the expected news of ditched aircraft — the good word of "Bombs Away."

At 1:21 the flash came: *Bombs Away . . . General conflagration . . . Flak moderate to heavy . . . Fighters none.*

The message was dramatic but cryptic. Just as the scoreboards on the ground told the incomplete story, so the radio report left much unsaid. It omitted the horror seen and the frenzy felt.

Blink, blink, blink . . . Faster than their eyes could count — up and down, column after column of small green lights blinking on and off. Every one of those blinking green lights on the instrument panels meant another incendiary bomb had left its station, was falling, was set to burst 2,000 feet above Tokyo and disintegrate into 38 separate balls of liquid, almost unquenchable fire.

A major crossed himself with his left hand — his right clutched the controls — and murmured, "This blaze will haunt me forever. It's the most terrifying sight in the world, and, God forgive me, it's the best."

A crew chief cracked jokes as a tear or two streamed down his face. It was a way to look brave. He was grateful that the danger of collision over the target was eliminated by the fierce light of the fires.

A colonel-pilot didn't think his in-

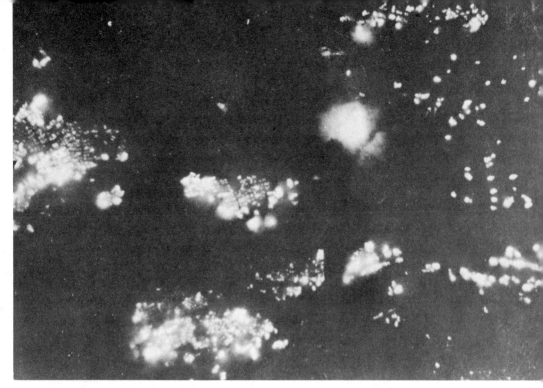

Tokyo by night at the beginning of an incendiary raid. Soon entire area will be a mass conflagration as fire spreads across the highly inflammable city.

Taken after the 300-plane raid of March 9, 1945, burned out (white) area shows the 16.7 square miles of Tokyo obliterated in this one attack.

tercom was on: "When I first heard we were to go in below 7,000, I didn't give the General much credit for that brain wave. It's against everything the ship is built for — but I'll fly these missions any day in the week. By God, you can see what you do. Seeing an enemy city burn to hell makes up for a lot of flak fright."

Many of these men had been attacking Japan since the previous November. In those four months, more than 800 men from the 73rd Wing alone had been killed. And during those costly raids they had seldom seen their target; too often weather had ruined their formation; too often their bombs had dropped uselessly into rice paddies.

But this was the payoff!

This time every man in the Superforts was able to look out and see Tokyo blazing wildly, burning, smoking, exploding. The planes filled with the stench of smoke which sifted in through the air vents, lifted a mile high by tornadic updrafts from the inferno below.

Gen. Tom Power had been chosen to lead the mission and to make a special report to General LeMay. After going in on his bomb run at 5,000 feet, Power went up to 10,000, then 20,000 feet, and flew back and forth across the target for almost two hours.

Many of the B-29's were carrying the largest bomb load ever taken to Japan, 18,000 pounds, twice what they could have carried if they had gone in at 30,000 feet, their usual altitude.

The M-69 incendiaries which they dropped broke up and scattered as they fell, so each plane was blanketing an area about 2,500 feet long and 500 feet wide with burning gasoline. The great heat of the fires helped spread them out, linking the burning areas into one tremendous fire. Tokyo was indeed highly inflammable; its firebreaks were unable to contain this conflagration.

Power and his crew found it difficult to judge the extent of the destruction because of the thick smoke from the spreading fires. However, they estimated the burning area to be 15 square miles — remarkably close to the actual figure of 15.8 square miles. Lt. Col. Harry Besse, the 314th Intelligence Officer, made sketches of what he saw for General LeMay.

Back in the tower at Isley Field the radio flashes added up to a happy conclusion: *The LeMay Plan had worked.*

But the final test would be the return of the B-29's to their bases in the Marianas — miles from the burning city. The hours were long that day. It wasn't until early in the afternoon that the last of the planes of the 73rd Wing returned to Saipan.

The 73rd crews piled out of their planes, many with faces of disbelief. They had been there, over Tokyo — at 7,000 feet, without guns! And now they were home safe. It was incredible. Their whole squadron was home — then their whole group. The entire wing lost just one plane — one plane missing, with no word received from it. Not counting aborts, 160 planes had taken off; 159 returned. The facts seemed wild, but they were true.

For Curtis LeMay, the hours of the mission had been agonizing ones and the loneliest ones of his life. While his crews in their giant planes were taking off, crossing the miles of ocean, and swinging low over Tokyo, he had betrayed his agitation only by constant pacing.

Now with Brig. Gen. Lauris Norstad, Chief of Staff from 20th Air Force Headquarters in Washington, LeMay received the special report from General Power, who landed at 10:00 A.M. THE PLAN HAD WORKED. There had been antiaircraft fire and innumerable searchlights, but Japanese defenses had soon fallen apart. Damage was many times greater than that inflicted during the raid of February 25. The feasibility of low-level bombing with incendiaries had been proven.

So at last the planes were back, the interrogations over, the reports in, the evaluations completed. Now LeMay knew and could speak. And he told newsmen: "I believe that all those under my command on these island bases have by their participation in this single operation shortened this war. To what extent they have shortened it no one can tell, but I believe that if there has been cut from its duration only one day or one hour, my officers and men have served a high purpose. They will pursue that purpose stubbornly. They are fighting for a quicker end to this war, and will continue to fight for a quicker end to it with all the brains and strength they have."

Immediately through LeMay's head ran other names: Nagoya, Osaka, Kobe.

He came to his next decision fast: "Carry out the remainder of the plan; devastate Japan's major industrial cities in the next days after and nights."

Nagoya was next!

"How soon?" the men asked. "How much time do we have?"

The answer: "Hit Nagoya *as soon as possible* — in one day at the most."

"One day! Hell, we can't get off the ground in one day. It'll take two days at the very least. It'll take . . ."

They were talking into thin air. LeMay had gone — back to his War Room, back to his maps, to sit, silent, chewing on an unlighted cigar and thinking.

That was that; that was an order. One day! Stretch it any way you want; double your shifts, whip everyone to a frenzy, work under floodlights during the dark Pacific night, but take no more than 24 hours.

As it turned out, only 29 hours separated the return from Tokyo from the takeoff to Nagoya. In that time small miracles were performed; the men with oil and grease on their hands did it. LeMay received constant progress reports:

"Nine engines have been changed, slow-timed and readied, sir."

LeMay puffed out a jet of smoke. "Double it."

"We've put four planes back in commission."

LeMay stared at the large wall map, highlighted in the darkened War Room. "They never should have been out of commission in the first place."

"Thirty-three planes have been repaired, sir."

LeMay went on reading a secret report from Washington.

"It took 3,000 man-hours to do that job, sir."

LeMay never answered.

"Every plane has been given a thorough inspection — whatever it needed: 100-hour inspection, 50-hour, 25-hour."

LeMay, lighting his cigar, paused long enough to nod.

If the men of the 21st Bomber Command hadn't understood the reason why it would have been worse. But behind LeMay's impassive face and grumbled answers lay an uncanny knowledge of men, planes, and the difficulties of the problems to be licked. It was just another instance of his knack of knowing his men's capabilities and their jobs better than they did themselves.

A grease-stained crew chief, gulping hot coffee on the flight line, said it: "We don't mind the day and night work, just as long as we can get a burned-out Jap city in return."

In the dusty ordnance dumps, GIs worked without stopping, loading bombs onto trucks, unloading them at the airplanes. There, on the hardstands, groups of four ordnance men assigned to load each ship, sweated with the plane's ground crew as they crammed the giant double bomb bays with 68 M-69 incendiaries and the Pathfinder ships with 184 smaller, brighter-burning, magnesium bombs which would light up a target.

Figures tell the work done by the ordnance companies. To "bomb up" *one* wing for *one* raid it took: 400 man-days to uncrate the incendiaries; 400 man-days to transport them from the dumps to the line; 600 man-days to load the bombs into the planes from the hardstands. In all, a total of 1,400 man-days — for one raid for just one wing! And this job of work was done through rain, heat and night, and often within 24 hours.

There were also casualties among the ordnance men and ground men during the fire blitz. Indeed, as many men were "killed in action" on the ground in the Marianas as died in the air over Japan.

Lifting bombs hour after hour can break a man's back. A bomb can slip and fall. It will crush your skull. Make a mistake about a fuse, and it's the last mistake you'll ever make.

The job done by the ground crews and service groups was epic. Their work was made up of small things — changing wheels, changing engines, changing cylinder heads, repairing fuel lines, replacing instruments, correcting malfunctions in the bomb racks, in the turrets, in the radio sets, in the radar equipment, in the hydraulic lines. The list was endless because in a B-29 there were 55,000 separate parts, every one of which could go wrong, each of which was, during these hectic days, subjected to untold strain.

Why all the urgency? LeMay reasoned this way: "Those cities wouldn't have been burned without our ground crews; we never could have sent our planes back up so fast if it hadn't been for their magnificent work. If we'd delayed, the Japs might have been more prepared. The ground crews get as much credit as any man in the entire command."

And so it took the crews 29 hours instead of 24 to get ready for the second fire-bomb raid, and on the afternoon of March 11th 313 Superforts were off for Nagoya, Japan's greatest warplane-producing center and third largest city. This time the B-29's were to carry 200 pounds of ammunition in the tail turret in case the Japanese

had learned that the Superforts were unarmed in the Tokyo raid.

Wild Japanese claims followed: 22 Superforts were shot down and 60 damaged. Actually 285 planes had reached the target and only one was lost, a plane that ditched shortly after takeoff.

The actual results fell short of those achieved at Tokyo. The American airmen had become overoptimistic and spaced their bombs farther apart, hoping to destroy a larger area. Because of this greater dispersal and the warning provided by the Tokyo raid, Nagoya fire fighters were better able to curb the conflagration. Only 2.05 square miles were destroyed by 1,790 tons of bombs. Clearly the way to burn down an area was to concentrate the fires, to make them so hot that nothing could put them out. The next raid would apply the concentration technique.

Before it took place, however, General LeMay sent this word to Japan:

View of daylight incendiary raid on Osaka from 20,000 feet up. Fire bombs are aimed at the harbor and dock area.

"All the Japanese have to look forward to is the total destruction of their industries, cities, and other vital targets devoted to their war efforts. If it is necessary, we will send 1,000 planes over the target."

Forty-eight hours later, on the night of March 13, 301 Superforts were airborne; 274 made it to Osaka. They dropped 1,732 tons of incendiaries and laid waste 8.1 square miles of the Empire's second largest city. Because of cloud cover over the target most of the bombs were dropped by radar.

Perhaps the most spectacular incident on this raid was the destruction of the 150-acre Osaka arsenal. Explosion after violent explosion threw up concussions so terrific they rocked 70-ton Superforts a mile up in the air. One of the 313th Wing B-29's named "Topsy-Turvy," was blown from 7,000 feet to 12,000 feet; the pilot recovered control and flew it home. Another B-29 "Jostlin' Josie" from the 73rd Wing, was hurled from 7,000 feet up to 10,000 feet, and then fell 2,000 feet before the pilot regained control. A ship commanded by Capt. Jack D. Nole caught several violent blasts. The first dumped the bombardier, Lt. John B. Allen, into the lap of the co-pilot; the second pitched him into the controls, the third threw the ship on its side and hurled Captain Nole from his seat. . . . Something big had been blown up a mile and a half below them.

Seventy hours later, on March 16, 334 planes were airborne; 307 reached

Kobe with 2,355 tons of incendiaries for the fourth giant incendiary raid on Nipponese cities within a week. Hitting docks, shipyards, an aircraft plant, and locomotive works, the incendiaries burned out 3 square miles, 21.4 per cent of the city; the fires started were visible 100 miles away.

On March 19, in the fifth massed strike by the 21st Bomber Command, the Superforts returned to Nagoya, burning out another 3.5 square miles and ending a ten-day fire blitz campaign that made history.

It tallied up like this:

Thirty-two square miles of Japan's four principal cities demolished.

Hundreds of vital war plants destroyed; hundreds of others put out of operation; gas, electricity, heat, light. water, transportation disrupted.

Countless Japanese dead.

Hundreds of thousands panic-stricken; millions realizing for the first time that the Empire was not winning a glorious victory.

These were the statistics from Japan. From the Marianas, there were different figures.

The ground crews had put in more than 300,000 man-hours; had loaded over 2,000,000 individual bombs; had loaded more than 10,500 gallons of gasoline; had sent over 1,500 Superforts to Japan. The air crews had flown 257,500 combat hours, suffered 156 casualties, and lost 21 aircraft.

The road to victory was getting shorter, the price for Pearl Harbor higher. The Superforts had come into their own. The once-glorious Empire was reeling from blows it had not counted on. How long could it withstand this kind of war from the air?

General LeMay had that answer too and he sent it to Washington, where preparations for a land invasion of Japan, estimating a million American casualties, were feverishly under way.

The Japanese would surrender, wrote LeMay, in less than six months without an American soldier setting foot on the homeland.

And this is exactly what happened. Little wonder Col. Pinky Smith called the sulky-looking cigar-smoking General LeMay "a machine or a god."

Yokohama, Japan, May 29, 1945. B-29's dropping hundreds of fire bombs to hit enemy installations below.

In the young hours of August 6, 1945, three silver B-29's traced an arc across the Pacific sky pointing toward Japan. They had left the darkness-enveloped airfield on Tinian in the Mariana Islands at 2:45 A.M. This was a highly secret special mission, the first real combat flight of the 509th Composite Group, an outfit which had been wrapped in mystery from its inception in the States. Since its arrival on Tinian, the men of the 509th had been teased by crews of other wings for the "soft, fat combat tour." The 509th had flown only practice and test missions up to now.

The target for the three sky-specks was Hiroshima, an ancient city in Japan and a major Japanese defense headquarters. Alternate targets, in case of bad weather over Hiroshima, were Kokura and Nagasaki. The population count of Hiroshima was normally much larger than the 245,000 souls it held on this morning, for thousands of families had evacuated to the country, fearful of the awesome fire-bomb raids which had laid waste Japanese metropolitan areas for the past six months. Indeed, the once great Empire now lay prostrate, its major cities gutted and burned out, its forces decimated in the field, and its borders surrounded by air and by sea. It was a besieged land like none other had ever been.

At nearly 200 miles per hour, high over the Pacific, the three four-engine giants nudged closer to their target. Leading was the Enola Gay, *commanded by Capt. Paul Tibbets. The two wingmen, one a photo ship,* No. 91, *and the other,* The Great Artiste, *flown by Maj. Charles W. Sweeney, carried instruments to be parachuted with the bomb drop.*

Far ahead the city of Hiroshima still slept. In a few hours it would begin to pulse with its normal daily activities. Aboard the aircraft, however, tension was building even at this early hour. Crew members had been told after takeoff, the specifics of things to come. They felt an awareness that something beyond their comprehension would happen with the release of that one bomb. And yet they knew not exactly what.

The first atomic bomb, dropped on August 6, 1945, was followed by the release of the second atomic bomb on August 9, 10:58 A.M. This second bomb fell from the open bays of the B-29 Bock's Car, *flown by Maj. Charles W. Sweeney and his crew. The city below was Nagasaki, located on the west coast of Kyushu and home of four large Mitsubishi aircraft plants. The primary target of* Bock's Car *had been Kokura and over it Sweeney had made several bomb runs but a thick cloud cover blanketing the city prevented assurance of accuracy. Reluctantly Sweeney turned the B-29 toward the alternate, Nagasaki, also nestling below an overcast. Running low on gas, a radar approach was made. At the last minute of the bomb run a hole opened in the clouds and through it the bombardier tumbled the bulbous-shaped object, the second and last atomic bomb to be dropped in anger.*

Although Sweeney immediately turned his plane up on the wing and

266

swerved away, five terrific shock waves rocked the aircraft with deadly impact, tossing it like a feather. Bock's Car landed on Okinawa with only a few gallons of fuel left in its tanks. It returned to the 509th base on Tinian by 11:39 that night.

The Dropping of the Atomic Bombs

A Picture Story

...tory's first atomic bomber, the B-29 Superfor-... ...Enola Gay, as it comes in for a landing on ...an Island, Marianas.

...w of the *Enola Gay*. Maj. Thomas W. Ferebee, ...bardier, and Capt. Paul W. Tibbets, Jr., pilot, ...d second and third from left, respectively.

The end of one age and the beginning of another. Mushroom cloud above the doomed city of Nagasaki.

The world's first nuclear bomb, "Little Boy," detonated in an air burst over the city of Hiroshima, Japan, at about 8:16 a.m., August 6, 1945.

"Fat Boy," the second and last atomic bomb to be dropped in anger, fell on Nagasaki, Japan, at 10:58 a.m., August 9, 1945.

A low, oblique view of part of the Hiroshima A-bomb destruction.

Cross-cut by hills and valleys, Nagasaki suffered less than flat Hiroshima.

On the morning of August 9, 1945, the inner council of the Japanese government was meeting to discuss surrender terms when the news of the atomic explosion over Nagasaki reached them. The Emperor and Premier Kantaro Suzuki had already decided to accept the surrender terms offered by the Potsdam Conference, so that the Russian entry into the Pacific War that day had little bearing on the events that were to quickly follow.

On August 10, the Japanese Cabinet met and unanimously concurred with the decision to end the war and the message was sent to the United States via the neutral Swiss government.

The American reply came on August 12 and on the 14th it was confirmed by the Japanese who were told to send representatives to General MacArthur's headquarters in Manila to work out specific details.

How would you go about making initial arrangements for this historic meeting? Well, here's how the man of action, General Douglas MacArthur, pushed aside prescribed channels of protocol and diplomacy to get the job under way in a hurry.

Direct Wire

WHEN General MacArthur wanted to send his first message to Emperor Hirohito following Japan's surrender, a problem arose as to the means of communicating it. If the message went through diplomatic channels at Berne [Switzerland], two days might be required for the transmission. The General preferred to send his message direct.

Maj. Gen. Spencer Akin, chief signal officer on General MacArthur's staff, asked Army Airways Communications System if it had a high-powered transmitter which could reach Japan.

"If the message is ready," replied Col. R. G. Nichols, commanding officer of the 68th AACS Group, "put it on GHQ teletype to WXXU and we'll send it out from there."

WXXU is the AAF weather station which re-broadcasts to the entire Southwest Pacific area weather information received from other AACS stations all over the Pacific. In the months before V-J Day this station had rather contemptuously been sending its weather information in the clear on the assumption that eliminating the necessity of elaborate coding and decoding more than outweighed any possible use the Japs were in position to make of weather data. It was a well-known fact that the Japs had been copying this free weather map of the Pacific every day. And this fact made it a sure bet that the Japs would pick up General MacArthur's message to the Emperor in the same way.

The message directed that the Japanese allocate one of their radio frequencies for direct communication with Allied Supreme Headquarters. Specifically, he suggested that Jap station JUM, which had been heard clearly in Manila, would be satisfactory.

Signaling Jap call signs — stations which had deliberately jammed our own frequencies in the past — the AACS station put the message on the air and repeated it at intervals of two hours. Then it sat by to monitor JUM. Soon the Jap reply was received on the frequency that General MacArthur had requested, and direct two-way communication was established between the two headquarters.

Copy of the original direct wire from General MacArthur to the Emperor of Japan initiating surrender arrangements.

GENERAL HEADQUARTERS

UNITED STATES ARMY FORCES→ PACIFIC

E   15 AUGUST 1945 FROM SIG

JUM V WXXU NR 1

FROM
COMMANDER FOR THE ALLIED POWERS

TO   THE JAPANESE EMPEROR

THE JAPANESE IMPERIAL GOVERNMENT

THE JAPANESE IMPERIAL GENERAL HEADQUARTERS

MESSAGE NUMBER Z1500   I HAVE BEEN DESIGNATED AS THE SUPREME COMMANDER

FOR THE ALLIED

POWERS PAREN THE UNITED STATES CMA THE REPUBLIC OF CHINA CMA THE

UNITED KINGDOM AND THE UNION OF SOVIET SOCIALIST REPUBLICS PAREN AND

EMPOWERED TO ARRANGE DIRECTLY WITH THE JAPANESE AUTHORITIES FOR

THE CESSATION OF HOSTILITIES AT THE EARLIEST PRACTICABLE DATE PD

IT IS DESIRED THAT A RADIO STATION IN THE TOKYO AREA BE OFFICIALLY

DESIGNATED FOR CONTINUOUS USE IN HANDLING RADIO COMMUNICATIONS

BETWEEN THIS HEADQUARTERS AND YOUR HEADQUARTERS PD YOUR REPLY TO THIS

MESSAGE SHOULD GIVE THE CALL SIGNS CMA FREQUENCIES AND STATION

DESIGNATION PD IT IS DESIRED THAT THE RADIO COMMUNICATION WITH MY

HEADQUARTERS IN MANILA BE HANDLED IN ENGLISH TEXT PD PENDING DESIGNATION

BY YOU FOR ABLE STATION IN THE TOKYO AREA FOR USE AS ABOVE

INDICATED CMA STATION JIG UNCLE MIKE ON FREQUENCY ONE THREE SEVEN

NAUGHT FIVE KILOCYCLES WILL BE USED FOR THIS PURPOSE AND WIA

MANILA WILL REPLY ON ONE FIVE NINE SIX FIVE KILOCYCLES PD

UPON RECEIPT OF THIS MESSAGE CMA ACKNOWLEDGE

MACARTHUR   58597 A C

Little did the 7th Air Force P-47 fighter pilots and ground crews on the tiny island of Ie Shima dream their base would one day suddenly become the center of world events. It did on August 19, 1945, for here on this Ryukyu coral atoll, located between Japan and the Philippine Islands, Japanese emissaries transferred from two twin-engine "Betty" bombers to a USAAF C-54 transport for the flight to General MacArthur's headquarters in Manila to iron out surrender terms.

And it was a humorous moment when the honorable Japanese pilot nervously taxied the big rising-sun bomber ignominiously into a ditch alongside the runway . . . Not one American stepped forward to help the embarrassed Japanese crewmen extricate their plane.

The Sun Also Sets

Clive Howard and Joe Whitley

ALL THROUGH the long, hot morning of August 19, the rumors traveled from group to group and from man to man. . . .

The Japs weren't going to surrender to us; we were going to surrender to them. . . .

It was a Jap trick — a sort of psychological booby trap contrived to throw us off guard while an enormous enemy fleet, hidden until now, sailed on Hawaii.

A few minutes after noon, a Marine radar operator sitting in a paneled truck on the northern tip of Okinawa saw a disturbance on the oscilloscope screen. Whatever caused it was 120 miles north of Ie Shima, moving toward the island with a speed that caused the pip to flare wildly up and down.

At 30 minutes past noon, from far out to sea there was the heavy drone of many airplane engines. The 55,000 men on Ie Shima shaded their eyes and looked to the north. The men who had been sitting or lying down got quickly to their feet.

Just breaking the horizon was a fleet of P-38's. As the planes sped closer, the men on Ie could make out two larger, plum-shaped planes locked in the center of the fighter formation.

As the planes sped closer, the P-38's swung off course and began to orbit the island.

The two larger planes held a course straight toward the island.

Then the first Jap bomber, painted white and with five green crosses (one under each wing, one on either side

271

and one on the upper tail fin), moved across the island of Ie Shima.

Except for the movement of eyes and the slow turning of heads as the Jap Betty passed overhead, the men gathered below were motionless and silent.

The second enemy plane flew over the island.

Three times the white Bettys circled and passed over the island, perhaps making certain of the white crosses painted on the runway below, perhaps waiting for the landing signal, perhaps hesitant.

Then the Japs flew out to sea, and still restricted to the immediate area of Ie Shima by the circling P-38's, began to turn toward the runway.

The first Betty touched its wheels cautiously to the coral and began rolling down the runway past the incredible number of suntanned, expressionless American faces.

As the plane flashed by, Lt. Bob George turned to Colonel McAfee.

"For three years I've been meeting up with Bettys," he said, "but this is the first time I've ever been glad to see one. Wonderful, isn't it?"

McAfee wasn't listening. He was staring apprehensively at the second bomber, which had sideslipped toward the landing strip at a crazy angle with its nose dropped far below the safe landing attitude. McAfee was thinking how disastrous it would be if the plane crashed on the strip, or, worse, if it plowed into the closely packed spectators.

The Jap pilot recovered at the last moment and bounced into a landing so sloppy that McAfee silently cursed him.

As the plane rolled past McAfee, he noticed for the first time the great, ugly splotches of brown showing through the white paint. To the end, the Japs had done things badly.

As the Bettys moved slowly back up the airstrip behind the "Follow Me" jeep which had sped out to meet them, a hatch above the pilot's compartment was pushed open and a Japanese head was thrust into the open.

"So that's what they look like," one man said. And then, aware of the critical stares of the men around him, he added, self-consciously, "I've never seen one before."

The Jap was wearing a leather flying helmet with fur earlaps turned up and, as he pulled off his flying goggles, the men at the edge of the strip saw he was wearing thick, horn-rimmed glasses. The Jap, apparently the copilot, signaled the jeep's course to the pilot below by banging on the fuselage with his open hand.

That, and the unsynchronized burbling of the Bettys' engines, were the only sounds disturbing the spontaneous silence.

The two planes halted about 100 feet from a C-54 Skymaster parked toward the seaward end of the strip — the transfer ship which was to carry the surrender delegation to MacArthur's headquarters in Manila.

For a few moments nothing happened. The military police, in rigid files on the east and west sides of the strip, stood stiffly at parade rest, the sun flashing from their bayonets. The men massed behind them were motionless and silent.

Then, a small hatch in the side of one of the Bettys was pushed open. An Army lieutenant, wearing an interpreter's armband, walked across the strip to the open hatch and talked into the airplane.

A thin man — tall for a Japanese — squeezed through the narrow opening and dropped to the runway. He wore a sports coat, a shirt open at the collar, tan shorts, white, knee-length stockings and white shoes. Heavy glasses and a small black mustache gave his face a rather quizzical expression.

The man took a few tentative steps forward and then, apparently noticing for the first time the mass of staring, silent Americans, halted in his tracks.

Through the same small door, and an identical opening in the second Betty, 14 Japanese army and navy officers and a second civilian made their way to the ground.

Most of them were short and round and wore horn-rimmed glasses under their peaked hats. All except the two civilians trailed great samurai swords from their left hips. A few carried hara-kiri knives.

The 16 Japs lined up under the broad wings of the transfer plane — their eyes cast resolutely down.

The 55,000 Americans looked on entranced, each man aware of his presence at a historic spectacle, but experiencing the soldier's ancient inability to regard himself as a participant in the drama of war.

One of them expressed in a soldier's simple terms the familiar, detached attitude of the spectator which each man was consciously experiencing: "It's like a dream," he said to no one in particular. "Like looking on something from another world."

Ie Shima's spectators to the first tangible evidence of final capitulation, the same men who had staged the Pacific's rowdiest, wildest victory celebration five days before, had not been briefed on their conduct before the enemy's generals and admirals.

The silence, the motionless staring as bit by bit the peace began to unfold, were spontaneous — the unanticipated reaction of men who had not expected to see this thing happen during their own lifetimes.

S/Sgt. Bob Price, who had worked his way closer to the Japs than most American soldiers were permitted, noticed that the uniforms of the high-ranking enemy officers were made of a cheap, sleazy green cotton. The leather boots and belts looked artificial. Most of the Japs carried their lunches wrapped in white paper and small tins filled with pastry. Price thought they looked strange and lonely, as if they had gotten all dressed up to impress us and it didn't quite come off.

"Or then again," Price began, "perhaps there is nothing in the Jap military code which tells a man what to wear to a surrender."

The Japanese aircrewmen, when they rolled out of the Bettys after the peace delegation, made a flashier but more comical impression. They wore gleaming, mahogany-colored leather flying jackets with hoods lined with white fur and knee-length flying boots. Dwarfed by the American interpreters around them, who wore rumpled khaki uniforms, the Jap crewmen looked like small, oriental versions of the Graustark soldier.

Standing 20 feet away from the Japanese officials now lined up under the Skymaster's wings, and towering over them even at that distance, Brig. Gen. Frederick H. Smith, an early fighter pilot in the Pacific, delivered brief instructions. He told the delegation it would proceed at once to Manila. He offered to house the Jap aircrewmen on Ie Shima until the delegation returned from Manila. The Japs listened without looking up from the runway, and with their heads turned slightly away from the American General. Lt. Gen. Kawabe Takashiro, leader of the Jap delegation, nodded grudgingly as Smith finished talking.

There was an awkward moment as the Jap emissaries, ready to board the Skymaster, looked around for their baggage. Takashiro, after pondering

Ie Shima. Glum after their cold reception, this part of the 16-man delegation provides an interesting facial study in defeat. Second from left is leader of the delegation, Lt. Gen. Kawabe Takashiro, Vice Chief of Imperial Staff.

the problem in surrender protocol for a few moments, said something over his shoulder to a lower-ranking officer, who — in the ancient custom of all the world's armies — passed the problem on down the line.

Watching the Jap pilots and enlisted men shuttling back and forth between the Bettys and the Skymaster with the delegation's luggage, Lt. Bob George was trying to make the spectacle fit into a pattern which for him had started at Makin Island and ended here on Ie Shima more than 70 missions later.

The tiny, spit-and-polish, comic-opera soldiers, struggling awkwardly under the weight of baggage as they scurried back and forth like brown beetles, looked not at all like the enemy — the ruthless, mighty aggressor who, early in 1942, was steamrolling unopposed through the Pacific.

The pilot was staring at the phenomenon, trying to bring into focus whatever it was that left him with no sensation of proximity to the enemy, when a Jap crewman inside the lead Betty moved to a glass blister opposite him.

The fighter pilot, staring at the Jap, felt the cold impact, the quick downward plunge of his stomach familiar to American airmen about to engage the enemy in combat. The spectacle on Ie Shima assumed its place in the pattern.

Somehow the Jap crewman, hunched over behind the glass blister and peering momentarily through the glass at the Americans, was a familiar enemy.

Their baggage finally assembled, and the delicate protocol problem settled in a manner which caused broad grins among the high-ranking American officers present, the 16 Japs queued up before the flight of landing steps wheeled up to the Skymaster.

A grizzled crew chief, noting the dispatch cases and portable typewriters of the two Jap junior officers at the end of the line, said derisively: "A couple of lousy T-5 clerks."

The Japs began climbing the long steep flight of steps. Each Jap officer was periled at every step by the samurai sword which clanged against the wooden framework and became entangled between his legs.

Standing close to the plane, S/Sgt. Bob Price said: "I'm praying. It would be hell if one of them slipped. It would be an international incident."

The Japs, to Price's great relief, made it safely, and the plane's big steel doors were slammed shut.

The transfer plane wheeled slowly down the runway past the white crosses. Then it parked at an angle for a few moments while the pilot revved up its four engines, and came back up the runway gathering speed. At 28 minutes past one o'clock, the plane pulled itself into the air.

The 55,000 Americans on Ie Shima, still entranced and silent, watched the Skymaster until it was out of sight, and then turned their attention to the two Bettys and the nine Jap crewmen left on the island. Through an interpreter, the Japs were directed to move their planes into revetments.

And in so doing, the Jap crewmen suffered further an ignominy which, to the American pilots, crew chiefs and line mechanics, was a sweeter remembrance than the submission of the Jap generals and admirals. The landing gear of the lead Betty, as the plane was being wheeled into a revetment, broke through the coral surface. The tire went almost out of sight.

The Americans pressed as close to the disabled Betty as the MP's would allow and, smiling openly, looked on as the Japs, sweltering in their high-altitude flying suits, struggled with the embedded landing gear. Nobody said a word. Nobody offered to help.

Finally, the Japs freed their plane and were rounded up and placed in command cars. The pilot of the lead Betty was led to a command car which had a provocative Varga girl painted on its side. He sat on the back seat with his possessions, wrapped in a bright silk scarf, placed beside him. With the white fur earlaps of his leather helmet turned up, the Jap pilot looked, to Sgt. Bob Frederick, "like a bewildered rabbit."

The procession of command cars and MP's jeeps had started to bore through the crowd when the Jap pilot remembered something. He ran back to the lead Betty, climbed inside and in a few minutes came back to the command car carrying three wilted bouquets — roses, pinks and larkspurs.

A technical sergeant Nisei inter-preter from Honolulu asked the pilot in perfect Japanese why the flowers. The pilot answered in perfect English, "Just because."

Then the Jap aircrews were gone and the only tangible evidence still remaining on the airstrip of the peace which had been so long in coming were the two Bettys, closely guarded by military police, and the flight of landing steps the Japs had climbed for the last lap of their ignominious journey.

For a long time, nobody moved from the airstrip. The men sat or stood just as they had all through the morning, talking quietly or not talking at all. Some lingered near the Bettys, as though reluctant to take leave of the visible reassurance that this dream was not false like all their other dreams of peace. A few men lingered near the landing platform, examining it with careful glances but not noticing that it was the exact companion of dozens of other landing platforms, at places like Hickam Field, Johnston Island, Kwajalein, Saipan.

Finally, as the sun — which looked that day like a bright, midwest harvest sun — was halfway down the sky, the men began drifting away from the airstrip. Some of them went to their tents to write letters which had been thought out and mentally written over and over again in that other lifetime before the morning of August 19. Others remembered there was a beer ration that day and it was the first time within the memory of any veteran that many men had to be reminded of it. Still others lay back on their cots, staring wordlessly at the canvas ceiling.

Hours after the Skymaster had flown the Japanese delegation off the island, a formation of P-47's from the 318th Fighter Group, which had been out on combat air patrol, came out of the setting sun and began letting down into the landing pattern.

Sitting under the wing of a parked Thunderbolt, where they had been talking quietly all afternoon, Colonel McAfee, Captain Dupuy and Lieutenant George watched the planes as, one by one, they landed and rolled to the end of the strip.

They watched the last plane as it turned off the airstrip and heard, as from a great distance, the quick gasp of its engine as the propeller turned over for the last time.

Then the airstrip was long and empty and quiet. The three men got slowly to their feet and began walking back toward their tents.

As they trudged along in the evening freshness, McAfee looked around the island and out over the Pacific as though he was seeing it all for the first, or perhaps the last time.

Far out to sea there was a tapering path of orange light — dark and diluted with the greenish-blue of the sea where the whitecaps began to move shoreward, stronger, brighter where it stretched beyond the tumbling horizon.

The sun had set.

The skies of the Pacific were quiet and peaceful again. The hostile jungles were quickly reclaiming the little pieces of civilization that had briefly touched down and then moved on. The seas lapped the shores at a thousand places with a sound that somehow was different now.

And in the councils of men around the world a strange new feeling of security, almost unbelievable, permeated the air. It was a security that was good but uneasy, uneasy because of what the war in the Pacific had wrought.

Air power had come into its own, and as decidedly as it had transformed Japan from pride, power, and prosperity into humiliating defeat and collapse, so it could do the same to any nation on earth.

Here, the Father of American air power, the builder of U.S. aerial might and the leader of its employment to victory in the Pacific, sums it all up.

Our Power to Destroy War

Gen. Henry H. Arnold

WE MUST look to the future. We have come victorious through the greatest war of all time. It was not a war which we sought, or for which we were ready, so not unnaturally we faced moments of great danger and deep discouragement. With enormous effort and at heavy cost we surmounted them. This is a proud and jubilant moment, but let us not forget that it is also a fateful moment. Today, in the hour of triumph when it is only human nature to be affected by sentiments of relief, optimism, and hope or wishful thinking, we must make decisions on which will depend to a great degree the permanence of peace, the fate of our country, and perhaps even the existence of human civilization. Our wartime responsibilities were heavy, but none of them was heavier than this responsibility that comes with peace.

With planes of the range of the B-17 and B-24 we knocked out German air power and enabled our ground-sea-air team to conquer Germany. With planes of the operational range of the B-29 we were able to bring about the surrender of Japan. For any consideration of the future it is vitally important that we understand exactly how that surrender was brought about.

I am not referring now to who won the war.

No one arm, no one service, no one of the United Nations could or would claim the credit for what everyone must now realize was a vast and well-coordinated joint effort. It took, working together, all arms of the U.S. services, all services of our fighting, cooperating Allies, and the enormous industrial powers of the United States.

Nevertheless the decisive part played by air power in the defeat of Japan without the necessity for an invasion of the home islands can scarcely be disregarded. A modern industrial nation such as Japan would not have admitted defeat at this stage of the war unless her industrial potential had been hopelessly weakened, the morale of her people seriously affected, and her isolation from the essentials necessary to wage war rendered virtually complete by blockade and the destruction of her navy and merchant fleet. The fanatical Japanese would never have offered to accept the crushing terms of the Potsdam ultimatum merely because the odds against them rendered "victory" of any sort impossible. The Japanese army, although it had been hurt, was still a powerful force capable of inflicting heavy casualties on an invading force. The kamikaze corps had shown its capabilities in the Philippines and Okinawa campaigns and was preparing for an even greater effort against an invading amphibious force. Yet the Japanese acknowledged defeat because air attacks, both actual and potential, had made possible the destruction of the enemy's capability and will for further resistance. It had long been thought

that it might be possible to bring about the defeat of Japan by air attack and blockade without the necessity of invasion, but war planners could never rely on victory without invasion. Though unprecedented in the history of warfare, this is what happened.

The destructive effects and increasing power of incendiary attacks on urban industrial areas, and high-explosive attacks on critical war industries, principally the oil industry and the aviation industry, were principal factors in breaking the Japanese will and ability to fight. A long series of air battles drove the Japanese air forces, for all practical purposes, out of the skies, not only in the vast controlled areas but over the homeland itself. Over the homeland, the Japanese were compelled to forego the defense of vital targets and yield air supremacy in an endeavor to recover enough to complete its destruction in a suicide role against an invading force. The destruction of the Japanese navy was completed. The Army Air Forces shared with surface craft, naval air and submarines in the sinking of nearly 600 Japanese combat vessels. Aircraft are officially credited with sinking more than 2,000,000 tons of Japanese merchant shipping, of 1,000 tons and over, although in this respect submarines are primarily responsible for the reduction of the operational merchant fleet of a once great maritime power to substantially less than 1,000,000 tons.

General Henry H. "Hap" Arnold, Commander of the Army Air Forces, chats with a Superfort crew chief on Guam during the strategic air offensive against Japan. Behind Arnold is General LeMay.

Finally, there is the air contribution to the blockade and strangulation of the home islands. With the destruction of the Japanese navy and the immobilization of the Japanese air forces, the U.S. and British land, sea, and air forces completed the blockade of Japan. The sea mining by B-29's immobilized hundreds of ships and sank dozens of others in the vital Shimonoseki Straits and later, coupled with aircraft and submarine attack, virtually cut off Korea and the mainland of Asia from the home islands through the mining of Korean and western Honshu ports.

The collapse of Japan has vindicated the whole strategic concept of the offensive phase of the Pacific War. Viewed broadly and simply, that strategy was to advance air power, both land- and carrier-based, to the point where the full fury of crushing air attack could be loosed on Japan itself, with the possibility that it would bring about the defeat of Japan without invasion and with the certainty that it would play an essential and vital role in preparation for and cooperation with an invasion. The entire island-hopping campaign in the Southwest and Central Pacific had as one of its principal objectives the acquisition of air bases ever closer to, and finally within range of, Japan. These bases were also vital as Navy supply and counting bases. They were essential in order to neutralize or knock out Japanese air strength, thus allowing the U.S. Navy as a whole, and particularly its offensive air power, to be brought within range of the home islands themselves — something which would invite ruinous losses as long as Japanese land-based air strength remained full and effective. Finally, the bases enabled us to defeat every effort of the Japanese army to stop the inevitable advance to the home islands in preparation for an invasion of Japan.

This, then, was how the surrender

Final action of the Pacific War — the signing of the surrender terms aboard the battleship *Missouri* in Manila Bay. Admiral Chester Nimitz is shown signing above.

of the Japanese was brought about. I wished to stress it, because the harnessing of the atom and its dramatic use as the climax of this campaign has tended to overshadow a most important point. When the atomic bomb was ready, we were in a position to deliver it, practically unopposed, to any point in Japan that we chose. The appalling effects of the delivery are shown in the Japanese Emperor's rescript announcing surrender.

"Should we continue to fight, it would . . . result in an ultimate collapse and obliteration of the Japanese nation."

This is true; but the Japanese situation was hopeless before that. There is reason to think that, from the Japanese standpoint, the atomic bomb was really a way out. Because the bomb was incredibly destructive, it was possible for the Emperor, without too much loss of face, to give up, as the only answer to this unheard-of development. The Japanese position was hopeless even before the first atomic bomb fell because the Japanese had lost control of their own air. They could not counter our air strikes, and so could not prevent the destruction of their cities and industries. They could not offer any effective opposition to the gathering of the immense forces of our land-sea-air team, which was preparing to descend on their coasts.

These are the facts about the fall of Japan that we must keep in mind if we are to maintain the peace we have won at such cost. This is the lesson:

At no time in the foreseeable future can there be any security for a nation which, through ignorance, negligence, or unpreparedness, allows itself to be put in that fatal position of Japan during the last year of this war.

EDITOR'S NOTE: There were none among the scores of defeated Japanese military and civilian leaders interviewed after the war who would disagree with "Hap" Arnold:

"If I were to give you one factor as the leading one that lead to your victory, I would give you the Air Force."
— *Admiral ISN Asami Nagano, Chief of Naval General Staff and Supreme Naval Advisor to the Emperor*

"It is my opinion that our loss in the air lost us the war."
— *Lt. Gen. Masakaza Kawabe, Commanding General Air, General Army*

"If I were to give the decisive factors in the war and the order of their importance I would place first the Air Force . . ."
— *Vice Admiral IJN Shigeru Fukudome, Chief of Staff Combined Fleet*

". . . the determination to make peace was the prolonged bombing by the B-29's."
— *Prince Fumimaro Konoye, Premier of Japan*

"Air was the branch of the United States services which contributed most to the defeat of Japan. The 5th and 13th Air Forces around the Solomons and New Guinea forced the Japanese air force to withdraw, and the B-29's from the Marianas wrought considerable damage on Japan. The defeat of the Japanese air force caused the final surrender of Japan."
— *Lt. Gen. Noburu Tazoe, Chief of Staff, Air General Army*

Graveyard of a war now past. Partially sunken monuments to heroism on both sides dot the beaches of Pacific islands. Above, Japanese troop transport protrudes bow-high on the beach at Guadalcanal.

". . . air power can be pushed up to within striking distance of Japan and its action against Japan in combination with other arrangements, *will be decisive.*"

BRIG. GEN. WILLIAM MITCHELL
U.S. Army Air Corps
October 24, 1924.

BOMBERS

TYPE	OVERALL DIMENSIONS	SPEED
Mitsubishi Kl.21 Type 97 (2b) "Sally" Heavy bomber	Span: 72' 9¾" Length: 52' 6" Height: 15' 11"	Max: 247 mph at 13,120 ft. Cruise: 236 mph
Mitsubishi G4M Type 1 "Betty" Heavy bomber	Span: 81' 8" Length: 64' 4¾" Height: 13' 5¾"	Max: 292 mph at 15,000 ft. Cruise: 196 mph
Mitsubishi Ki.67 Type 4 HlRY4 "Peggy" Attack bomber	Span: 73' 9¾" Length: 61' 4¾" Height: 15' 9"	Max: 334 mph at 19,980 ft. Cruise: 248.5 mph
Nakajima Kl.49 Type 100 "Helen" Heavy bomber	Span: 66' 7" Length: 53'	Max: 304.5 mph
Mitsubishi G3Ml-3 Type 96 "Nell" Attack bomber	Span: 82' Length: 52' 6" Height: 12' 4"	Max: 230 mph at 10,000 ft. Cruise: 161 mph
Kawanashi H8Kl-4 Type 2 "Emily" Patrol bomber	Span: 13' 3" Length: 84' Height: 20'	Max: 251-285 mph at 10,000 ft. Cruise: 170 mph
Kuwasaki Kl48 Type 99 "Lily" Light bomber	Span: 57' Length: 40' 6"	Max: 313 mph

AIRCRAFT — PACIFIC WAR

BOMB LOAD	POWERPLANT	ARMAMENT	RANGE
1,654.1-2,205.1 lbs.	Two Mitsubishi Ha. 101 type 100 14-cylinder radial, 1,490 h.p. each	Five to six 7.7 mm machine guns	Max: 1,677.7 mi. with max. bomb load
2,000 lbs. or one large torpedo	Two Kasei radials with 1,530-1,870 h.p. each	Six 7.7 mm machine guns plus .20 mm tail cannon	Max: 2,671.9 mi.
2,000 lbs.	Two Mitsubishi Ha. 104 18-cylinder twin row radials with 2,000 h.p. each	Four 12.7 mm machine guns, two 20 mm cannon	Max: 2,360 mi. with bomb load of 1,764 lbs.
1,654 lbs.	Two Mitsubishi Ha. 109 radials with 1,570 h.p. each	Five 7.7 mm machine guns, one 20 mm cannon	Max: 1,491 mi. Normal: 1,000 mi.
2,200 lbs. or one torpedo	Two Kinsei double radials with 1,000 h.p. each	Seven 7.7 mm machine guns	Max: 2,796.2 mi. Normal: 1,615 mi.
4,411 lbs.	Four Kasei radials with 1,530-1,850 h.p. each	Two 20 mm cannon, several 7.7 mm machine guns	Max: 4,412 mi. Normal: 2,000 mi.
1,102.7 lbs. bombs	Two Ha. 115 radials with 1,000 h.p. takeoff each	Four 7.7 mm machine guns	1,491 mi.

FIGHTERS — FIGHTER BOMBERS — ATTACK BOMBERS

TYPE	OVERALL DIMENSIONS	SPEED
Mitsubishi Zero — Sen "Zero" ("Zeke") Ftr-Ftr/bomber	Span: 36' 1" Length: 29' 8¾" Height: 11' 5¾"	Max: 334 mph at 16,570 ft. Cruise: 207 mph Climb: 19,685'/7 min. 7 sec.
Kawasaki Hien Type 3-1A "Tony" Fighter	Span: 39' 4" Length: 29' 4" Height: 12' 1"	Max: 348 mph at 16,409 ft. Cruise: 215 mph Climb: 16,400'/8 min.
Kawanashi Sniden 21 "George" Ftr-Ftr/bomber	Span: 39' 3¼" Length: 30' 8" Height: 13'	Max: 370 mph at 18,370 ft. Cruise: 219 mph Climb: 19,685'/7 min. 50 sec.
Kuwasaki Ki.45 Toryu "Nick" Night fighter	Span: 49' 5¼" Length: 36' 1" Height: 12' 1¾"	Max: 340 mph at 22,965 ft. Cruise: 236 mph Climb: 16,400'/7 min.
Nakajima Ki.43 Hayabusa Type 1 (2B) "Oscar" Ftr-Ftr/bomber	Span: 35' 6¾" Length: 29' 3" Height: 10' 1½"	Max: 320 mph at 19,680 ft. Cruise: 214 mph Climb: 16,400'/5 min. 47 sec.
Nakajima Ki.44 Shoki "Tojo" Ftr-Ftr/bomber	Span: 30' 10" Length: 24' 2"	Max: 376 mph at 17,060 ft. Cruise: 248-273 mph Climb: 16,700'/4 min. 17 sec.
Nakajima Ki.84 Hayate "Frank" Ftr-Ftr/bomber	Span: 37' Length: 32' 3" Height: 11' 2"	Max: 388 mph at 19,680 ft. Cruise: 254 mph Climb: 16,400'/5 min. 59 sec.
Nakajima J1N1-S Gekko "Irving" Escort fighter	Span: 55' 8½" Length: 39' 11½" Height: 13' 1½"	Max: 315 mph. Cruise: 186 mph Climb: 9,840'/5 min. 1 sec.
Rikugun Ki.4b "Dinah" Armed recon	Span: 62' 4" Length: 46' 7⅝"	Max: 391 mph at 27,230 ft. Cruise: 217 mph Climb: 19,685'/9 min. 3 sec.
Nakajima B6N1-2 Type 97 Carrier attack	Span: 48' 6" Length: 35' Height: 14'	Max: 299-300 mph Climb: 16,400'/10 min.

BOMB LOAD	POWERPLANT	ARMAMENT	RANGE
Two 66 lb. bombs	One Nakajima Sakae radial with 1,130 h.p.	Two 7.7 mm machine guns, two 20 mm cannon	Max: 1,130 mi. at 152 mph, 875 mi. at 212 mph
None	One Kawasaki Ha. 40 type 2 liquid-cooled inverted V 12 cylinder with 1,160 h.p. takeoff	Two 20 mm cannon, two 12.7 mm machine guns	Max: 1,118 mi.
1,250 lbs. bombs	One Nakajima-Homare 18-cylinder radial with 1,990 h.p. takeoff	Four 20 mm cannon, two 7.7 mm machine guns	Max: 1,069 mi.
None	Two Mitsubishi Ha. 102 type 1 14-cylinder radials with 1,080 h.p. takeoff each	One 37 mm cannon, two 20 mm cannon	Max: 932 mi. Normal: 732 mi.
1,150 lbs. bombs	One Nakajima Ha. 115, 14-cylinder twin radial with 1,130 h.p. takeoff	Two 12.7 mm machine guns	Max: 1,865 mi. with external fuel tank Normal: 1,006 mi.
Two 220 lb. bombs	One Nakajima Ha. 109 14-cylinder radial with 1,520 h.p. takeoff	Four 12.7 mm machine guns	497 mi.
1,100 lbs. bombs	One Nakajima Ha. 45/11, 18-cylinder radial with 1,900 h.p. takeoff	Two 12.7 mm machine guns, two 20 mm cannon	Max: 1,815 mi. with external fuel Normal: 1,025 mi.
None	Two Nakajima Sakae 21, 14-cylinder radials with 1,130 h.p. takeoff each	Four 20 mm cannon	Max: 2,485.4 mi. Normal: 1,360 mi.
Two 550 lb. bombs	Two Mitsubishi Ha. 214 18-cylinder radials with 1,970 h.p. takeoff each	One .57 mm cannon, two 20 mm cannon, one 12.7 mm flex. machine gun	Max: 2,485 mi. with external fuel
1,764 lbs. bombs or one torpedo	One Kasei radial with 1,870 h.p. takeoff	Three 7.7 mm machine guns	652-1,087 mi.

TYPE	OVERALL DIMENSIONS	SPEED
Suisei D4Y1-3 Model 12 "Judy" Carrier dive bomber	Span: 37' 10"	Max: 361 mph Cruise: 205 mph
Kawanishi PiY3S "Frances" Night ftr/bomber	Span: 65' 7½" Length: 49' 2½" Height: 14' 8½"	Max: 325 mph at 17,720 ft. Cruise: 230 mph Climb: 16,400'/4 min. 23 sec.
Aichi (Q3A2) Type 99 "Val" Carrier dive bomber	Span: 49' 8" Length: 34' 9" Height:	Max: 266 mph Cruise: 205 mph
Mitsubishi J2M3 Raiden 21 "Jack" Fighter	Span: 35' 5" Length: 32' 7" Height: 12' 8"	Max: 338 mph at 7,875 ft. Cruise: 219 mph Climb: 9,840'/2 min. 56 sec.

TRANSPORTS

TYPE	OVERALL DIMENSIONS	SPEED
Mitsubishi Ki57 Type 100 "Topsy"	Span: 74' Length: 52' 8" Height: 16'	Max: 266 mph Cruise: 193 mph Ceiling: 23,000 ft.
Nakajima Ki34 Type 97 "Thora"	Span: 65' 4" Length: 50' Height: 13' 7"	Max: 230 mph Cruise: 217 mph

PRINCIPAL ALLIEI

BOMBERS

TYPE	OVERALL DIMENSIONS	SPEED
Boeing B-29 "Superfortress" Very long range (ULR) heavy bomber	Span: 141.3'	Max: 358 mph at 30,000 ft. Cruise: 230 mph at 20,000 ft.

BOMB LOAD	POWERPLANT	ARMAMENT	RANGE
1,103 lbs.	One Atsuta water-cooled engine with 1,400 h.p. takeoff	Three 7.7 mm machine guns	942.6 mi.
1,764 lbs. bombs	Two Mitsubishi Kasei 14-cylinder radials with 1,850 h.p. takeoff	Three 20 mm cannon	1,380.7 mi.
823 lbs. bombs	One Kinsei radial with 1,300 h.p. takeoff	Three 7.7 mm machine guns	838 mi.
132 lbs. bombs	One Mitsubishi MK4R — Akasei 23a — 14-cylinder radial with 1,820 h.p. takeoff	Four 20 mm cannon	655 mi. with droppable tank

CAPACITY	POWERPLANT	RANGE	CREW NO.
Cargo: 6,900 lbs. Passengers: 20	Two Mitsubishi Type 97 Ha. 5 14-cylinder radials with 850 h.p. each	1,240 mi.	4
Cargo: 3,080 lbs. Passengers: 5 to 8	Two Nakajima Ha1B 4-cylinder radials with 650 h.p. each	1,570 mi.	2

AIRCRAFT — PACIFIC WAR

BOMB LOAD	POWERPLANT	ARMAMENT	RANGE
Max: 20,000 lbs. Normal: 10,000 lbs.	Four Wright cyclone radials, 2,200 h.p. each	Twelve 0.50 cal. machine guns, one 20 mm cannon	Max: 5,600 mi. or 3,250 mi. with 20,000 lb. bomb load

BOMBERS (Cont.)

TYPE	OVERALL DIMENSIONS	SPEED
*Consolidated B24D "Liberator" Long range (LR) heavy bomber	Span: 110' Length: 99' Height: 18'	Max: 313 mph at 25,000 ft. Cruise: 233 mph
Boeing B-17E "Flying Fortress" Long range (LR) heavy bomber	Span: 103' 9" Length: 73' 10" Height: 19' 2"	Max: 317 mph at 25,000 ft. Cruise: 195-273 mph
North American B-258 "Mitchell" Medium range (M) bomber	Span: 67' 7" Length: 51' Height: 15' 4"	Max: 281 mph at 15,000 ft. Cruise: 248 mph
Douglas A-20g "Havoc" Medium range (M) bomber	Span: 61' 4" Length: 48' Height: 17' 7"	Max: 339 mph at 12,000 ft. Cruise: 272 mph
Lockheed PVI "Ventura" Medium range (M) naval bomber	Span: 65' 6" Length: 51' 9" Height: 13' 2"	Max: 312 mph at 13,200 ft. Cruise: 164 mph
Consolidated PBY-5 "Catalina" Navy patrol bomber	Span: 104' Length: 63' Height: 22' 4'	Max: 178 mph at 7,000 ft. Cruise: 107 mph

*Navy Designation, PB4Y-1

FIGHTERS — FIGHTER BOMBERS — ATTACK BOMBERS

TYPE	OVERALL DIMENSIONS	SPEED
Bell P-39D "Aircobra" Air Force ftr-ftr/bomber	Span: 34' Length: 30' 3" Height: 10' 10"	Max: 368 mph at 13,800 ft. Cruise: 213 mph Rate/climb: 2,720'/1 min.
Curtis P-40K "Warhawk" Air Force ftr-ftr/bomber	Span: 37' 4" Length: 33' 4" Height: 12' 4"	Max: 362 mph at 15,000 ft. Cruise: 290 mph Climb: 15000'/7.5 min.
Lockheed P-38G "Lightning" Air Force fighter	Span: 52' Length: 37' 10" Height: 9' 10"	Max: 400 mph at 25,000 ft. Cruise: 340 mph Climb: 20,000'/8.5 min.

BOMB LOAD	POWERPLANT	ARMAMENT	RANGE
Max: 12,800 lbs. Normal: 5,000 lbs.	Four Pratt Whitney radials, 1,700 h.p. each	Ten 0.50 cal. Browning machine guns	Max: 3,600 mi. or 2,100 mi. with bomb load
Max: 5,000 lbs. Normal: 4,000 lbs.	Four Wright cyclone radials, 1,200 h.p. each	Thirteen 0.50 cal. Browning machine guns	Max: 3,300 mi. or 2,000 mi. with 4,000 lb. bomb load
Max: 4,000 lbs. Normal: 3,000 lbs.	Two Wright cyclones, 1,700 h.p. each	Thirteen 0.50 cal. Colt Browning machine guns. "H" models had 75 mm cannon and four .50 caliber machine guns nose	Max: 2,450 mi. or 1,560 mi. with 3,000 lb. bomb load
Max: internal 2,000 lbs. Max: external 2,000 lbs.	Two Wright double cyclones, 1,600 h.p. each	Nine .50 cal. Colt Browning machine guns	Max: 1,090 mi. with 2,000 lb. bomb load
Max: 2,010 lbs. or one torpedo	Two Pratt Whitney radials; 2,000 h.p. each	Four .50 cal. and two .30 cal. machine guns	Max: 1,660 mi. with six 325 lb. depth charges or 1,360 mi. with one torpedo
Max: 1,000 lbs. or 2 torpedoes or three 325 lb. depth charges	Two Pratt Whitney radials, 950 h.p. each	Three .30 cal. and two .50 cal. machine guns	2,535 mi. patrol, or 1,405 mi. with four 325 lb. depth charges, or 2,145 mi. with 2,000 lbs. bombs

BOMB LOAD	POWERPLANT	ARMAMENT	RANGE
500 lb. bomb	One Allison V in-line Engine, 1,150 h.p. at 13,800'	One .37 mm nose gun, four .30 cal. wing guns, two .50 cal. nose guns	Max: 1,595 mi. ferry, or 800 mi. with 500 lb. bomb
500 lb. bomb	One Allison V in-Line, 1,325 h.p. takeoff	Six .50 cal. wing guns	Max: 1,600 mi. or 350 mi. with 500 lb. bomb
Two 1,000 lb. bombs in place of droppable fuel tanks	Two Allison V in-Line, 1,325 h.p. takeoff each	One 20 mm cannon, four .50 cal. machine guns	Max: 2,400 mi. at 203 mph with external fuel tanks, 350 mi. at 310 mph

TYPE	OVERALL DIMENSIONS	SPEED
Republic P-47N "Thunderbolt" Air Force ftr-ftr/bomber	Span: 42' 7" Length: 36' 1" Height: 14' 8"	Max: 467 mph at 32,500 ft. Cruise: 300 mph Climb: 25,000'/14.2 min.
North American P-51H "Mustang" Air Force ftr/bomber	Span: 37' Length: 33' 4" Height: 13' 8"	Max: 487 mph at 25,000 ft. Cruise: 380 mph Climb: 30,000'/13.5 min.
Douglass SBD-3 "Dauntless" Navy dive bomber	Span: 41' 6" Length: 32' 8" Height: 13' 7"	Max: 250 mph at 16,000 ft. Cruise: 152 mph Climb: 1,190'/1 min.
Curtis SB2C-1 "Helldiver" Navy dive bomber	Span: 44' 9" Length: 36' 8" Height: 13' 2"	Max: 281 mph at 12,400 ft. Cruise: 152 mph Climb: 1750'/1 min.
Gruman TBF-1 "Avenger" Navy torpedo bomber	Span: 54' 2" Length: 40' Height: 16' 5"	Max: 271 mph at 12,000 ft. Cruise: 145 mph Climb: 1430'/1 min.
Gruman F4F-4 "Wildcat" Navy fighter	Span: 38' Length: 28' 4" Height: 11' 10"	Max: 318 mph at 14,400 ft. Cruise: 155 mph Climb: 1,950'/1 min.
Vought F4U-1 "Corsair" Navy ftr-ftr/bomber	Span: 41' Length: 33' 4" Height: 16' 1"	Max: 417 mph at 19,900 ft. Cruise: 182 mph Climb: 2,890'/1 min.
Gruman F6F-3 "Hellcat I" Navy fighter	Span: 42' 10" Length: 33' 7" Height: 13' 1"	Max: 375 mph at 17,300 ft. Cruise: 160 mph Climb: 3,500'/1 min.

TRANSPORTS

TYPE	OVERALL DIMENSIONS	SPEED
Douglas C-47 "Skytrain" "Gooney Bird"	Span: 95' Length: 64' 4" Height: 16' 10"	Max: 230 mph Cruise: 150 mph Ceiling: 24,000 ft.
Curtiss-Wright C-46 "Commando"	Span: 108' Length: 76' 4" Height: 21' 8"	Max: 264 mph Cruise: 160 mph Ceiling: 25,000 ft.

BOMB LOAD	POWERPLANT	ARMAMENT	RANGE
Three 1,000 lb. bombs	One Pratt Whitney radial, 2,800 h.p. at 32,500 ft.	Eight .50 cal. machine guns, ten 5 in. rockets	Max: 2,200 mi. or 800 mi. with 2,000 lbs. bombs
Max: Two 1,000 lb. externally carried bombs	One Allison V in-Line, 1,380 h.p. takeoff	Six .50 cal. machine guns plus 2 bombs or ten 5 in. rockets	Max: 2,400 mi. with two external tanks or 850 mi. with two 1,000 lb. bombs
1,000 lbs.	One Wright radial with 1,000 h.p. takeoff	Two .50 cal. fixed machine guns, two .30 cal. flexible machine guns	Max: 1,580 mi. or 1,345 mi. with 1,000 lb. bomb load
1,000 lbs.	One Wright radial with 1,700 h.p. takeoff	Four .50 cal. machine guns, two .30 cal. flexible guns	Max: 1,895 mi. or 1,750 mi. with 1,000 lb. bomb load
2,000 lbs.	One Wright radial with 1,700 h.p. takeoff	One .30 cal. fixed, one .50 cal. flexible	Max: 1,450 mi. or 1,215 mi. with one torpedo
None	One Pratt Whitney radial with 1,200 h.p. takeoff	Six .50 cal. wing guns	Max: 1,100 mi. Normal: 770 mi.
2,000 lbs. bombs or eight 5-inch rockets	One Pratt Whitney radial with 2,000 h.p. takeoff	Six .50 cal. wing guns	Max: 2,220 mi. Normal: 1,015 mi.
None	One Pratt Whitney radial with 2,000 h.p. takeoff	Six .50 cal. wing guns	Max: 1,590 mi. Normal: 1,090 mi.

CAPACITY	POWERPLANT	RANGE	CREW NO.
Max. cargo: 10,000 lbs. Normal: 7,500 lbs. Passengers: 21	Two Pratt Whitney radials, 1,200 h.p. each	2,125 mi.	4-5
Cargo: 15,000 lbs. Passengers: 50	Two Pratt Whitney radials, 2,000 h.p. each	Over 1,400 mi.	4

TYPE	OVERALL DIMENSIONS	SPEED
Douglas C-54 "Skymaster"	Span: 117' 6" Length: 93' 9" Height: 27' 6"	Max: 300 mph Cruise: 185 mph Ceiling: 30,000 ft.
Waco CG-4A Glider	Span: 83' 8" Length: 48' 8"	Max: 180 mph Cruise: 150 mph

CAPACITY	DIMENSIONS	RANGE	CREW NO.
Cargo: 32,000 lbs. Passengers: 50	Four Pratt Whitney radials, 1,450 h.p. each	Over 2,000 mi.	6
Cargo: 4,000 lbs. Passengers: 15	None		2

Index